THE Weekend Woodworker ANNUAL

1994

THE Weekend Woodworker ANNUAL

1994

Quick and Easy Country Projects

Selected by the Editors of Rodale Books

Illustrations by Sally Onopa

Rodale Press, Emmaus, Pennsylvania

The authors and editors who compiled this book have tried to make all the contents as accurate and as correct as possible. Plans, illustrations, photographs, and text have all been carefully checked and cross-checked. However, due to the variability of local conditions, construction materials, personal skill, and so on, neither the authors nor Rodale Press assumes any responsibility for any injuries suffered, or for damages or other losses incurred that result from the material presented herein. All instructions and plans should be carefully studied and clearly understood before beginning construction.

This book is being simultaneously published by Rodale Press as a book entitled *The Weekend Woodworker®: Quick and Easy Country Projects.*

If you have any questions or comments concerning this book, please write to:
Rodale Press, Inc.
Book Readers' Service
33 East Minor Street
Emmaus, PA 18098

Executive Editor: Margaret Lydic Balitas
Managing Editor: Jeff Day
Editor: Bob Moran
Writers: Kenneth S. Burton, Jr.,
   Bob Moran, David Page, Christopher Semancik
Copy Manager: Dolores Plikaitis
Copy Editor: Nancy N. Bailey
Office Manager: Karen Earl-Braymer
Administrative Assistant: Susan Nickol
Editorial Assistance: Deborah Weisel

Art Director: Michael Mandarano
Book Designer: Robert E. Ayers,
   PUBLICATION DESIGN
Book Layout: Peter A. Chiarelli
Cover Designer: Darlene Schneck
Photographer: Mitch Mandel

Cover Projects: The projects shown on the cover include (clockwise from upper left): Tilt-Top Table/Bench (page 2), Schoolmaster's Desk (page 10), Chimney Cabinet (page 114), Cobbler's Bench (page 22), and One-Door Milk Paint Cabinet (page 94).

ISBN 0–87596–619–5 hardcover
ISSN 1058–4072

2 4 6 8 10 9 7 5 3 1 hardcover

CONTENTS

Special Techniques

Contributing Craftsmen

Phil Gehret (Chimney Cabinet, Slant-Front Cabinet, Corner Shelf Unit, Cherry Wall Shelves, Shelf with Pegs, Sconce, Bootjack, Towel Rack, Treenware)

Darwin Jack (Trestle Table)

Brian and Faith Johnson (Bookcase)

Fred Matlack (Magazine Rack)

Bob Moran (Window Valance, Kitchen Shelves)

Butch Roller (Pie Safe)

INTRODUCTION

This book assumes that woodworking as a hobby is supposed to be enjoyable. It assumes that the first reason for making, say, an end table, is that you are proud of your craftsmanship and get real, sensual pleasure from working with wood. What you do with the table when you have finished making it is important but secondary.

The 40 projects that we've assembled here were chosen with these priorities in mind. They were chosen to be fun to make, and then to be useful to have. We've focused on country furniture, specifically on genuine antique country furniture, because it's fun to make and also happens to be quite useful.

You won't need an acre of shop space or a fortune in cast iron to enjoy these projects; the dairy farmer or miller's son who made the original a century ago did it with pretty basic hand tools. The step-by-step instructions that we've given assume that you have a table saw and a router but no other power tools.

If, on the other hand, you own a variety of machines, great; use them when appropriate.

To help make your woodworking a pleasure, we've tried to eliminate many of the frustrations that can crop up during a project. Toward this end, much of the needed information can be found in more than one place. For example, you can see how a project goes together in both an exploded view and a conventional two-dimensional drawing; you can find most dimensions in both the drawings and in the cutting list.

We've also included some jigs and techniques that are particularly well suited to today's home woodworking shop; that is, they are simple to make and use, economical of time and materials, and work well without your having to spend a week getting used to them. Check out "Edge-Gluing" on page 6 and "Cutting Tenons" on page 60 for examples of these techniques.

Enough said. Go do it.

PART ONE

TABLES

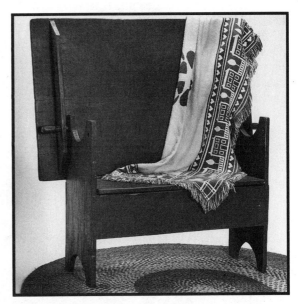

TILT-TOP TABLE/BENCH

The most striking feature of this table is its economy of design. A few boards, nails, and screws create a table, a bench, and a chest. There are no complicated mechanisms to give it this versatility, just simple geometry. Perhaps because they are so simple, tables like this survive over the years. In today's household the tilt-top table allows a dining room or family room to provide either table space or increased open space and seating; the room can host either a sit-down meal or a party for lots of people.

Make the table from any reasonably stable wood. The pictured table is a mix of pine and oak. Hand-plane marks are

still visible in the boards, under the red paint. If your room is large enough, you can make the table more versatile by increasing the size of the tabletop. An increase of 4 to 6 inches in each direction is good. Too large a top will make the bench unstable.

1 Select the stock and cut the parts. Edge-glue narrower stock as necessary to obtain the widths required, then cut the ends, stretchers, seat, hinge board, chest bottom, and supports to the dimensions specified by the Cutting List. See page 6 for more on edge-gluing. Since none of the parts require perfectly uniform thickness, feel free to hand plane them for an historically accu-rate hand-planed feel and look. Prepare the top last, even after constructing the base if you want.

2 Notch the ends for the stretchers. The stretcher boards provide lateral strength for the table and form the sides of the chest. They fit in notches in the edges of the ends. Lay out the notches, marking the depth of the notch with a marking gauge. Saw the ends of each notch with a handsaw, then saw along the notch on the waste side of the layout lines with a coping saw or saber saw. Clean up and flatten the sawn surface with a coarse file or bullnose plane. The stretchers should fit snugly into the notches.

CUTTING LIST

Part	Dimensions
Ends (2)	$1'' \times 14\frac{1}{4}'' \times 29''$
Stretchers (2)	$\frac{3}{4}'' \times 7\frac{3}{4}'' \times 36\frac{3}{4}''$
Bottom supports (2)	$\frac{3}{4}'' \times 1'' \times 34\frac{1}{2}''$
Chest bottom	$\frac{7}{8}'' \times 12\frac{3}{4}'' \times 34\frac{1}{2}''$
Seat supports (2)	$\frac{1}{2}'' \times 3'' \times 12\frac{1}{2}''$
Hinge board	$\frac{7}{8}'' \times 3\frac{1}{2}'' \times 34\frac{3}{4}''$
Seat	$\frac{7}{8}'' \times 12'' \times 34\frac{1}{2}''$
Battens (2)	$1'' \times 3\frac{1}{4}'' \times 27\frac{1}{2}''$
Tabletop	$\frac{3}{4}'' \times 29\frac{1}{2}'' \times 46\frac{3}{4}''$
Hinge pins (4)	$1\frac{3}{8}''$ dia. $\times 6''$

Hardware

3d and 6d cut box or fine finish nails. Available from many building-supply stores and from Tremont Nail Company, P.O. Box 111, Wareham, MA 02571; (508) 295–0038. Item #CX6 or #CE6.
1 pair butt hinges, $2'' \times 1\frac{1}{2}''$, open
#10 $\times 2''$ flathead wood screws

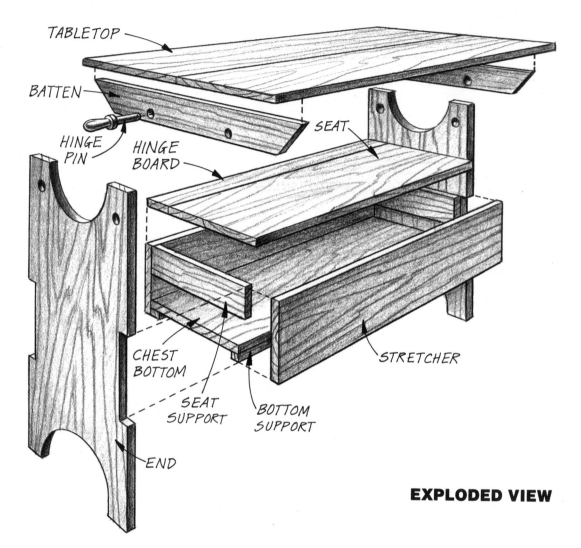

TABLETOP

BATTEN

HINGE PIN

HINGE BOARD

SEAT

CHEST BOTTOM

SEAT SUPPORT

BOTTOM SUPPORT

STRETCHER

END

EXPLODED VIEW

3 Make the cutouts in the table ends. The top and bottom of the ends have semi-circular cutouts. These form the table feet and add visual interest when the tabletop is tilted up. The top rear corners of the ends are rounded to allow the top to tilt. Lay out the cutouts and rounded corners, then saw them with a coping saw or saber saw.

Clean up the sawn edges with files and sandpaper.

4 Attach the stretchers to the ends. Predrill for four 6d cut finish nails in both ends of both stretchers. Sand the table ends and stretchers. Stand the ends on edge on the workbench and nail a stretcher into the notches, making certain that the table ends are parallel to each other and at right angles to the stretchers. Turn the assembly over and install the second stretcher in the same way.

5 Attach the bottom support strips and chest bottom. Glue and clamp the two bottom support strips inside the lower edge of each stretcher. The bottom of the original table simply sets in place on the support strips. You'll have a steadier table and less danger of the bottom bowing or cupping if you screw it to the supports.

6 Nail the seat supports to the table ends. The seat supports fit between the stretchers with ¼ inch of clearance to allow for shrinkage. Place the assembled table base on end on the workbench. Nail one of the seat supports in place with 3d cut nails. Turn the assembly over and nail the other support in place.

7 Attach the hinge board. The hinge board has a ⅛-inch-radius bead along the hinged edge. Rout the bead with a beading bit in a table-mounted router. Lay out and cut the hinge mortises on the beaded edge of the board.

Put the hinge board in place on the stretcher and support boards. Drill for four 6d nails through the hinge board into the stretcher and one into each support board. Sand the hinge board, then glue and nail it in place.

SHOP TIP: Butt hinges are available in a variety of designs; the correct mortise depth depends on the design. To determine the correct depth, hold the hinge in its closed position with the leaves parallel to each other. With some hinge designs the leaves will be touching each other when they are parallel but with other designs they will be a small distance apart. Measure from the outside of one leaf to the outside of the other leaf while they are parallel. From this measurement subtract the amount of clearance that you want between the door and the piece that the door hinges to: ¹⁄₁₆ inch is a good amount for most applications. Divide the remainder by 2. This is the depth of the mortise for each leaf. Scribe the depth onto the stock with a marking gauge.

8 Install the seat. The seat fits between the table ends with ⅛ inch of clearance at each end. It hinges to the hinge board. Before attaching the seat, round-over the top of the front edge with a ⅜-inch roundover bit in your router.

Center the seat between the ends, mark the location of the hinge-board mortises on the seat, and cut mortises to match. Sand the seat before installing the hinges.

9 Cut the battens and screw them to the tabletop. Saw the

(continued on page 8)

EDGE-GLUING

Edge-gluing is the process of gluing narrow boards edge to edge in order to make wide boards. You can do an excellent job of preparing the edges with a table saw and a hand plane. The homemade clamps described below work at least as well as expensive bar clamps.

To get strong and durable glue joints, your wood should be well adjusted to the humidity of your shop. To achieve this, bring it into the shop several weeks before using it. Stack it on a flat surface, off the floor, with sticks of uniform thickness between layers of boards in the stack. This allows air to circulate around each board. Place the sticks about 16 inches apart, directly over the sticks in the layer below.

1 **Make the clamps.** Each clamp consists of two wooden bars, two carriage bolts with wing nuts, and a wedge, as shown in the drawing.

Rip the bars from the best 2 × 4s you can find. Lay out the bolt holes on a plywood template the length and width of the bars. Tape the template to a bar and drill ⅜-inch holes through both the template and the bar at each layout mark. Then tape the template to each remaining bar in turn, line up the bit with the holes now in the template, and drill the holes in the remaining bars. Wax the bars thoroughly to prevent glue from sticking to them.

Saw the wedges out of hardwood and plane out the saw marks.

The ⁵⁄₁₆-inch-diameter carriage bolts should be 3½ inches longer than the thickness of the boards you want to clamp.

2 **Prepare the edges.** The edges that you will glue together must be as straight, as square to the board faces, and as smooth as you can make them. This involves sawing them straight and square and then planing them smooth.

Check that your table-saw blade is sharp and truly perpendicular to the saw table and that the fence is truly parallel to the blade. Rip the edges to be glued and check that they are straight with a long straightedge.

Check that the edge of your plane iron is straight and polished to the sharpest edge you can achieve. Adjust the plane to take the thinnest possible shaving that will remove all of the saw marks in one stroke. Check that the blade protrudes a uniform amount from the sole of the plane across the width of the plane. In one long sweep of the plane, take a shaving off of the entire edge of a board. You're done. If you try to take a second stroke, or touch up this part or that, you'll wind up getting the edge out of square or not straight. Then you'll have to go back to the saw and start over.

3 **Lay out the clamps.** Insert two bolts in one bar from each clamp. Space the bolts slightly farther apart than the width of the

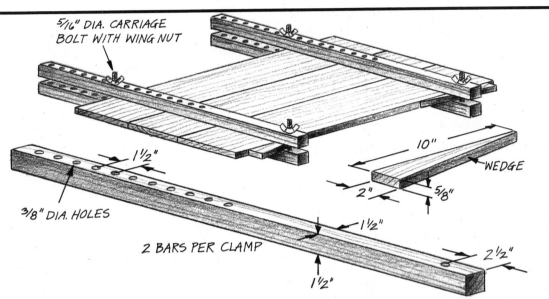

5/16" DIA. CARRIAGE BOLT WITH WING NUT

1 1/2"

3/8" DIA. HOLES

2 BARS PER CLAMP

10"

WEDGE

2"

5/8"

1 1/2"

1 1/2"

2 1/2"

panel. Lay out these bars on your workbench, parallel to each other, a foot or so apart, with the bolts sticking up.

4   Apply the glue. If a glue-up requires more than two joints, do it in stages so the glue won't dry out before assembly. Apply a small bead of glue to the edges to be joined, then brush out the beads. Use a small, disposable plumber's flux brush to spread the glue and work it into the surfaces.

5   Clamp the joint. Assemble the boards between the bolts in the clamp bars. Install the second bar and wing nuts for each clamp. Turn the nuts snug enough to keep the edges of the boards aligned but not so tight that the clamp can't move sideways. Insert a wedge between

an edge of the assembled panel and a carriage bolt on each clamp. Work all of the wedges in as tight as you can get them by hand while keeping the clamps perpendicular to the joints. Glue should begin to squeeze out of the joints. Now tap the wedges further. The clamp will tend to move so that it's no longer perpendicular to the joints. Let it. This angling of the clamps applies tremendous pressure and makes the clamps easy to disassemble. When all of the clamps are tight (great hammer blows are not required), let the glue dry.

To remove the clamps after the glue is dry, tap the clamps back toward a position perpendicular to the joints. The wedges will then come loose. Remove the wedges, the wing nuts, the top bar, and the glued-up panel.

ends of the battens to 45 degrees, as shown in the *Side View.* Drill three shank holes and counterbores for #10 screws in the edge of each batten. The counterbores must be 1¾ inches deep in the 3¼-inch-wide battens for the 2-inch screws to reach ½ inch into the tabletop. Make the shank holes near the ends slightly oversize to allow some seasonal movement in the tabletop.

With the tabletop centered and square on the base, clamp the battens in position on the underside of the top. Leave ⅛-inch to ¼-inch clearance between the battens and the table ends. Turn the tabletop over and mark the screw locations on the underside. Remove the battens and drill ½-inch-deep pilot holes.

Sand the top and the battens, then screw the battens in place. If you like, glue the center 3 or 4 inches of each batten but no more.

10 **Drill holes for the hinge pins.** Lay out the hinge pin holes on the inside of the table ends. Put the tabletop on the base and shim it up off the base about the thickness of a couple of business cards. Clamp one of the battens to the adjacent table end. Bore the ¾-inch holes through the table end and batten. To prevent tear-out on the outside of the batten, clamp a scrap of wood where the hole will exit. Drill both holes at one end of the table, then repeat the procedure at the other end.

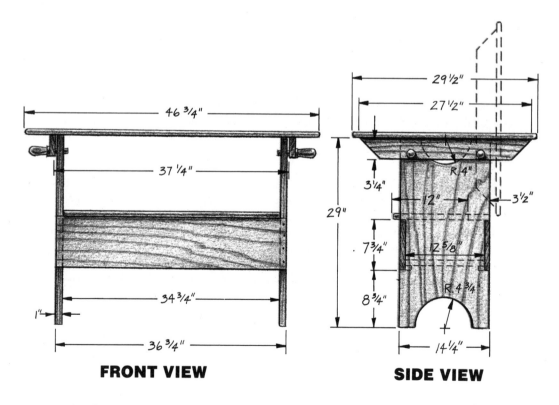

FRONT VIEW   **SIDE VIEW**

11 **Make the hinge pins.** The table in the photo has holes for four pins, two to hinge the top and two to lock it. The locking pins have long since been lost. You can turn the pins on a lathe if you have one, or shape them with a drawknife and spokeshave. The *Hinge Pin Detail* shows the shape. If you're shaping them by hand, consider starting with lengths of wooden closet pole. Put a very slight taper on the shafts of the pins so the pin will wedge tight in the batten while still turning in the hole in the table end. Test them and sand the pins or holes to get a proper fit. The top should tilt without loosening the pins.

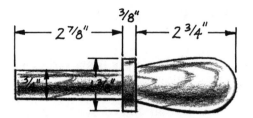

HINGE PIN DETAIL

12 **Complete the tilt-top table/ bench.** Tables get a lot of use and abuse so their finish needs some thought. For an historically accurate reproduction, use red milk paint. It's quite durable and ages nicely. See page 100 for more information. If you prefer a natural finish, you can use a modern polyurethane or a traditional oil. The polyurethane gives a durable surface film but when the film isn't durable enough the resultant scratches look pretty bad and are a nuisance to touch up. The oil finish will mark up more easily but the wear doesn't usually look so bad and touching up with a bit more oil is easy. You might also consider using just paste wax on the bare wood. If you're thinking of stain, keep in mind that a scratch through stain sticks out like a sore thumb.

One final thought on this table design: If the tabletop gets to looking pretty bad, just pull the pins and take the top back to the shop for planing, sanding, and refinishing.

SCHOOLMASTER'S DESK

This style of desk has a variety of names. Some would call it a stand-up desk, or a tall desk, since it's too tall to use with a chair. You could sit at it with a tall stool but most people will find it comfortable to use while standing. Other folks might call it a schoolmaster's desk since the style was found at the head of classrooms early in this century. It's about the right width for a birch rod!

A tall desk like this can be quite handy in the home. In a large kitchen it can hold the telephone, directories, writing paper, pens and pencils and provide an excellent surface for taking notes. The sloping lid will hold an open tele-

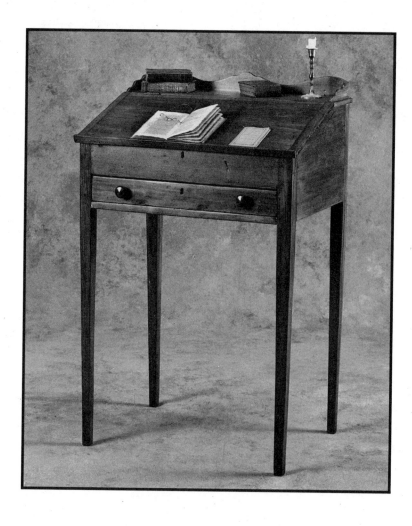

phone directory or cookbook. In an entry or foyer the desk would provide an impressive place for a guest book, and nobody would notice if the sloping lid were hiding gloves and earmuffs.

The plans and step-by-step instructions reflect a few minor changes from the original. The inside of the desk shows signs that it once had built-in shelves. You could easily add small

EXPLODED VIEW

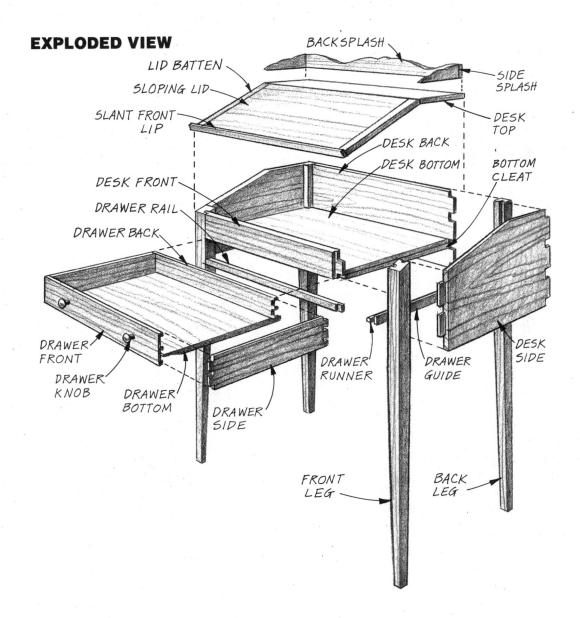

BACK SPLASH

LID BATTEN

SLOPING LID

SLANT FRONT LIP

SIDE SPLASH

DESK TOP

DESK BACK

DESK BOTTOM

BOTTOM CLEAT

DESK FRONT

DRAWER RAIL

DRAWER BACK

DRAWER FRONT

DRAWER KNOB

DRAWER BOTTOM

DRAWER SIDE

DRAWER RUNNER

DRAWER GUIDE

DESK SIDE

FRONT LEG

BACK LEG

CUTTING LIST

Part	Dimensions
Front legs (2)	$1\frac{7}{8}'' \times 1\frac{7}{8}'' \times 43\frac{1}{2}''$
Back legs (2)	$1\frac{7}{8}'' \times 1\frac{7}{8}'' \times 48\frac{1}{8}''$
Desk front	$\frac{3}{4}'' \times 4\frac{7}{8}'' \times 30\frac{1}{4}''$
Desk back	$\frac{3}{4}'' \times 13\frac{3}{4}'' \times 30\frac{1}{4}''$
Lid battens (2)	$\frac{3}{4}'' \times 1\frac{1}{4}'' \times 15\frac{3}{4}''$
Desk sides (2)	$\frac{3}{4}'' \times 13\frac{3}{4}'' \times 21\frac{1}{4}''$
Drawer rail	$1'' \times 1\frac{7}{8}'' \times 30\frac{1}{4}''$
Desk bottom	$\frac{3}{4}'' \times 21\frac{3}{4}'' \times 30\frac{1}{4}''$
Sloping lid	$\frac{3}{4}'' \times 15\frac{3}{4}'' \times 31''$
Tenon pegs (18)	$\frac{1}{4}''$ dia. OR $\frac{1}{4}''$ square $\times 1''$
Bottom cleats (2)	$\frac{3}{4}'' \times 1\frac{1}{8}'' \times 19''$
Desk top	$\frac{7}{8}'' \times 8\frac{3}{4}'' \times 33''$
Backsplash	$\frac{3}{8}'' \times 3'' \times 32''$
Side splashes (2)	$\frac{3}{8}'' \times 2\frac{1}{4}'' \times 8\frac{1}{8}''$
Slant front lip	$\frac{5}{16}'' \times 1\frac{1}{8}'' \times 33''$
Drawer front	$\frac{3}{4}'' \times 3\frac{3}{8}'' \times 27\frac{15}{16}''$
Drawer sides (2)	$\frac{1}{2}'' \times 3\frac{3}{8}'' \times 21''$
Drawer back	$\frac{1}{2}'' \times 2\frac{3}{4}'' \times 27\frac{15}{16}''$
Drawer bottom	$\frac{1}{2}'' \times 20\frac{3}{4}'' \times 27\frac{3}{8}''$
Drawer guides (2)	$1\frac{1}{8}'' \times 1\frac{3}{4}'' \times 19''$
Drawer runners (2)	$\frac{5}{8}'' \times \frac{3}{4}'' \times 20''$
Drawer knobs (2)	$1\frac{3}{4}''$ dia. $\times 2\frac{1}{8}''$

Hardware

1 pair brass butt hinges, $2'' \times 1\frac{1}{4}''$, open. Available from Woodcraft Supply, P.O. Box 1686, Parkersburg, WV 26102-1686; (800) 225–1153. Item #16Q42.

4d finish nails, $1''$

1 friction lid support. Available from Woodcraft. Item #13L31.

shelves and a center divider if you like. The slant top and drawer both have locks that we have omitted. You're welcome to add locks of your choice. The lid of our antique is held open by a stick of wood pivoting on a screw on one side of the desk. It's a crude and somewhat precarious arrangement so we've specified a commercial lid support.

Our desk is made entirely of clear pine but any good furniture wood is suitable.

1 Select the stock and cut the parts. If you surface your own wood, you can build the desk out of 8/4 (eight-quarter) and 4/4 (four-quarter) stock. Rip the legs slightly oversize out of unsurfaced 8/4 stock. As you plane the legs to the dimensions specified by the Cutting List, keep in mind that the legs will be tapered on their inner surfaces. Knowing that the tapered portions can be left rough at this stage may make it easier to get 1⅞ inches out of 8/4 stock. Rip the drawer rail, drawer guides, and knob blanks from 8/4 stock and surface them.

Set aside the thickest, flattest, 4/4 stock for the desk top since it should have a finished thickness of ⅞ inch. Then select 4/4 stock for the ¾-inch-thick parts, edge-gluing as needed to make up the required widths. See "Edge-Gluing" on page 6 for more information. Resaw the thinner parts from

either 4/4 or 8/4 stock. With the exception of the drawer bottom, all of the thinner parts are narrow enough to resaw with a sharp, thin-kerf, rip blade on the table saw. You can substitute ¼-inch plywood for the drawer bottom. Saw and plane all the desk parts except the drawer parts to the dimensions given in the Cutting List.

2 Cut mortises in the legs for the front, side, and back tenons.
The simplest way to cut mortises in the home shop is with a plunge router, a fence attachment, and a spiral upcut bit. Begin by laying out all of the mortises *and* the corresponding tenons as shown in the *Leg Joinery.* Lay out the locations

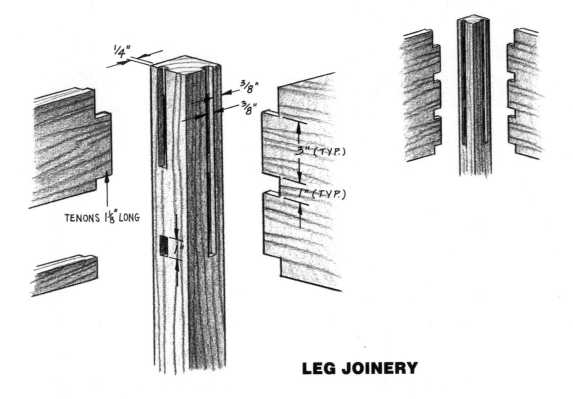

TENONS 1⅛" LONG

¼"

3/8"

3/8"

3" (TYP.)

1" (TYP.)

1"

LEG JOINERY

of the tenon pegs at this time, too. The two back legs are interchangeable but the front legs are mirror images of each other. Label all four legs for their position in the desk. When you've laid everything out, double-check by holding the tenons up to the mortises.

The length of the haunch grooves is the same as the width of the adjoining part. Rout the groove ⅜ inch wide by ¼ inch deep with a ⅜-inch-diameter spiral upcut bit. If you're unsure of your ability to keep the router steady on the 1⅞-inch width of the legs, clamp a second leg alongside the one you're routing. Guide the cut with the fence attachment running along the outside surface of the leg.

Adjust the router to cut the mortises 1³⁄₁₆ inch deep. This makes the mortises ¹⁄₁₆ inch deeper than the length of the tenons. Don't change the setting of the router fence. Rout the mortises in a series of passes, then square the ends of the mortises and haunches with a chisel. See page 18 for a similar mortising technique that uses a shop-made jig to steady the router.

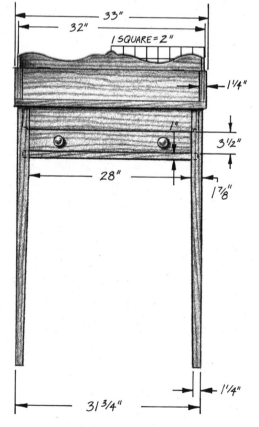

FRONT VIEW

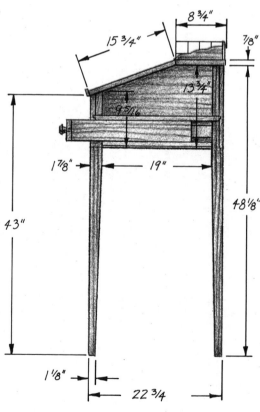

SIDE VIEW CROSS SECTION

3 Cut the desk bottom grooves.
The desk bottom separates the
drawer compartment from the compartment under the sloping lid. It fits into
grooves in the front and back. Rout the
3/8-inch-deep grooves in several passes
of increasing depth with a 1/4-inch-
diameter straight bit. Lay out the
grooves as shown in the *Bottom Groove
Detail* and guide the router with its fence
attachment.

4 Make the grooves in the lid battens. Battens help to hold the sloping lid flat. They join the lid with a
tongue and groove. Rout the 1/4-inch-
deep grooves in the battens with a 1/4-
inch-diameter straight bit. Don't try to
hold the router steady on the 3/4-inch-
wide edge of the battens. Clamp the battens between a couple of scraps of
squared-up 8/4 stock so you have a
broad, flush surface for the router. Center the groove in the edge of the battens.

5 Cut the tenons on the sides,
back, front, and drawer rail.
Perhaps the safest and easiest way to
cut tenons on wide parts such as these
is with a hand-held router. The first step
is to cut a rabbet along the end forming
one big tenon, then cut away parts of
the one big tenon to form smaller tenons
and haunches.

Clamp one of the parts to your
workbench with the outer surface facing
up and the end hanging over the edge of
the bench. Chuck a fairly large diameter
straight bit in the router. Adjust the
fence so the bit will cut just up to the
shoulder line. Adjust the depth of cut so
a 3/8-inch-thick tenon will be left after
cutting the rabbet. Take a series of cuts

starting at the end of the board and cutting closer to the shoulder with each
pass. The fence will prevent cutting past
the shoulder line, leaving a nice straight
shoulder. Cut rabbets on both ends of
the front, back, and sides.

Hold the tenon pieces in position
against their corresponding leg mortises
to check the location of the haunches.
Saw the sides of each tenon with a back
saw, then saw the ends of the haunches
between the tenons with a coping saw.
Make sure that no parts of the haunches
are longer than the depth of the haunch
groove.

6 Cut the tongues on the desk
bottom and sloping lid. Cut
these tongues the same way you cut the
tenons on the front, back, and sides.
The only differences are the dimensions.
The tongue on the sloping lid is formed
by *two* rabbets, one on each side.

7 Assemble the sloping lid. The
battens help prevent the lid from
cupping but they can cause more problems than they cure if they are glued

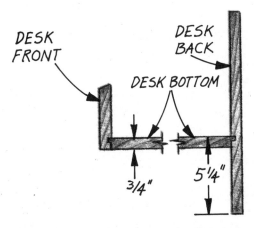

BOTTOM GROOVE DETAIL

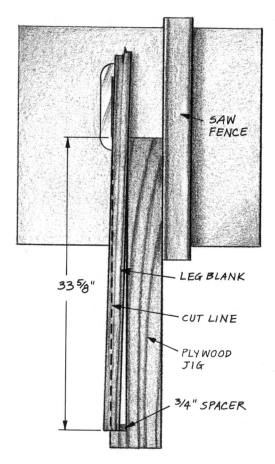

33 5/8"

SAW FENCE

LEG BLANK

CUT LINE

PLYWOOD JIG

3/4" SPACER

TAPER DETAIL

a straightedge, then saw the tapers with a tapering jig as shown in the *Taper Detail*. Clean up the cut with a hand plane.

9 **Saw the slope on the front legs, front, and sides.** The sloping lid is 20 degrees from horizontal. Adjust the tilt of the table saw to this angle and crosscut the tops of the front legs, as shown in the *Side View Cross Section*.

Assemble the four legs to the front, rail, side, and back pieces without glue. A band clamp will hold the assembly securely. Lay out the bevel on the front and the slope on the sides.

Disassemble the parts, then rip the bevel on the front and plane it smooth. While the saw is set up at this angle, rip the same bevel on the upper edge of the sloping lid. Adjust the tilt of the table saw back to square and adjust the miter gauge to 20 degrees from square. Cut the slope on the sides staying well outside the line, then plane to the line.

10 **Notch the corners of the desk bottom.** The desk bottom must fit around the legs at the corners. Lay out the notches, then saw them with a handsaw.

11 **Assemble the desk.** You've already laid out the locations of the tenon pegs. Prick a hole at these locations with an awl or small nail so the locations won't get sanded away. Sand the parts, but avoid the mortised surfaces of the legs. Glue and clamp the front and back legs to the desk sides. Insert the desk bottom into the front and back grooves, then glue and clamp the desk front, drawer rail, and back between the two side units. Don't glue the tongues on the desk bottom into the grooves.

continuously to the lid. To prevent cracking the lid in dry weather, glue only the middle 2 or 3 inches of each batten to the lid. At the ends, nail through the edge of the batten into the lid with a 4d finishing nail. Set the nail heads and fill the holes.

8 **Cut the taper in the legs.** The taper in the legs begins at the bottom edge of the sides, back, and drawer rail. Only the inside surfaces of the legs taper. Lay out the taper in each leg with

12 **Peg the tenons in the legs.** Drill ¼-inch-diameter, 1-inch-deep peg holes in the legs, through the tenons, where you've laid them out. Peg the tenons with ¼-inch dowels, or with ¼-inch square pegs made from the same wood as your legs. Bevel the leading edge of the pegs slightly, apply glue, and drive the pegs into the drilled holes. Then saw and sand them flush with the surface of the legs.

13 **Glue the bottom cleats to the desk sides.** The desk bottom is now held along its sides but not at its ends. Cleats glued to the desk sides support the ends of the bottom as shown in the *Drawer Support Detail.* Glue the cleats to the desk sides but not to the desk bottom so the bottom is free to shrink in dry weather. Apply glue somewhat sparingly to the cleats and clamp them in place, tight against the bottom. If you don't have clamps with deep enough throats, nail or screw the cleats in place.

14 **Cut the backsplash dadoes and attach the top.** The three backsplash pieces fit in ⅜-inch-wide by ⅛-inch-deep dadoes in the desk top. Rout these dadoes with a straight bit, then square the ends.

The desk top is glued and nailed to the sides and back. Predrill the nail holes inside the dadoes so they will be hidden. Sand the desk top, then glue and nail it to the sides and back.

15 **Make and attach the backsplash.** Lay out the curves of the backsplash parts from the *Front View* and *Side View Cross Section.* Saw them out with a coping saw. Clamp the two sides together and saw them as one to get a perfect match between them. Smooth the sawn edges with files and sandpaper, then sand the surfaces. Glue and clamp them into the dadoes on the desk top. When the glue has dried, round the edges slightly and smooth the joint between the back- and side splash pieces with sandpaper.

16 **Attach the lip to the desk lid.** The lip at the bottom edge of the lid serves as a stop for pencils or papers. Sand the lip, rounding-over the top edge slightly, then glue and clamp it to the edge of the lid.

17 **Hinge the slant lid to the desk.** Mortise the hinges into the desk top. Adjust the depth of the mortises to allow for only a minimal clearance between the top and the lid. Adjust the width of the mortise so the plane of the upper surface of the top passes through the hinge pin. This position minimizes the projection of the hinge barrel above the desk surface while still allowing the lid to open fully. Screw the hinges to the top.

Set the desk lid in place and mark the hinge positions on the top edge. Mortise the lid for the hinges and screw them in place.

18 **Cut the drawer parts.** Measure the drawer opening in the assem-

(continued on page 20)

PLUNGE-ROUTING MORTISES

A good mortise-and-tenon joint requires a mortise with smooth, flat, parallel sides. Meeting these requirements with mallet and chisel is time-consuming, even with years of experience.

The need for well-cut mortises is perhaps better appreciated by restoration specialists than furniture makers. The restorer is asked to fix joints that have failed. Very often he discovers cracked and crumbly glue in the joint. It would be easy to blame the glue but the prob-

lem is really with the joint. Glue cracks and crumbles only when it is much too thick, indicating a poorly fitting joint. Such joints are occasionally found on furniture made by old masters, an indication that even with years of experience a good hand-cut mortise-and-tenon joint is not a sure thing.

The modern plunge router is capable of routing extremely accurate mortises, over and over again. The smooth, flat sides and uniform width of routed mortises win half of the battle

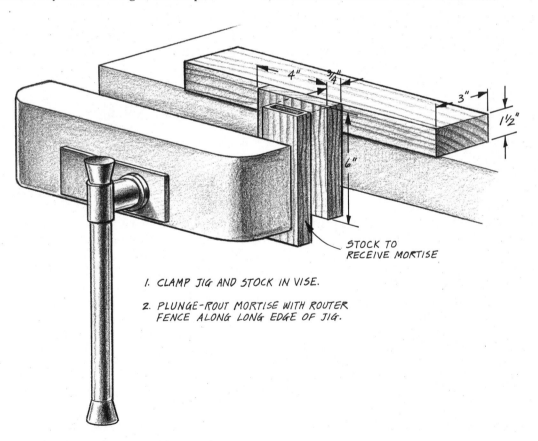

STOCK TO RECEIVE MORTISE

1. CLAMP JIG AND STOCK IN VISE.

2. PLUNGE-ROUT MORTISE WITH ROUTER FENCE ALONG LONG EDGE OF JIG.

for outstanding mortise-and-tenon joints. The other half is, of course, the tenons. (See page 60 for how to win that half of the battle.)

There are two secrets to successful mortising with a plunge router. The first is providing a broad platform for the router base. Trying to keep a router stable on a narrow edge is an invitation to disaster. A simple, easily made jig provides the needed stability.

The second secret is the selection of router bits. The bit of choice must plunge cleanly and easily and must pull the chips and shavings up, out of the mortise. Spiral upcut bits meet these requirements.

The mortising jig, in its simplest form, is shown in the drawing. The jig simply drops in position over the fixed face of a woodworking vise. The horizontal part, or table, provides a secure platform for the router. The rear edge of the table provides a smooth runway for the router's fence. The vertical part, or face, is clamped to the stock in the vise and ensures that the table will be perpendicular to the face of the stock and, therefore, that the mortise will be perpendicular to the edge of the stock.

If you want a more sophisticated jig, you can lengthen the table. The longer table provides room to clamp stops that limit the travel of the router. These, and stops to position the stock, can speed up mortising identical parts.

Spiral upcut bits, which are identical to machinist's end mills, are widely available from woodworking tool sources. These bits plunge cleanly and aggressively. The shearing action of the spiral produces smooth surfaces and the spiral lifts waste out of the cut just like an auger bit. Most spiral upcut bits are high-speed steel, not carbide. They will give long service

between sharpenings if you take care not to overheat them. To keep the bit cool, take shallow enough cuts that you can feed the cut fairly rapidly without too much force.

Cutting a mortise is a simple seven-step process.

1. Lay out the length and width of the mortise.
2. Clamp the stock in the jig in the vise so the mortise surface is flush with the jig table.
3. Select a spiral upcut bit the same diameter as the width of the mortise and chuck it in the router.
4. Adjust the router fence to position the bit between the laid-out sides of the mortise.
5. Adjust the maximum plunge depth to the depth of the mortise and adjust the depth turret to cut the mortise in at least three equal passes.
6. Plunge to the full depth of the mortise at the two ends of the mortise.
7. Remove the waste between the end holes in successive passes of increasing depth.

There you have it: a clean, accurate mortise, albeit with rounded ends. If the joint is blind, round the edges of the tenon to match the mortise. A sharp chisel is usually the best tool for this.

If you're making through mortise-and-tenon joints in a traditional design, you may want to square the ends of the mortise with a narrow chisel instead of rounding the edges of the tenon.

bled desk and, if it differs from the drawing, adjust the drawer part sizes so the drawer will fit the opening. Plane the stock and saw the parts to size. Edge-glue boards to get sufficient width for the drawer bottom, or make the bottom out of ¼-inch hardwood plywood.

19 **Cut the dovetails in the desk drawer.** The drawer in the original desk has traditional handcut dovetail joints, half-blind where the sides join the front, and through dovetails at the back. The dimensions of these dovetails are shown in the *Drawer Detail*, if you want to reproduce them exactly. If you would like the strength of a dovetailed drawer but are not concerned with historical accuracy, cut the joints with a router as explained in "Routing Dovetails" on page 36.

20 **Cut the bottom groove and assemble the drawer.** Rout a ¼-inch by ¼-inch drawer bottom groove in the front and sides. Make sure the groove is positioned within the tails on the sides so it won't show from the outside of the assembled drawer.

If your drawer bottom is ½-inch solid wood, plane a broad chamfer on its front and side edges so it will fit the bottom grooves. Sand the inside surfaces of the drawer parts, then glue and clamp the dovetails together. Slide the bottom into its grooves and secure it with two or three 1-inch nails into the back. Check the drawer for twist and, if necessary, clamp it to a flat surface while the glue dries.

21 **Install the drawer guides and runners.** Check that the drawer

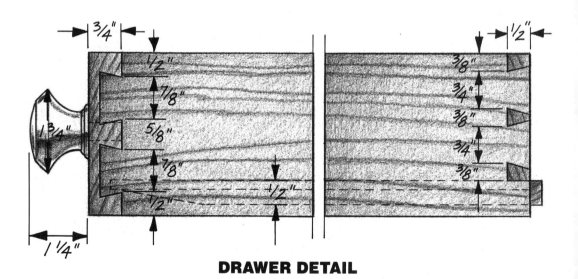

DRAWER DETAIL

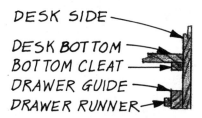

DRAWER SUPPORT DETAIL

guides fit between the legs, flush with the drawer opening. Then glue the guides to the desk sides, flush with the bottom edge of the sides as shown in the *Drawer Support Detail*. Check that the drawer runners will be flush with the top surface of the drawer rail at the same time that they are flush with the bottom edge of the guides. Then glue them to the guides.

22 **Turn and attach the drawer knobs.** If you have a lathe and want to turn the drawer knobs to match the original, follow the shape shown in the *Drawer Detail*. The original knobs have ⅜-inch-diameter stems, which are glued into holes in the drawer face. If you buy similar knobs, they will probably attach with a screw. When drilling the drawer front for either the knob stem or screw shank, back up the hole with scrap wood to prevent tear-out when the bit exits. Sand the outside of the drawer and try its fit in the opening. Sand or plane as necessary for an easy sliding fit, then install the knobs.

23 **Install the lid support and complete the desk.** Install the lid support according to the manufacturer's instructions.

Finish sand the desk, softening hard edges on all the upper parts that the user will feel but maintaining a crisp appearance elsewhere, especially on the legs.

Remove the hardware and dust the desk thoroughly with a tack cloth.

For a durable clear finish, apply three coats of a penetrating oil or two coats of a brushing lacquer or polyurethane.

COBBLER'S BENCH

A cobbler's bench is truly a thing of the past. Amateur weavers and spinners, woodworkers, and even blacksmiths are often happy to use century-old tools and furniture of their trades. But there aren't many amateur cobblers.

In a room furnished with antiques, or antique reproductions, however, the cobbler's bench has a unique place. It is one of very few nineteenth-century furniture items that functions well as a coffee table. The bench is a reasonable height and a good length and width for a coffee table. The drawer can keep magazines or a telephone directory instead of ham-

mers, punches, and other tools for leather-working. Fill the nail trays on top with after-dinner mints.

The original bench was made from various hardwoods. The seat, sides, cleats, and drawer front are hard maple, the legs and drawer knob are oak, and the hidden parts of the drawer are poplar. All the visible parts are a deep reddish brown.

1 **Select the stock and cut the bench parts.** If you want to be fussy and build a reproduction that will

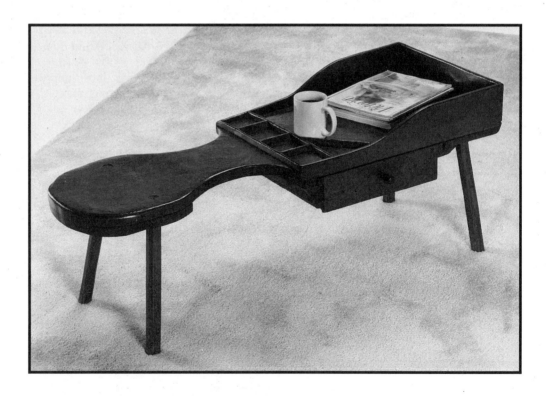

EXPLODED VIEW

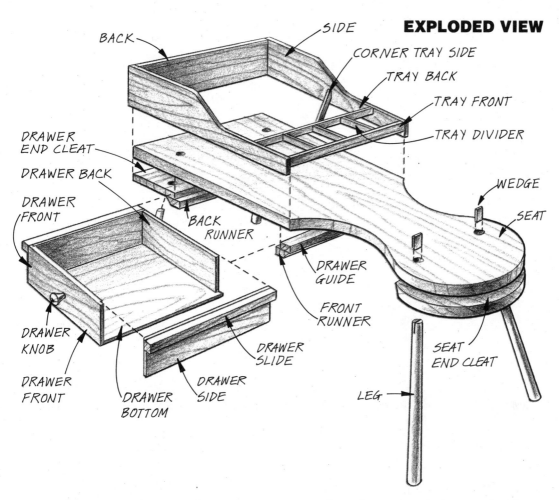

BACK

SIDE

CORNER TRAY SIDE

TRAY BACK

TRAY FRONT

TRAY DIVIDER

DRAWER END CLEAT

DRAWER BACK

DRAWER FRONT

BACK RUNNER

WEDGE

SEAT

DRAWER GUIDE

FRONT RUNNER

DRAWER KNOB

DRAWER FRONT

DRAWER BOTTOM

DRAWER SIDE

DRAWER SLIDE

SEAT END CLEAT

LEG

fool a museum curator, find wide boards for the seat and drawer bottom. Otherwise, edge-glue to obtain the necessary width. "Edge-Gluing" on page 6 provides helpful information. If you buy your lumber surfaced, substitute ¾-inch-thick stock for the parts listed as ⅞ inch thick. You can also change the thickness of the seat if necessary but it will look a bit anemic if you use stock only ¾ inch thick. If you redesign the drawer so the bottom fits in a groove, you can substitute ¼-inch plywood for the bottom.

Saw the surfaced stock to the dimensions specified by the Cutting List. Leave the tray parts as one long piece for the time being and saw the four wedges from scrap when you need them.

2 Cut out the seat. Lay out the shape of the seat right on the stock. The shape tapers from 15½ inches wide at the drawer end to 12¾ inches wide at the sitting end. Lay out the leg holes be-

CUTTING LIST

Part	Dimensions
Seat	1¹⁄₁₆″ × 15½″ × 45½″
Seat end cleat*	⅞″ × 12½″ × 10¾″
Drawer end cleat*	⅞″ × 15½″ × 7″
Legs (4)	1¼″ × 1¼″ × 14⅝″
Wedges (4)	³⁄₁₆″ × 1″ × 1½″
Drawer sides (2)	⅜″ × 3⅛″ × 14¼″
Drawer bottom	⅜″ × 14¼″ × 14¾″
Drawer front	¾″ × 3½″ × 14¾″
Drawer back	½″ × 3⅛″ × 14″
Drawer knob	⅞″ dia. × 2″
Drawer slides (2)	⅝″ × ¹³⁄₁₆″ × 14½″
Drawer guide	⅞″ × 1⅜″ × 14¾″
Front runner	⅞″ × 1¹⁵⁄₁₆″ × 14½″
Back runner	⅞″ × 2¼″ × 15½″
Sides (2)	½″ × 4½″ × 24½″
Back	½″ × 4½″ × 16½″
Tray front	½″ × ⅝″ × 13¾″
Tray dividers (3)	½″ × ⅝″ × 5″
Tray back	½″ × ⅝″ × 14″
Corner tray side	½″ × ⅝″ × 7¾″

Hardware

3d and 6d fine cut finish nails. Available from many building-supply stores and from Tremont Nail Company, P.O. Box 111, Wareham, MA 02571; (508) 295–0038.

*The grain of the cleats should go in the direction of the shorter dimension, not the longer dimension.

fore you cut the seat to shape. The layout will be easier while the stock is square.

The seat will be awkward to handle on a band saw. Saw it out with a saber saw if you have one, or with a coping saw. If you want to duplicate the original exactly, saw the curved portions at a 2-degree undercut angle. Hand plane or joint the straight tapered edges. Leave the curved parts rough for the time being.

3 **Attach the cleats to the seat.** Temporarily clamp the seat end cleat to the seat. Trace the seat onto the cleat. The drawer end cleat is flush with the outside surface of the sides and back in the completed bench. Hold the back in position and clamp the drawer end cleat to the seat flush with the back. Now hold the sides in position and trace their outer edges onto the cleat.

Saw both cleats to shape, undercutting 2 degrees, and plane the edges of the drawer end cleat. Glue and clamp both cleats to the underside of the seat. When the glue is dry, smooth the curved edges at the sitting end of the seat with rasps and sandpaper.

4 **Drill the leg holes.** The legs splay out at 7 degrees when viewed from either the front or the end of the bench. That works out to a 10-degree splay angle when viewed obliquely. To drill the leg holes, make a guide by cross-cutting a scrap of 1 × 4 at 10 degrees

from square. Position the guide on edge along the splay line shown in the *Top View*. Align a 1-inch auger or spade bit parallel to the angled end of the guide to drill the leg hole. Clamp a piece of scrap wood to the bottom of the seat to prevent tear-out when the bit exits. Drill all four leg holes this way.

5 **Shape the legs.** The legs taper slightly. They are 1¼ inches square at the bottom and 1-inch diameter (round) at the top. First, lay out a 1-inch

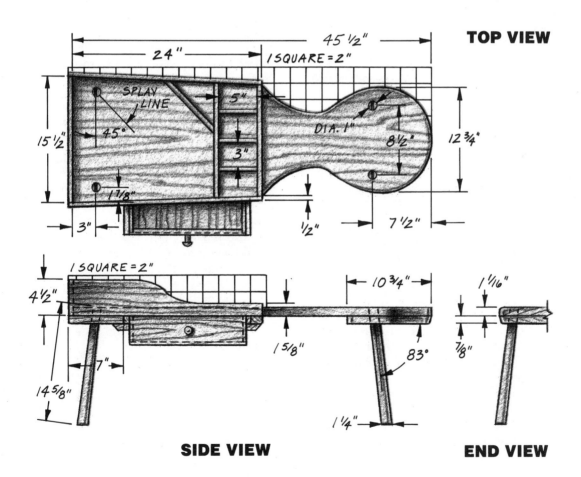

TOP VIEW

SIDE VIEW

END VIEW

circle centered on the top end of each leg. Plane all four sides to taper to a 1-inch square circumscribing the circle. Complete the shaping with a drawknife and spokeshave. The four edges of the finished legs should have a small round-over at the bottom, say a ⅛-inch radius, gradually increasing to a ½-inch-radius roundover at the top, forming the 1-inch-diameter tenon. The top 2 inches should be cylindrical, that is, without taper.

Saw a 1½-inch-deep slot in the top of each leg for the wedges that hold the legs in the seat.

6 Attach the legs to the seat. Turn the seat upside down on your workbench. Glue the legs into the leg holes with the wedge slots perpendicular to the length of the seat as shown in the *Top View.* When oriented in this direction, the wedges won't split the seat. Turn the assembly over, apply glue to the wedges, and hammer them into the slots. When the glue has dried, trim the legs and wedges flush with the surface of the seat.

Stand the bench upright on a flat surface. Place shims under the legs as necessary to level the seat. Hold a piece of ¼-inch or ⅜-inch-thick stock on the flat surface with the edge against the side of a leg and trace a line on the leg parallel to the flat surface. Repeat, tracing lines on all four sides of all four legs, then hand saw the legs to these lines. Chamfer the bottom edges of the legs slightly with a block plane.

7 Make the drawer. The tool drawer under the cobbler's bench is of simple construction, as shown in the *Drawer Detail.* The sides and bottom join the front in rabbets, the back simply butts the sides, and the bottom overlays the sides and back. These joints are glued and nailed with 3d nails.

Adjust a combination blade in the table saw to a height of ½ inch and, with multiple passes, crosscut a ⅜-inch-wide rabbet in the ends of the drawer front. Cut the rabbet for the drawer bottom in the same manner, sliding the drawer front along the saw fence. Drill a ⅝-inch hole in the center of the drawer front for the knob.

Glue and nail the drawer sides into the rabbets on the ends of the drawer front. Glue and nail the drawer back between the two sides, and nail the bottom to the assembly. If you make certain the bottom is square, attaching it will square up the drawer.

8 Attach the drawer knob and slides. The drawer knob can be turned on a lathe, but the knob on the original was whittled by hand to the shape shown in the *Drawer Detail.* You can also buy simple wooden knobs. Glue the drawer knob in the hole in the drawer front. If the fit is not snug, cut a slot in the shaft and wedge it in place.

Glue and clamp the drawer slides to the top outside edges of the drawer. The ¹³⁄₁₆-inch-wide surface of the slides goes against the drawer sides.

9 Fit the drawer guide and runners to the seat. Turn the bench upside down. The drawer end cleat serves as one drawer guide, as shown in

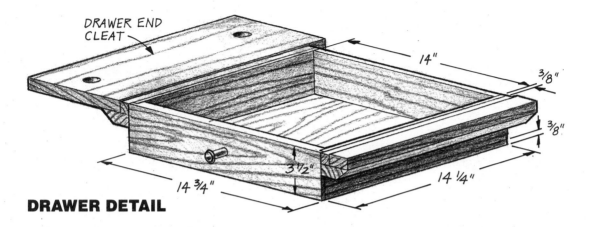

DRAWER END CLEAT

14"

3/8"

3/8"

14 1/4"

3 1/2"

14 3/4"

DRAWER DETAIL

the *Drawer Detail*. Position the drawer on the seat, against the cleat, with 1/16-inch spacers between the cleat and the slide. Position the other guide along the other slide, again with 1/16-inch spacers. Nail the guide to the seat with 6d nails, gluing the middle 3 to 4 inches.

Bevel an edge of each runner, then glue and nail the runners to the guides, again with 6d nails. Where the cleat serves as the guide, glue only the center 3 to 4 inches. Keep a 1/16-inch space between the runners and the drawer sides. When you remove the spacers, the drawer should slide easily.

10 **Attach the drawer stop.** The drawer can open to either side of the bench. If you omit the stop, you can make the drawer reversible but then you must stop the drawer yourself every time you close it. Make the 1/4-inch × 3/8-inch × 4 1/2-inch stop from scrap wood. To install it, close the drawer, position the stop so it touches the back of the drawer, and glue and nail it to the underside of the seat.

11 **Cut out and attach the sides and back.** Lay out the pattern on one of the sides. Tape or clamp the two sides together and cut out both at one time with a coping saw. Smooth the sawn edges with files and sandpaper, then separate the two sides.

Glue and nail the sides to the seat with 3d nails, then nail the back to the end of the seat and to the sides. Glue only the middle 3 or 4 inches of the back to allow seasonal movement of the seat.

12 **Install the tray parts.** These pieces create small compartments for the cobbler's nails and tacks. The sides of the tray parts on the original are beveled slightly. You can bevel them with a hand plane or spokeshave.

Trim the tray front to fit between the sides, then nail it in place with 3d nails. Predrill the nail holes to prevent splitting the small parts. Bevel the ends of the tray dividers to match the bevel on the sides of the front and back, then glue and nail them in place. Trim the tray back to fit and nail it in place. The remaining piece, the corner tray side, fits at an angle as shown in the *Top View*. Miter the ends at 45 degrees and nail it in place.

Now sand the top edges of all of the dividers. Keep in mind that these compartments were for nails and tacks so the edges, especially on the side toward the sitting cobbler, would receive a lot of wear. Reproduce this wear with coarse sandpaper, then smooth the edges out with finer sandpaper.

13 **Complete the cobbler's bench.** Soften all the edges of the bench with files and sandpaper, especially the edges of the seat and sides.

You can apply whatever finish will best suit your use for the bench, including a stain if you like. If you really want to create an authentic-looking finish, apply boiled linseed oil and put the bench where it will receive the maximum amount of direct sunlight. Give it another light rubbing with linseed oil every month or two and put it back in the sun. Over time the linseed oil will darken quite a bit, more on areas that receive the most light and less on areas that are more shaded. The visual effect of these naturally modulated tones is virtually impossible to duplicate with stains and will give the bench the appearance of a genuine antique.

SINGLE-DRAWER END TABLE

Country pine furniture, when left unpainted for many years, achieves a rich golden tone known as "pumpkin pine." This table has that color, as you can see in the photo on the back cover.

A small table like this has much to recommend it. It is very versatile because of its size. It will work well as a telephone table, a bedside table, a lamp table, a hall table, or an accent piece. The drawer adds to the table's usefulness.

The table is made entirely of pine. The top, curiously, is only ⅜ inch thick, and although you could make it thicker, it looks appropriate as is.

1 **Select the stock and cut the parts.** Although the original table is pine, almost any species of wood will make a fine table. Poplar is a good choice if you want to paint the table. Cut the parts to the dimensions specified by the Cutting List. Edge-glue boards as needed to make the top and drawer bottom. "Edge-Gluing" on page 6 gives detailed instructions. Since thin panels like the tabletop can easily cup in a short period of time, you might want to build the base before making up the thin top. Make the drawer bottom from ¼-inch plywood instead of solid wood if you prefer.

2 **Cut the mortises for the sides and back.** Lay out the mortises for the sides and back on all of the legs as

shown in the *Mortise-and-Tenon Details*. Rout the mortises as explained in "Plunge-Routing Mortises" on page 18. Square the ends of the mortises with a chisel.

EXPLODED VIEW

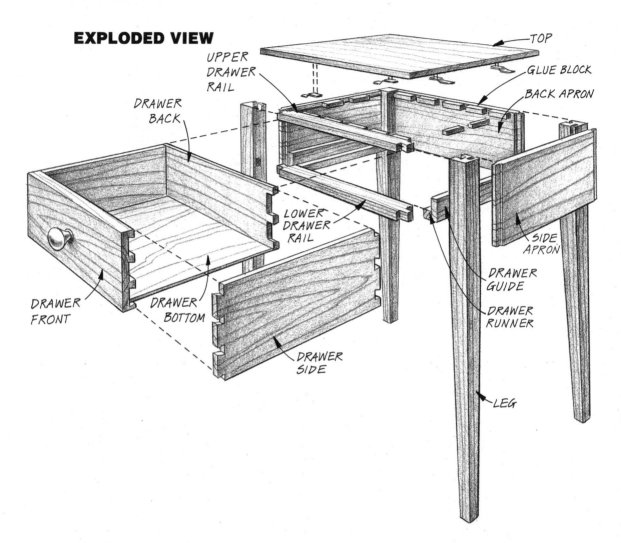

TOP

UPPER
DRAWER
RAIL

GLUE BLOCK

BACK APRON

DRAWER
BACK

LOWER
DRAWER
RAIL

SIDE
APRON

DRAWER
GUIDE

DRAWER
RUNNER

DRAWER
FRONT

DRAWER
BOTTOM

DRAWER
SIDE

LEG

3 **Mortise the front legs for the lower drawer rail.** Lay out and cut the mortises for the lower drawer rail the same way you cut the mortises for the sides and back. Notice, however, in the *Mortise-and-Tenon Details,* that these mortises are wider.

4 **Cut the upper drawer rail dovetails.** The upper drawer rail joins

each front leg with a single dovetail, as shown in the *Top View.* Lay out the dovetails on the drawer rail. Crosscut the dovetail shoulders on the table saw. Use the miter gauge and position the cuts with a stop block or the rip fence to keep the shoulders aligned. Clamp the drawer rail in a vise and saw the sides of the tails with a dovetail saw.

Trace the dovetails onto the top ends of the front legs with a layout knife.

Saw and chisel out the ⅝-inch-deep sockets. Since you can only saw part of the depth of the layout lines, you may find it helpful to remove some of the waste from the socket with ½-inch brad point drill bit. Check the fit of the dovetails in the sockets and pare the parts as necessary for the best fit.

5 **Taper the table legs.** Lay out the taper on the two inside surfaces of each leg with a straightedge and sharp pencil. The taper stops 21½ inches from the bottom of the legs. If you'd rather

avoid the exercise required to hand plane the entire tapers, make a simple tapering jig as shown in the *Taper Detail* and remove most of the stock on the table saw. Hand plane the final surfaces.

6 **Tenon the side and back aprons and lower drawer rail.** Double check that the dimensions of the mortises in the legs match those in the *Mortise-and-Tenon Details,* then lay out the apron tenons. Cut the tenons on the table saw as described in"Cutting Tenons" on page 60.

CUTTING LIST

Part	Dimensions
Sides aprons (2)	⅞″ × 6⅜″ × 14½″
Back apron	⅞″ × 6⅜″ × 16½″
Lower drawer rail	¾″ × 1½″ × 16½″
Upper drawer rail	⅝″ × 1½″ × 16¼″
Legs (4)	1½″ × 1½″ × 28″
Drawer guides (2)	⅝″ × 2″ × 13″
Drawer runners (2)	¾″ × ¾″ × 13″
Top	⅜″ × 16¼″ × 18⅝″
Glue blocks* (5)	⅝″ × ⅝″ × 2″
Glue blocks* (9)	½″ × ½″ × 2″
Drawer bottom	⅜″ × 14⅜″ × 14⁹⁄₁₆″
Drawer sides (2)	⅜″ × 4⅞″ × 14⅞″
Drawer front	⅞″ × 4⅞″ × 14¹⁵⁄₁₆″
Drawer back	⅜″ × 4⅛″ × 14¹⁵⁄₁₆

Hardware

8 tabletop fasteners.* Available from The Woodworker's Store, 21801 Industrial Blvd., Rogers, MN 55374-9514; (612) 428–3200. Item #70409.

2 wire nails, 1″

1 drawer knob, 2″ dia. Available from The Woodworker's Store. Item #23119.

*The top may be fastened with either glue blocks or tabletop fasteners but both are not required; see Step 8.

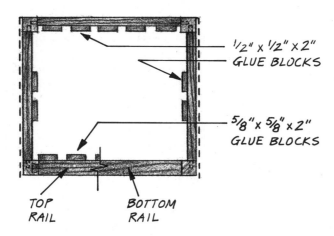

1/2" x 1/2" x 2" GLUE BLOCKS

5/8" x 5/8" x 2" GLUE BLOCKS

TOP RAIL

BOTTOM RAIL

TOP VIEW (TOP REMOVED)

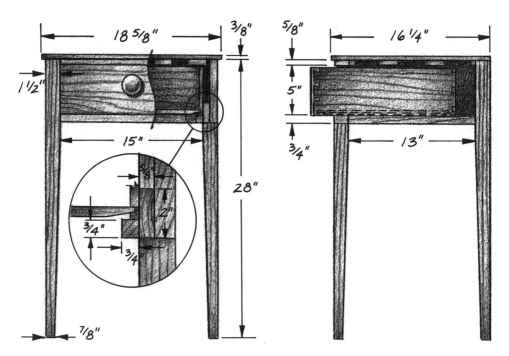

18 5/8"

3/8"

1 1/2"

15"

28"

7/8"

5/8

3/4"

2"

3/4

FRONT VIEW

5/8"

16 1/4"

5"

3/4"

13"

SIDE VIEW CROSS SECTION

SHOP TIP: The resin in pine and some other softwoods will bleed indefinitely if it has not been "set" (crystallized) by high enough kiln temperatures. To avoid problems, avoid buying from a stack if any of the boards show signs of flowing pitch. Pine that has been properly kiln dried for interior use should have no flowing pitch and should not feel tacky.

7 **Assemble the table.** Sand the exterior surfaces of the table parts but not the joints. Clamp each side apron to the corresponding front and back legs. Next, clamp the bottom drawer rail and back apron to the two side assemblies. Finally, clamp the top drawer rail dovetails down into their sockets. Check that the entire table is square by measuring diagonally from corner to corner on each side. If the diagonals on a side are equal, that side is square. Trim tenon shoulders as necessary to make the entire table square, then reassemble it with glue and clamp it.

8 **Install the drawer guides and runners.** Check the fit of the drawer guides. They should fit easily between the front and back legs and their inner surface should be flush with the inner surfaces of the legs. Trim them if necessary. Glue and clamp them to the

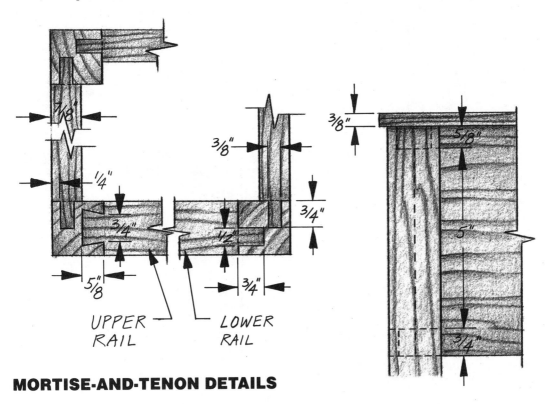

MORTISE-AND-TENON DETAILS

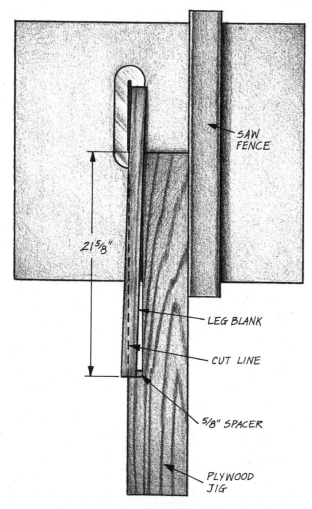

TAPER DETAIL

SAW FENCE

21⅝"

LEG BLANK

CUT LINE

5/8" SPACER

PLYWOOD JIG

9 Attach the tabletop. In today's centrally heated houses, the humidity can vary significantly from season to season. This causes expansion and contraction across the grain of wide pieces of wood like tabletops. The construction of the original antique table shown in the photo doesn't allow for these changes; the top is solidly fastened on all sides with glue blocks as shown in the drawings.

To duplicate the original exactly, glue and clamp the ⅝-inch-thick glue blocks to the back edge of the upper drawer rail. Then glue and clamp the ½-inch glue blocks to the inside of the aprons, flush with the top edge, as shown in the drawings. When these are dry, glue and clamp the top in position.

To allow for seasonal movement in today's typical household, fasten the top down with tabletop fasteners instead of glue blocks, as shown in *Top Fastener*. You can rout the slots for the fasteners with a 3⁄32-inch slotting cutter and arbor,

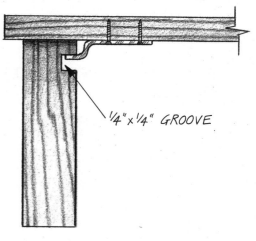

¼" x ¼" GROOVE

TOP FASTENER

inner surfaces of the side aprons, flush with the bottom edges of the aprons.

Check the fit of the drawer runners. They should be flush with the top surface of the lower drawer rail and flush with the bottom edge of the drawer guides. Trim them if necessary, then glue and clamp them to the guides.

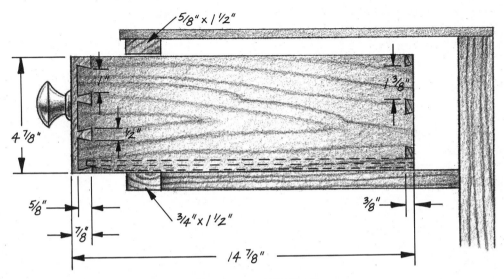

DRAWER DETAIL

or you can cut them with a biscuit joiner. The biscuit-joiner slot is more than $3/32$ inch wide but only the $7/16$-inch dimension shown in the drawing is critical. Use two fasteners on each of the four sides.

A third alternative for fastening the top is to make wooden tabletop fasteners similar in function to the metal ones shown in the drawing.

10 **Cut the drawer dovetails.** The drawer in the original table has traditional hand-cut dovetail joints, half-blind where the sides join the front, and through dovetails at the back. The dimensions of these dovetails are shown in the *Drawer Detail* if you want to reproduce them exactly. If you would like the strength of a dovetailed drawer but are not concerned with historical accuracy, cut the joints with a router as explained

in "Routing Dovetails" on page 36. In this case you will need to adjust the length of the sides and, depending on what dovetail templates you own, you may need to adjust the thickness of the sides and back.

11 **Cut the drawer bottom dado.** If you hand-cut the drawer dovetails to the dimensions in the *Drawer Detail*, the tails on the sides will cover the ends of the drawer bottom groove in the drawer front. In this case you can cut the drawer bottom groove in the drawer front and sides with a $1/4$-inch dado cutter on the table saw.

If you cut the dovetails with a router jig, however, the groove in the drawer front may need to be blind on

(continued on page 38)

ROUTING DOVETAILS

There are two approaches to cutting dovetails with a router. The first approach is very efficient, making a strong joint quickly with a simple jig, but is limited to uniformly spaced half-blind dovetails. This approach is particularly well suited for joining drawer sides to their fronts and backs.

The second approach is more versatile, making variably spaced through or half-blind dovetails, but requires a more complex and costly jig and more steps in the operation. This approach is well suited for exposed joinery as frequently found in the corners of a blanket chest.

The explanations that follow deal only with the first approach, and only with the basic principles. Many router makers sell a jig taking this approach and each has minor features that are unique. The basic principles remain the same in all of them.

To understand the efficiency of routing half-blind dovetails, imagine a dovetail joint as shown in (1) of *Routing Tails and Sockets To-*

gether. Pull the joint apart and fold the vertical part down 180 degrees. Hold the tails up to the sockets as shown in (2) and notice how the cuts needed to make both pieces are very similar. By aligning the end of the tail piece with the surface of the socket piece, and offsetting the socket piece, as shown in (3), both the pins and the sockets can be cut in a single operation.

The router jig performs two essential functions. It clamps the two pieces in the correct relationship to each other and it holds a template in position on the clamped pieces. The router uses a template guide to follow the template while making the cuts.

The following steps will guide you through the process. Begin with test cuts to properly adjust the depth of cut of the router.

1 **Arrange the parts.** Keeping track of which parts go where is not difficult if you remain organized. Position the parts on your

ROUTING TAILS AND SOCKETS TOGETHER

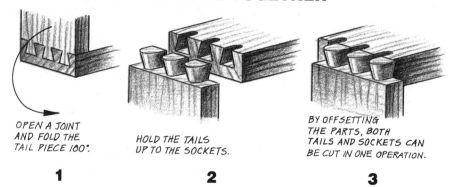

OPEN A JOINT AND FOLD THE TAIL PIECE 180°.

HOLD THE TAILS UP TO THE SOCKETS.

BY OFFSETTING THE PARTS, BOTH TAILS AND SOCKETS CAN BE CUT IN ONE OPERATION.

1   **2**   **3**

workbench the way you intend them to go together. Take them two parts at a time as you go through the following steps, cut the joint, then put them back in position.

2 Clamp the two halves of a joint in the jig. Choose two parts to be joined. Hold them in their final joined position, then turn the joining corner inside out. This is their position for cutting the joint. Clamp the tail piece vertically in the dovetail jig with the joint end uppermost. Clamp the socket piece horizontally in the jig with the joint end butted against the tail piece. Readjust the tail piece so the joint end is flush with the upper surface of the socket piece. Fit the template to the jig, resting on the stock, and tighten its fasteners.

3 Rout the joint. Starting at the left, guide the router so the template guide follows the first opening in the template. This will cut a socket and one side of a tail. Follow the opening all the way to the end. Then follow the

opening back out, around the end of the finger to the right, keeping the guide in contact with the rounded end of the finger, then into the second opening. Continue, keeping the guide in contact with the fingers, until you have finished the last side of the last tail, beyond which there is no socket.

4 Adjust the depth of cut. The depth of cut of the router adjusts the fit of the joint. Socket depth and tail length are always equal. When this dimension is correct the joint fits perfectly as shown in (1) of *Adjusting the Fit of the Joint*. If the depth is too great, as shown in (2), the joint won't go together. If it's too shallow, as shown in (3), the joint will be loose. Remember: Deep is tight, shallow is loose. An adjustment of $\frac{1}{64}$ inch makes a big difference in the fit of the joint. Retest each adjustment by cutting a full joint of at least three tails. When the test parts require a firm push but not pounding, cut the joints for your project.

ADJUSTING THE FIT OF THE JOINT

PROPER DEPTH OF CUT
PRODUCES PERFECTLY
FITTING JOINTS.

IF DEPTH IS TOO
GREAT, THE JOINT
WON'T GO TOGETHER.

IF DEPTH IS TOO
SHALLOW, THE JOINT
WILL BE LOOSE.

1   **2**   **3**

both ends. A blind groove will be easier to cut with a router, preferably a plunge router.

Cut the drawer bottom grooves as appropriate, then hand plane a bevel on the front and sides of the drawer bottom so it fits the grooves.

12 **Assemble the drawer.** Sand the drawer parts. Glue the drawer sides, front, and back together on a flat surface. Check that the assembly is square by checking that the diagonals are equal. Slide the drawer bottom in place from the back and nail through the bottom into the drawer back. A couple of 1-inch wire nails should suffice.

The knob specified in the Cutting List is the same diameter as the knob on the original but doesn't project as far from the front of the drawer. If you use this knob, drill a screw hole in the center of the drawer front for the knob screw.

If you turn your own knob to the shape shown in the *Drawer Detail,* include a ½-inch-diameter tenon on the knob and drill a matching hole in the center of the drawer front. Screw or glue the knob to the drawer front.

13 **Apply the finish.** To stay true to the period of the original table, you can apply an oil or a shellac finish. First give the table a final sanding. Then apply several coats of a linseed or tung-oil finish, or brush on several coats of shellac. The shellac dries fast and applies easily. If you're more concerned with serviceability than historical accuracy, you could apply a polyurethane. A milk-paint finish would be in character and give good service, even though this particular table shows no sign of ever having been painted. For more on milk paint, see page 100.

MILLER'S DESK

This desk, found in a barn in rural Berks County, Pennsylvania, is a style that was often used for record keeping in mills and feed stores. It would work well as a kitchen desk or as a stand for a dictionary, an open cookbook, or a guest book.

The construction is fairly simple: dado and rabbet joints held together with glue and finish nails and a few wood screws. The plans provided here reflect a few minor changes to suit today's standard lumber sizes and methods of work. The desk in the photo is made of mahogany and is finished with brick red paint. Suit your own taste in choosing a wood and a finish.

1 **Cut the parts to size.** Edge-glue narrower boards as necessary to obtain the widths specified by the Cut-

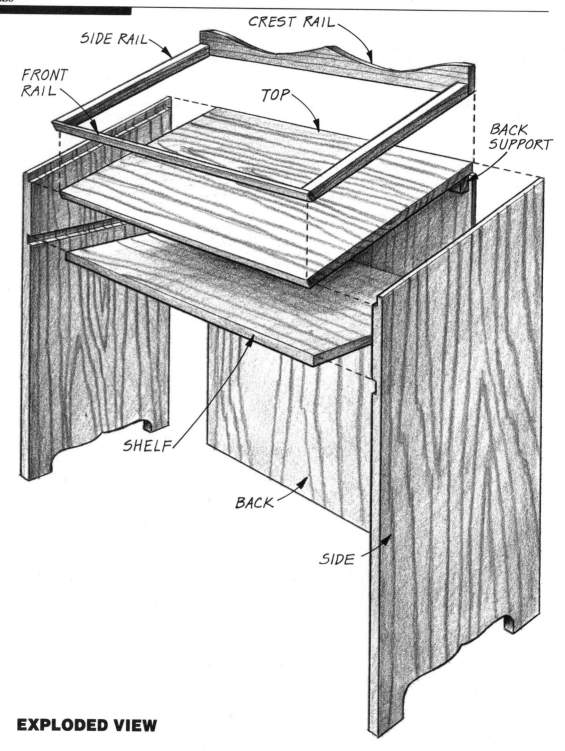

SIDE RAIL

CREST RAIL

FRONT RAIL

TOP

BACK SUPPORT

SHELF

BACK

SIDE

EXPLODED VIEW

ting List, then cut all of the parts to the sizes listed. See page 6 for more on edge-gluing. Make the back from ¼-inch hardwood plywood and all of the other parts from solid lumber.

2 **Cut the sides to shape.** The sides are angled to hold the slanted top as shown in the *Side View*. Lay out the angle from the dimensions given, set the table-saw miter gauge to the angle, and saw the angle on both side pieces.

Lay out the shape of the foot cutouts in the sides as shown in the *Side View*. Make the cutouts with a coping saw or a saber saw, then smooth the sawed edges with scrapers and sandpaper.

3 **Dado and rabbet the sides.** The shelf fits into dadoes in the sides;

SHOP TIP: To set a miter gauge to an angle that you've laid out on the stock, place the miter gauge upside down on the stock. Hold the miter-gauge fence against the edge of the stock while aligning the miter-gauge bar with the cut line, then tighten the knob. The cut must be made with the layout line down. You'll need to extend the layout line around the edge of the stock in order to have a mark for lining up the blade.

the top and back fit into rabbets. To cut these joints, set up a ¾-inch-wide dado blade on the table saw. Set the depth of cut to ⅜ inch. Make a test cut to be sure the shelf fits in the dado snugly. Cut the dadoes for the shelf as shown in the *Side View*. Be sure to make a left

---

CUTTING LIST

Part	Dimensions
Sides (2)	¾″ × 17″ × 33¼″
Shelf	¾″ × 16¾″ × 29¾″
Top	¾″ × 18″ × 29¾″
Back*	¼″ × 29¾″ × 32½″
Back support	¾″ × 1″ × 29″
Crest rail	¾″ × 2½″ × 30½″
Side rails (2)	¾″ × 1″ × 16⅞″
Front rail	½″ × ¾″ × 30½″

Hardware

4d finish nails
4 flathead wood screws, #6 × 1¼″
#4 × ¾″ flathead wood screws

*Use hardwood plywood.

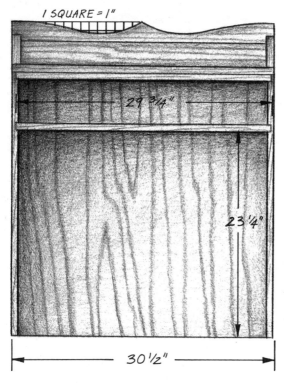

FRONT VIEW

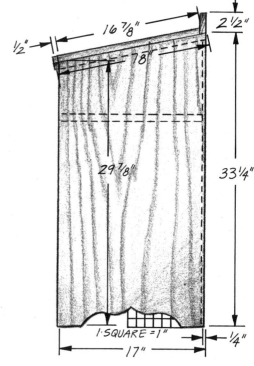

SIDE VIEW

and right side; the two are mirror images of one another.

Fit a rabbeting auxiliary fence to the rip fence as explained in "Cutting Rabbets with a Dado Cutter" on the opposite page. With the depth of cut still at ⅜ inch, adjust the fence to cut a full ¾-inch-wide rabbet. Cut the rabbets for the top by running the angled end of each side along the fence, past the blade. Move the fence over to cover all but ¼ inch of the cutter when cutting the rabbets for the back.

4 Bevel the top and the back support. The back edge of the top is beveled as shown in the *Cross Section at Back*. Tilt the table-saw blade to 79 degrees. Guide the top along the rip fence to make the cut. While the saw is set to this angle, bevel one edge of the back support and one edge of the crest rail as shown in the drawing.

5 Assemble the desk. Sand the sides, shelf, top, and back. Assemble the sides, shelf, and top without glue to make sure they will go together correctly. When you are sure the pieces all fit, disassemble them. Apply glue to the dadoes and rabbets and clamp the parts back together. Reinforce the joints with

CUTTING RABBETS WITH A DADO CUTTER

Cutting rabbets with a dado cutter may seem stone simple at first blush but can get a bit involved. If all of the pieces that need a rabbet are of the same width and the sides are parallel, it's a simple matter to guide one edge of the stock against the table-saw fence while cutting the rabbet in the other edge.

But if the pieces are of varying width, or are tapered, you will need to cut the rabbet in the edge that is against the fence. To keep the dado cutter a safe distance away from the steel fence, attach an auxiliary fence with a cutout to the saw fence.

Make the auxiliary fence out of ¾-inch-thick hardwood plywood or a straight-grained piece of stable hardwood like poplar or cherry. Make it the length and height of your table-saw fence. If your fence is predrilled for auxiliary fence bolts, fasten the new fence to the table-saw fence with stove bolts and wing nuts. If it isn't predrilled, you may be able to drill it yourself, or you can clamp the auxiliary fence in place.

To lay out the cutout, install the new fence and mount your dado cutter on the saw arbor. Adjust the depth of cut to the maximum, then bring the fence right up alongside the dado cutter. Mark the maximum cutting circle of the dado cutter on the auxiliary fence. Remove the auxiliary fence and saw to the line with a coping saw or band saw.

You can now safely rabbet the edge of stock that is against the fence while protecting both the steel fence and the dado cutter. You can also cut rabbets that are narrower than the dado cutter by adjusting the fence to house part of the dado cutter width; just be careful not to house so much of the cutter that it touches the steel fence where you can't see it.

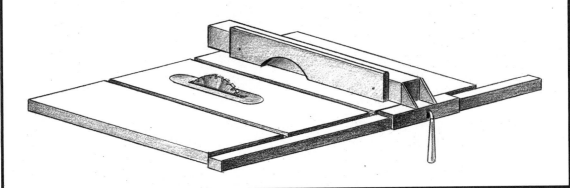

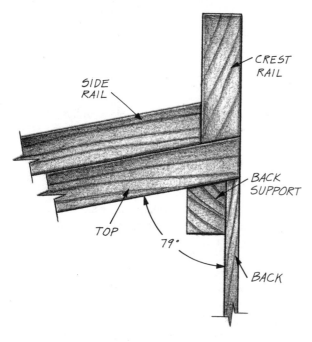

CROSS SECTION AT BACK

finish nails. Measure the diagonals to make sure the desk is square. Apply glue to the beveled edge of the back support, center it under the back edge of the top, and screw it in place with #6 × 1¼-inch flathead wood screws. Set the desk aside while the glue dries.

6 **Make and attach the rails.** Saw the crest rail to the shape shown in the *Front View*. Smooth the sawn edges with scrapers and sandpaper, then glue and clamp it in place along the back edge of the top. Hold the side rails and front rail in place to make sure they will all fit as shown in the drawings, then glue and nail the side rails to the sides. Finally, fit the front rail snugly against the side rails and glue and nail it to the top.

7 **Attach the back and apply a finish.** Put the back panel in place and secure it to the sides and along the shelves with #4 × ¾-inch flathead wood screws. Apply a finish appropriate for your intended use. If you decide to paint it like the original, see "Milk Paint" on page 100.

TAVERN TABLE

Taverns are not a particularly forgiving environment; only the strongest of their furniture makes it to the antique market. The table in the photo survived. Broad aprons join the stout legs with ½-inch-thick tenons. Stretchers further reinforce the legs. But even the thick top has one side broken off.

There were many serious demands on a tavern table. It had to accommodate the pints or quarts of a variable number of patrons but could not waste the proprietor's floor space. And it had to be as stable as possible to remain upright among patrons who might not. The oval top of this example gives it flexibility; a rectangular top of the same size is only inviting to four. Yet the table, 25 inches wide and 31 inches long, is quite compact. The relatively low height and flared legs give it good stability.

Diane Windle of Log Cabin Antiques in Parkesburg, Pennsylvania, who owns the table, rather likes the broken top. With one side gone, the table fits right up against a wall. When making your own table, you can make the top a complete oval or cut it off as shown in the *Top View.* Either way you'll have a useful table that your great-grandchildren will be able to gather 'round after a hard day's work at the blacksmith shop.

Make the table from pine or fir to match the original or from a hardwood like cherry, maple, or oak to match the rest of your tavern.

1 Cut the stock to size. Edge-glue 6/4 (six-quarter) stock to obtain the 25-inch width of the tabletop. (For more on edge-gluing, see page 6.) The legs will come easily from 8/4 (eight-quarter) stock and the remaining parts will come from 4/4 (four-quarter) stock if you buy your wood unplaned and do your own surfacing. If you're using dressed stock, 4/4 boards will be $^{13}/_{16}$ inch thick at best. A few minor adjustments to the dimensions will allow you to use it instead of the ⅞-inch stock specified. When cutting the parts to the dimensions specified by the Cutting List, cut the aprons and the short stretchers about ¼ inch longer than listed. Cut the long stretcher about 1 inch longer than listed.

EXPLODED VIEW

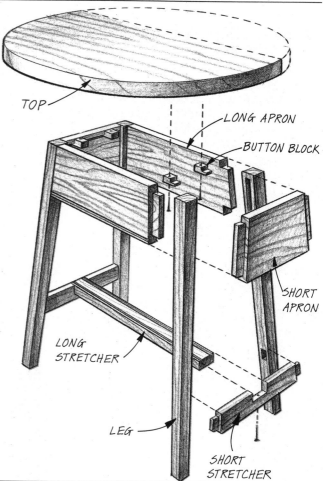

TOP

LONG APRON

BUTTON BLOCK

SHORT APRON

LONG STRETCHER

LEG

SHORT STRETCHER

CUTTING LIST

Part	Dimensions
Legs (4)	$1\frac{5}{8}'' \times 1\frac{5}{8}'' \times 25\frac{3}{8}''$
Short aprons (2)	$\frac{7}{8}'' \times 5\frac{3}{8}'' \times 13\frac{3}{4}''$
Long aprons (2)	$\frac{7}{8}'' \times 5\frac{3}{8}'' \times 20''$
Short stretchers (2)	$\frac{7}{8}'' \times 1\frac{5}{8}'' \times 16\frac{7}{8}''$
Long stretcher	$\frac{7}{8}'' \times 1\frac{3}{4}'' \times 24''$
Button blocks (4)	$\frac{3}{4}'' \times 1\frac{1}{4}'' \times 2''$
Top	$1\frac{3}{8}'' \times 25'' \times 31\frac{1}{4}''$

Hardware

2 flathead wood screws, #8 × 1¼″
4 flathead wood screws, #8 × 1½″

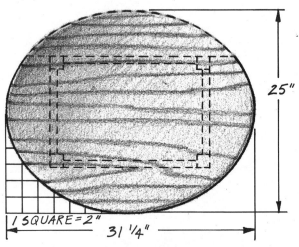

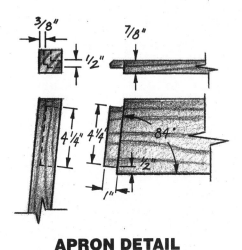

TOP VIEW

APRON DETAIL

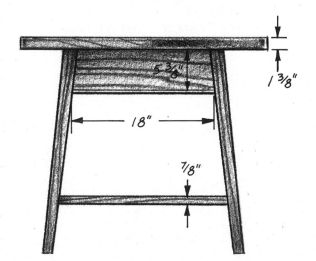

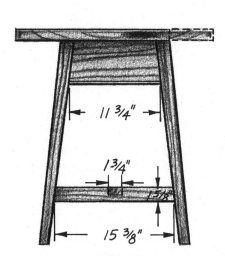

FRONT VIEW

SIDE VIEW

2 **Mortise the legs.** Before laying out the mortises, it's necessary to establish a finished cut end from which to measure. Tilt the table-saw blade 6 degrees and adjust the miter gauge to 6 degrees from square. Trim one end of each leg at these settings. This trimmed end will be the bottom of each leg. Lay out the mortises on the legs as shown in the *Apron Detail* and the *Stretcher Detail*. Check the *Exploded View* for the location of the stretcher

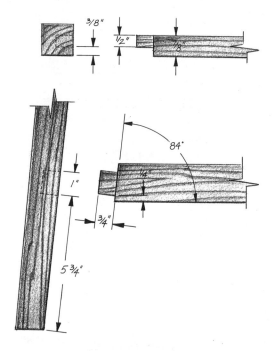

STRETCHER DETAIL

splay of the legs. Cut the ends of the aprons first, at an 84-degree angle. The bottom edge of the short aprons should be 13¾ inches long; the long aprons should be 20 inches long, measured the same way.

Cut the long side of the tenons with a dado cutter on the table saw. Set the depth of cut to slightly less than ⅜ inch. Position the rip fence so that it's 1 inch from the left (outside) of the blade to act as a stop. With the miter gauge adjusted to 6 degrees from square, test cut a board the same thickness as the aprons. Check the fit in a mortise. Adjust the thickness of the tenon by raising or lowering the blade. When test pieces fit nicely in your mortises, cut tenons on the ends of the aprons. You'll have to readjust the miter gauge to 6 degrees from square in the opposite direction after cutting one mortise on each apron. Cut the cheeks and shoulders at the ends of the tenons with a dovetail saw.

mortises to make sure you have two pairs of legs, not four identical ones. Cut the mortises as explained in "Plunge-Routing Mortises" on page 18. Square the ends of the mortises with a chisel.

3 Taper the legs. The legs taper from 1⅝ inches square at the top to 1¼ inches square at the bottom. Saw the taper on the outside, unmortised surfaces of the legs using a tapering jig as shown in the *Taper Detail*. Plane out the saw marks.

4 Tenon the aprons. The ends of the aprons, and the shoulders of the tenons, are at an 84-degree angle from the bottom edge. This determines the

5 Tenon the short stretchers. If the angles on the ends of the aprons are not exactly 84 degrees, the length of the short stretchers will vary from the dimensions in the drawings. To lay out the tenons on these stretchers, first assemble (without glue) the short aprons to the legs. Clamp the assemblies so they're solid. Hold, or clamp, the stretchers to the leg assemblies; center them from end to end and center them on the stretcher mortises. Scribe the shoulder lines where the edges of the legs meet the stretchers. Then lay out the remainder of the tenons as shown in the *Stretcher Detail* and cut the tenons with a dovetail saw.

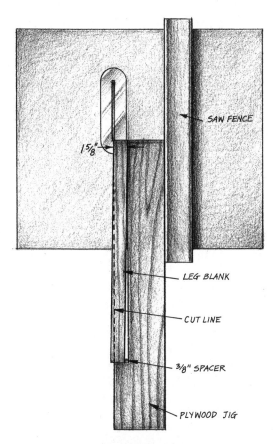

1 5/8"

SAW FENCE

LEG BLANK

CUT LINE

3/8" SPACER

PLYWOOD JIG

TAPER DETAIL

SHOP TIP: If you need to preserve maximum thickness when surfacing stock, rip and crosscut it to the approximate dimensions of the project parts before you surface it. This minimizes the amount of warp in the individual pieces and allows you to get a smooth surface with less stock removal. If you'll still have trouble keeping the thickness you need, smooth the front surface before you smooth the back. You can leave blemishes on the back if necessary in order to preserve thickness.

each short stretcher, drill and countersink a shank hole for a #8 flathead wood screw up into the cutout. Place the long stretcher in the cutouts, mark it for correct length, and cut it to length on the table saw.

7 **Bead the stretcher and aprons.** The original table is beaded along the edges that could be expected to re-

6 **Cut the long stretcher joints.** The long stretcher fits into cutouts in the short stretchers. Assemble (without glue) the legs, all four aprons, and the short stretchers. Clamp all the joints tight. Center the long stretcher on the short stretchers, then scribe the ends of the cutouts in the short stretchers from the long stretcher. Lay out the remainder of the cutouts from the *Lap Joint Detail* and make the cutouts with a dado cutter on the table saw.

From the center of the underside of

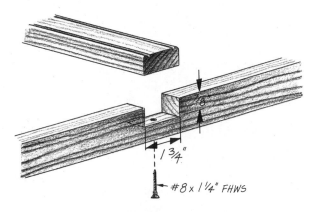

1 3/4"

#8 x 1 1/4" FHWS

LAP JOINT DETAIL

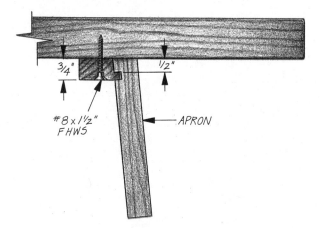

3/4"   1/2"

#8 x 1½"
F H W S

APRON

BUTTON BLOCK DETAIL

ceive abuse. These include the top edges of the long stretcher and the lower edges of the aprons. Cut these beads with a beading bit in a table-mounted router.

8 **Groove the aprons.** The inside top edges of the short aprons require a groove for the button blocks. Cut these grooves with a ¼-inch straight bit in a table-mounted router as shown in the *Button Block Detail.*

9 **Assemble the understructure.** Sand all the pieces. Glue and clamp the table together. Because the legs are splayed, you may need to place wedge-shaped clamping blocks between the clamps and the wood. Glue and screw the long stretcher into its notches in the short stretchers. Use 1¼-inch screws. When the glue dries, trim the tops of the legs flush with the tops of the aprons with a back saw.

10 **Shape and attach the top.** Cut the top to the shape shown in the *Top View.* Ease the edges slightly with files and sandpaper. Sand the whole top and place it upside down on your bench. Center the leg assembly upside down on top of it.

Saw tongues on the button blocks as shown in the *Button Block Detail.* Make sure the grain runs in the 2-inch direction. Drill and countersink a shank hole for a #8 screw in each block. Place the tongues in the grooves in the aprons, one block near each leg. Screw the blocks to the tabletop with #8 × 1½-inch flathead wood screws.

11 **Finish the table.** Finish the table to meet the demands that you'll place on it. For the kind of service that the table was designed to withstand, Behlen's Rockhard Tabletop Varnish would be a good choice. If you anticipate a tamer existence, a wide variety of finishes will give good service.

CANDLE STAND

An antique dealer in Dublin, Pennsylvania, found this small table at an estate auction. The auctioneer judged that it was made in the late 1800s, but beyond that its history is unknown. It's made of pine and still shows marks from the maker's plane. The construction is not very sophisticated, the whole table

being nailed together, but it's durable enough to be in good shape after more than a century.

An interesting feature of the table is a small hidden shelf under the top. The shelf is readily accessible from underneath, so it's doubtful that it was meant to conceal valuables. It was probably

EXPLODED VIEW

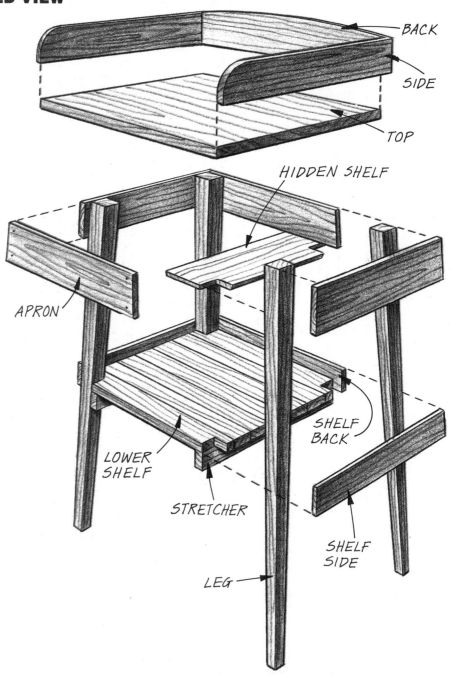

BACK

SIDE

TOP

HIDDEN SHELF

APRON

SHELF BACK

LOWER SHELF

STRETCHER

SHELF SIDE

LEG

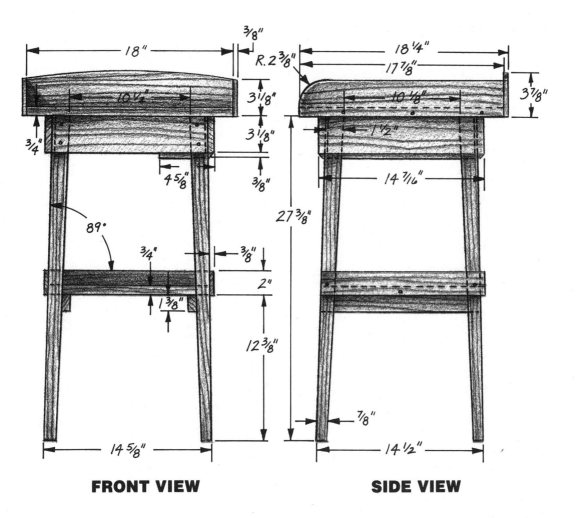

FRONT VIEW

SIDE VIEW

used as a place for spare candles. Whatever its original purpose, the shelf is a nice detail.

1 Cut the pieces to size. Saw all of the parts to the sizes specified by the Cutting List, allowing enough extra to smooth out the sawn surfaces. You can resaw thicker boards to make the ⅜-inch-thick pieces. The top and shelf

can be glued up from narrower boards. Or you can make each of them from just two wider boards and nail them in place side by side without gluing them together. That's how the original was built.

2 Taper the legs. The legs are tapered on their two inside surfaces as shown in the *Taper Detail*. Make a tapering jig from a piece of plywood as

CUTTING LIST

Part	Dimensions
Legs (4)	1½″ × 1½″ × 27½″
Aprons* (4)	¾″ × 3⅛″ × 15″
Stretchers (2)	¾″ × 1⅜″ × 14″
Lower shelf	¾″ × 14″ × 14⅛″
Shelf sides (2)	⅜″ × 2″ × 14⅜″
Shelf back	⅜″ × 2″ × 14⅞″
Hidden shelf	⅜″ × 4⅝″ × 14⅜″
Sides (2)	⅜″ × 3⅛″ × 18¼″
Back	⅜″ × 3⅞″ × 18¾″
Top	¾″ × 17⅞″ × 18″

Hardware

1½″ cut finish nails. Available from many building-supply stores and from Tremont Nail Company, P.O. Box 111, Wareham, MA 02571; (508) 295–0038. Item #CE-4.

*Trim to finish length during construction.

shown in the drawing. Hold the leg against the jig (and the jig against the saw fence) as you saw them.

3 **Rabbet the aprons.** The aprons are rabbeted where they join the legs as shown in the *Exploded View.* Lay out the rabbets as shown in the *Apron Detail.* Mark the center of the boards first, then measure out from the center as shown. Note that these rabbets are cut across the aprons at an 89-degree angle.

Set up as wide a dado blade as possible on the table saw. Adjust the depth of cut to ³⁄₁₆ inch. Set the miter gauge at an 89-degree angle to the blade. Cut a rabbet on one end of each apron, then reset the miter gauge at a 91-degree angle and cut the second rabbet on each apron.

4 **Cut the front and rear aprons to length.** Hold a leg in place in one of the rabbets in the front apron. Mark the apron for length along the outside of the leg, then cut it to length on the table saw. Repeat to cut both ends of both the front and rear aprons to length.

5 **Join the front and rear aprons to the legs.** Sand the legs and aprons. Position two of the legs in the rabbets of the front apron. Make sure that two of the tapered surfaces of the legs face each other and that the other two face away from the apron. Check that the bottoms of the legs are spaced apart as shown in the *Front View,* then glue and nail the front apron to the legs. Use two nails per leg and predrill the holes with a ³⁄₃₂-inch drill bit. Glue and

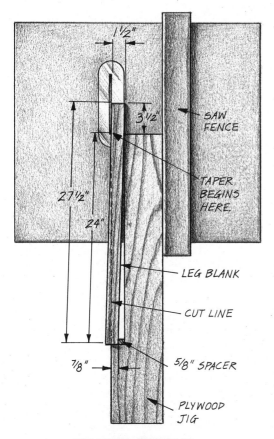

TAPER DETAIL

1½"

3½"

SAW FENCE

TAPER BEGINS HERE

27½"

24"

LEG BLANK

CUT LINE

7/8"

5/8" SPACER

PLYWOOD JIG

nail the rear apron to the other two legs in the same way.

6 **Cut the side aprons to length.** Hold a side apron in place between the front and rear leg assemblies. Mark its length along the front and rear aprons. Repeat with the other side apron. Cut both aprons to length on the table saw.

7 **Attach the side aprons.** Glue and nail the side aprons in place between the front and rear leg assemblies. Again, check that the legs are correctly spaced at the bottom and use two nails per leg.

8 **Attach the stretchers.** Sand both stretchers. Mark the stretcher location on the inside of each leg as shown in the *Front View.* Apply glue to the stretchers, then nail them to the legs.

9 **Notch and attach the lower shelf.** To lay out the leg notches on the lower shelf, hold it in place on top of the stretchers and mark where the inner surfaces of the legs contact the shelf. You'll have to cant the opposite edge up at an angle because the shelf won't fit until the notches are cut but that shouldn't matter. Once you have the locations of both sides of all four notches marked in this manner, use a square to lay out the sides of the notches. Saw out the notches with a backsaw or coping saw. Sand the shelf and put it in place on the stretchers. Predrill and nail the shelf down with three or four nails per stretcher.

10 **Miter and attach the shelf sides and back.** Tilt the blade on the table saw to 45 degrees. Cut one end of each shelf side and both ends of the shelf back at 45 degrees as shown in the *Exploded View.* If you want to, you can cut these miters at an 89-degree angle from the edge, similar to the rabbets in the aprons. If you do, though, you'll

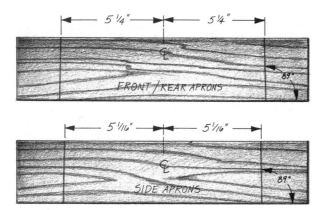

APRON DETAIL

then glue and nail it in place under the aprons.

12 Shape the sides and back. The front corners of the sides are rounded as shown in the *Side View.* Lay out the curves with a compass and cut them with a coping saw. The back has a slight arch to it. Mark the center of the piece along its top edge. Mark the ends 3⅛ inches up from the bottom edge. Flex a yardstick until it connects the three points in a smooth curve, then have a helper trace the curve with a pencil. Saw along the line with a coping saw and smooth all the curves with sandpaper.

13 Assemble the sides, back, and top. Sand the top. Assembling the sides and back at the top is similar to assembling the shelf sides and back. Miter the ends of the sides and back, then nail them to the top as shown in the *Exploded View.* To attach the top, first position it on the table as shown in the *Front View* and *Side View,* then nail it to the aprons.

be building a more nicely joined table than the original.

Sand the pieces, then attach them to the table. Align one of the shelf sides with the bottom of the shelf. Hold the shelf back in place to help position the shelf side from front to back. When it's in place, nail it to the shelf and legs as shown in the *Side View.* Position the shelf back and nail it in place, then attach the final shelf side.

11 Cut and attach the hidden shelf. Notch the hidden shelf to fit around the legs the same way you notched the lower shelf. Bevel the three outside edges of the shelf to a 45-degree angle on the table saw. Sand the shelf,

14 Finish the table. Examine the assembled table and touch up as necessary with sandpaper. Then stain and finish it. The table shown is stained a medium walnut brown and finished with several coats of satin varnish.

TRESTLE TABLE

This cherry coffee table, while not an antique, borrows its lines from country work tables. Tables meant strictly for dining were of less robust construction but the usual country table had to serve a variety of purposes. A table that wouldn't stand up under a side of pork was in the way when it was most needed. In designing this table, Darwin Jack of Oelwein, Iowa, has captured the flavor of the country table while suiting the needs of today's home.

The style is called a trestle table from the arrangement of legs and stretcher that form the understructure. Traditionally, the stretcher tenon was pinned to the leg assembly with a wedge so that the table could be disassembled and put out of the way when not in use.

1 **Select your stock and cut it to size.** Hardwoods and softwoods are both appropriate for a table of this design. With careful selection and planning, the entire table can be made from 8/4 (eight-quarter) stock. Keep in mind that if necessary the middle planks in the glued-up top can show saw marks on the bottom surface. Edge-glue the tabletop as described on page 6, then plane all of the parts to the required thickness and cut them to the dimensions specified by the Cutting List.

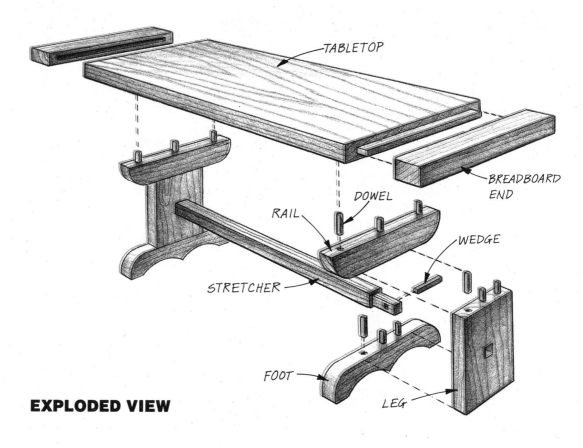

TABLETOP

BREADBOARD
END

DOWEL

RAIL

WEDGE

STRETCHER

FOOT

LEG

EXPLODED VIEW

CUTTING LIST

Part	Dimensions
Tabletop	1¾″ × 18″ × 44½″
Legs (2)	1½″ × 6¼″ × 8¾″
Stretcher	1¼″ × 1⅝″ × 40¾″
Wedges (2)	½″ × ⁹⁄₁₆″ × 3¼″
Feet (2)	1½″ × 2¾″ × 13¾″
Rails (2)	1½″ × 2¾″ × 13¾″
Dowels (18)	½″ dia. × 1⅞″
Breadboard ends (2)	1¾″ × 2¾″ × 18″

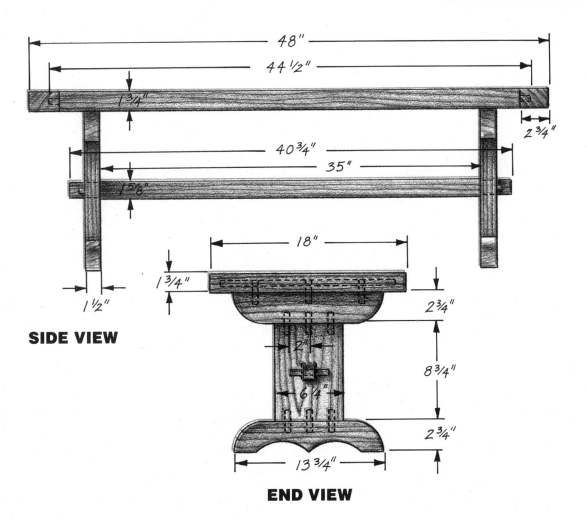

SIDE VIEW

END VIEW

2 **Cut the stretcher mortises in the legs.** The stretcher joins the legs with a through mortise and tenon. The tenon shoulders are quite shallow so care must be exercised to avoid making the mortises too large. Lay out the mortises in the centers of the legs. The dimensions are given in the *Stretcher Joint Detail*. Drill out the bulk of the mortises, preferably on a drill press, then trim the sides with a sharp chisel. Trim from both sides of the legs to avoid splitting out edges of the mortises.

3 **Cut the tenons on the stretcher.** Lay out the tenons on the stretcher to match the mortises. Cut the tenons on the table saw as described on page 60.

(continued on page 62)

CUTTING TENONS

Strong and durable glued mortise-and-tenon joints require a very good fit between the mortise and the tenon. You can achieve the needed accuracy in mortises by cutting them with a plunge router as explained on page 18. You can cut equally accurate tenons with a well-tuned table saw, a shop-made tenoning jig, and an accurate spacer.

A well-tuned table saw is essential for accurate work. For cutting tenons, the blade must be truly perpendicular to the saw table, the fence must be truly parallel to the blade, and the blade must be sharp. If your saw isn't in this condition, get out your saw manual and fix it.

A tenoning jig is a simple device to hold stock perpendicular to the saw table while feeding it accurately through the blade. The drawing shows an easy-to-make, easy-to-use, and reliable jig. Make the base, brace, and upright from particle board. Make the fence from solid wood. Make sure the edges of the base are parallel and the corners of the brace are square.

The use of a spacer to shift the tenoning jig between cheek cuts is one of the easiest and most accurate ways of cutting tenons on the table saw. The spacer must be as wide as the thickness of the tenon plus the width of a saw kerf. One nice feature of using spacers is that you can adjust them in very fine increments by adding (or removing) masking tape from them.

The drawing shows a spacer with cleats on the ends that keep the spacer properly posi-tioned alongside the tenoning jig. Cut the spacer from a stable piece of straight-grained hardwood. It's better to make it ever-so-slightly too narrow rather than too wide. Naturally, the sides must be parallel.

With your saw in tune and your jig and spacer ready, you can cut tenons. Begin by laying them out to match the mortises that they must fit into. Lay them out with a marking gauge. Label the surface from which you will gauge the cheek cuts. This surface is known as the reference surface and is usually the surface that is most visible in the finished project. Lay out identical tenons on several pieces of scrap as well. Be sure to mark a reference surface on these, too.

Install a sharp, smooth-cutting rip blade on the saw, adjust the depth of cut to the length of the tenons, and check that the blade is perpendicular to the table.

Clamp one of the scrap pieces in the tenoning jig with the reference surface against the upright. Make sure it is flush with the bottom of the base and tight against the fence.

Place the spacer alongside the jig and the two against the fence. Adjust the fence so the saw blade lines up on the waste side of the cheek mark closest to the reference surface. Turn on the saw and slide the jig and stock along the fence making the first cheek cut in the scrap. Remove the spacer and make the second cheek cut.

Saw off the cheek waste and test the tenon in the mortise. You'll only be able to stick a corner of the tenon in the mortise, of

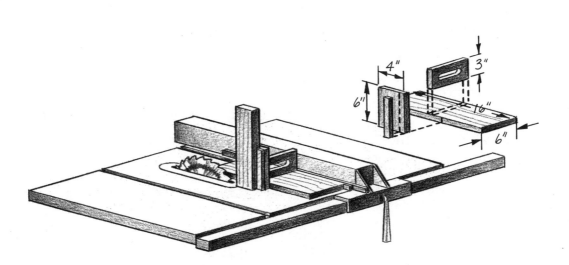

course, because you haven't cut the tenon edges yet. If the tenon is too tight, cut a new, slightly narrower spacer and try again. If you're lucky, the tenon is slightly too loose. Add layers of masking tape to the corner of the tenon until the fit is snug but not tight. Apply the same number of layers of tape to the spacer.

Now repeat the operation with a second piece of scrap. If the tenon still doesn't fit quite as well as you'd like, remove or add a layer of tape to the spacer to fine-tune it. Cut all of the identical parts without changing the setup.

Cut the edges of the tenons with the same basic procedure but don't fuss to get a perfect fit. The edge of the tenon is opposite end grain in the mortise so you won't get a good bond no matter how well the parts fit.

To saw the shoulders, first change to a smooth-cutting crosscut blade. Check that the miter-gauge fence is perpendicular to the miter-

gauge groove. Clamp a stop block to the saw fence well in front of the blade. Adjust the blade height to the depth of the shoulder. Place one of your tenon parts against the miter-gauge fence with the blade lined up on the waste side of the shoulder mark. While holding the part against the miter-gauge fence, pull the part and miter gauge back until the part is in line with the stop block on the saw fence. Move the saw fence over until the stop block touches the end of the tenon. Clamp the fence. To saw the shoulders, butt the tenon against the stop block, then hold it against the miter-gauge fence while pushing it over the blade. Check that the corner between the cheek cut and the shoulder cut is clean and square and adjust the blade height if necessary. It's better to score the tenon slightly than to have a ridge in the corner.

4 **Cut the wedges and their mortises.** Since the wedges taper slightly, the mortises must have one slightly angled side. Make the wedges first, to the dimensions in the *Stretcher Joint Detail*. Fit the tenons through their mortises in the legs. Mark where the tenons protrude from the outside surfaces of the legs, then lay the wedges on top of the tenons, tight against the legs. Mark where the outer edges of the wedges cross the tenons. These marks will be slightly angled because of the taper of the wedges. Disassemble the stretcher from the legs, then square down the sides of the tenons from your marks on the top surface. Complete the layout as shown in the *Stretcher Joint Detail*.

Drill out the wedge mortises from the smaller end, where the wedge will exit, and then widen the other side while squaring up the corners and smoothing the sides.

5 **Shape the feet and rails.** Lay out one of the foot scallops on a piece of stiff paper, then trace it onto the feet. Lay out the rounded ends of the feet and

rails in the same way. You can cut these curves with a coping saw and patience but a band saw would be a lot easier, especially if you're building the table out of a hardwood. Smooth the cuts with a rasp and sandpaper.

6 **Assemble the legs, feet, and rails.** Lay the parts out flat on the workbench and center the rails and feet on the legs. Mark the edges of the legs on the rails and feet. Lay out centers for three ½-inch dowel holes on both ends of both legs. One hole should be centered in the end, the other two should be 2 inches away. Transfer these locations to the rails and feet. Bore all of the dowel holes 1 inch deep.

Sand the legs, rails, and feet. Saw 12 dowels, 1⅞ inch long each, from a length of ½-inch dowel stock. Chamfer the ends of the dowels and saw or plane a groove or flat on the side of each so air and excess glue can escape. Glue the dowels into the legs, spread glue on the ends of the legs, and assemble the rails and feet to the legs. Clamp the assemblies and let the glue dry.

STRETCHER JOINT DETAIL

7 **Attach the breadboard ends.** Breadboard ends on a tabletop are quite traditional but seldom stay glued for very long. With changes in humidity, the top expands and contracts across its width more than the breadboard ends change in length. It is therefore important that the mortise and tenon fit quite well; when the glue comes unstuck, you want the parts to stay well aligned.

Rout the mortise in the breadboard ends first. Use a ½-inch-diameter

SHOP TIP: You can transfer hole positions with commercial dowel centers. You can also do it with small finish nails. When using dowel centers, you bore one dowel hole first, place the appropriate size dowel center in the bored hole, bring the two parts together, and press them so the points on the dowel centers mark the second piece.

To transfer centers with small finish nails, you must transfer the centers before boring either hole. First cut the heads off of the nails. Select a bit the same diameter as the nails. Drill holes in one of the pieces to a depth slightly less than the length of the nails. Insert the nails, blunt end first, into the holes. Bring the two parts together and press them so the points on the nails mark the second piece. Remove the nails and bore the dowel holes.

straight or spiral upcut bit and rout the mortises 1 inch deep. Stop the mortises 1 inch from the ends.

Cutting the tenons on the table saw would be awkward because of its size. It would be easier to cut them with a router. This is done by routing rabbets from both top and bottom surfaces of the tabletop. Clamp a straightedge across the tabletop to guide the edge of your router. Position it so the bit can come no further than 1 inch from the end of the tabletop. Set the depth of cut to just a hair under ⅝ inch; you want to be able to trim the tenon to fit the mortise. Rout both sides of both tenons, then cut the

shoulders at the ends with a back saw. These shoulders should be at least 1⅛ inches wide so the tenon has some expansion room in the mortise. A shoulder plane is quite handy for trimming the tenons to a perfect fit in the mortises but you can do as well with a sharp chisel and a little more time.

Sand the top and breadboard ends, then glue and clamp them together. If (or when) the glue bond eventually breaks, secure the breadboard ends by installing a single ¼-inch-diameter dowel locking the tenon into the mortise. Installed blind from the bottom surface, it will never show.

8 Assemble the table. Wedge the stretcher to the leg assemblies. Lay the tabletop upside down on a padded work surface. Position the trestle assembly on the underside of the top and mark the location of the rails. Lay out dowel holes in the rail and tabletop the same way you laid out the holes in the legs and rails. The dowel locations are shown in the *End View.* Bore the dowel holes 1 inch deep.

Sand all the parts, then glue the trestle assembly to the tabletop.

9 Apply your finish. Remember that this is a coffee table when selecting a finish. Use a finish such as polyurethane that resists water and alcohol. Apply as many coats to the bottom of the tabletop as you do to the top so that moisture content change in the wood will be uniform on both surfaces.

PART TWO

GARDEN PROJECTS

BUCKET BENCH

Bucket benches went hand in hand with dry sinks. They stored the buckets, jars, and crocks of water hauled in from the spring or well. Typically, the bucket bench sat on the back porch, or in the corner of the kitchen.

This bench was assembled with screws and cut nails. The wood is oak, with pine drawer sides and back. The boards that make up the drawer compartment are excessively thick, perhaps because the maker had no thinner stock and didn't want to plane off ½ inch of oak by hand. Feel free to use thinner boards if you wish, adjusting the width of the drawer box side as appropriate. Other parts listed in the Cutting List as $^{13}/_{16}$ inch or $^{7}/_{8}$ inch thick could be made from ¾-inch-thick stock with little effect on the appearance and no other dimensional changes needed.

You'll notice from the drawings that

the lower shelf simply butts the lower sides. You can make a stronger bucket bench if you rout a ¼-inch-deep dado in each lower side for the lower shelf to fit into. If you do this, increase the length of the lower shelf by ½ inch to keep the same overall dimensions. The bench in the photo was decoratively painted.

1 **Select the stock and cut the parts.** Cut all of the parts to the dimensions given in the Cutting List, edge-gluing as necessary to get sufficient

width. See page 6 for tips on edge-gluing. The width of the lower back boards can vary as long as they total 20¼ inches in width.

2 **Cut the curve in the upper side boards.** The upper sides have a curved front edge, as shown in the *Side View.* Lay out the curve on both pieces and saw it with a coping saw, a portable jigsaw, or a band saw. File and sand the curves smooth, rounding the edges slightly.

CUTTING LIST

Part	Dimensions
Upper sides (2)	$^{13}/_{16}" \times 7" \times 13^{1}/_{4}"$
Upper back board	$^{13}/_{16}" \times 7^{7}/_{8}" \times 38^{3}/_{8}"$
Upper shelf	$^{7}/_{8}" \times 14" \times 40^{5}/_{8}"$
Lower sides (2)	$^{13}/_{16}" \times 12^{3}/_{4}" \times 23^{3}/_{8}"$
Lower shelf	$^{13}/_{16}" \times 12^{3}/_{4}" \times 34^{3}/_{8}"$
Lower back boards (4)	$^{7}/_{8}" \times 5^{1}/_{16}" \times 36"$
Drawer box side	$1^{1}/_{8}" \times 12^{3}/_{4}" \times 5"$
Drawer box bottom	$1^{1}/_{8}" \times 12^{3}/_{4}" \times 7"$
Drawer sides (2)	$^{3}/_{8}" \times 3^{3}/_{4}" \times 11^{3}/_{4}"$
Drawer front	$^{3}/_{4}" \times 3^{3}/_{8}" \times 6^{1}/_{8}"$
Drawer back	$^{3}/_{8}" \times 3^{3}/_{8}" \times 6^{1}/_{8}"$
Drawer bottom	$^{3}/_{8}" \times 6^{1}/_{8}" \times 11^{3}/_{4}"$
Drawer face molding	$^{1}/_{4}" \times 5/_{8}" \times 24"$
Drawer stop	$^{3}/_{4}" \times 3/_{4}" \times 4"$

Hardware

Cut nails
9 flathead wood screws, #10 × 1¾"
6 flathead wood screws, #10 × 1½"
6 oak plugs for #10 screw counterbores
¾" brads
1 metal drawer knob, ¾" × 1"

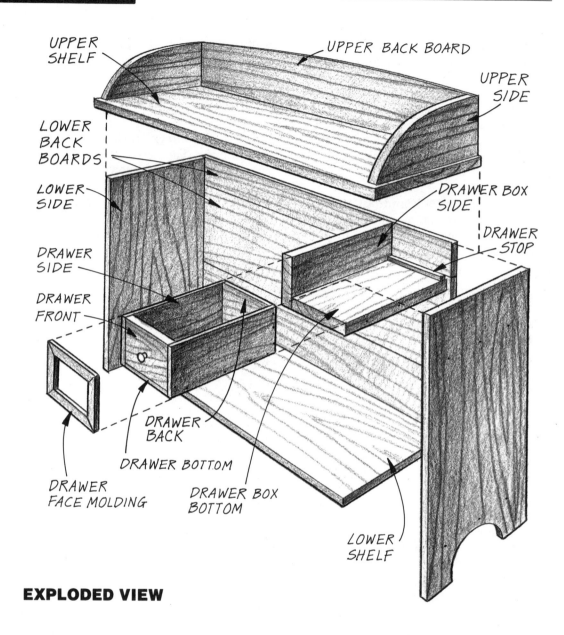

UPPER
SHELF

UPPER BACK BOARD

UPPER
SIDE

LOWER
BACK
BOARDS

LOWER
SIDE

DRAWER BOX
SIDE

DRAWER
STOP

DRAWER
SIDE

DRAWER
FRONT

DRAWER
BACK

DRAWER FACE MOLDING

DRAWER BOTTOM

DRAWER BOX
BOTTOM

LOWER
SHELF

EXPLODED VIEW

3 **Cut the curve in the upper back board.** Bend a thin strip of straight-grained scrap to lay out the ⅞-inch rise along the length of the back board. Drive a brad or clamp a block at each end of the back board where the curve begins. Push the strip of scrap against the brads and continue pushing, bending the strip,

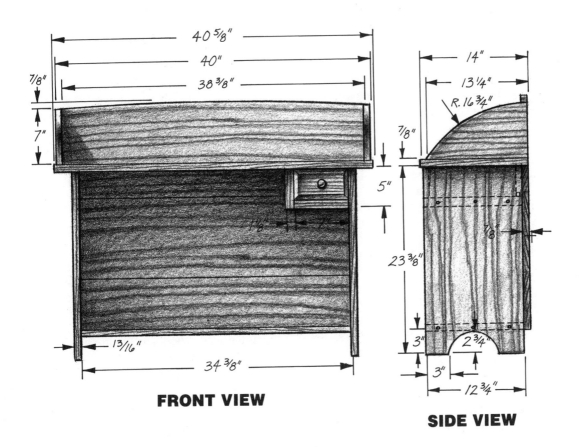

FRONT VIEW

SIDE VIEW

until the scrap reaches the edge of the board at the middle. Use a pencil to trace along the bent strip, then saw the curve. Smooth the curve as you did for the upper sides.

4 **Attach the upper sides to the upper back board.** Sand the parts. Nail the upper sides to the upper back board. Oak is a hard wood so it's a good idea to predrill for all of the nails used in the assembly. You can use glue in this joint if you like but oak is not the best wood for gluing and end grain is difficult

as well so don't expect much from glue in these joints.

5 **Attach the back-board assembly to the upper shelf.** Position the back-board assembly on the upper shelf as shown in the *Front View* and *Side View* and mark its position. Guided by these marks, drill shank holes for #10 wood screws through the shelf. Three 1¾-inch screws for each side and three along the back are sufficient. Countersink the holes from the bottom.

Clamp the back-board assembly in

position on the upper shelf, then drill pilot holes in the sides and back in line with the shank holes in the upper shelf. Screw and glue the upper shelf to the back board but omit the glue between the shelf and the sides.

6 **Cut out the foot in the lower sides.** Lay out the foot cutout shown in the *Side View* in each side, then saw to the layout as you did for the previous curves. Smooth the cutout somewhat but the edge won't be seen so it doesn't need to be perfectly smooth.

7 **Assemble the lower unit.** Sand the parts, then glue and nail the lower shelf to the two sides. Predrill the nail holes.

Lay this lower unit face down on your bench and check to make certain the unit is square and flat. Then nail the lower back boards to the back edges of the sides and shelf. Again, predrill the nail holes.

8 **Attach the upper and lower units.** Center the upper shelf unit on the lower unit. Lay out and drill nail

SHOP TIP: Rout small or thin pieces of molding on the edge of a larger piece of stock, then rip the piece you need from the edge. The larger piece of stock is more stable and safer to handle.

holes through the upper shelf into the lower sides, then nail the upper unit to the lower unit. From the back, drill and nail at an angle through the upper shelf into the lower unit back board. Two or three nails are enough; just be sure you miss the screws that hold the upper shelf to the upper back board. Keep the angle steep so the nails don't come out the front face of the back board.

9 **Install the drawer box.** Glue and nail the drawer box side to the drawer box bottom. Clamp this unit in position on the assembled bench and drill counterbores, shank, and pilot holes through the upper shelf and lower sides into the drawer box. Three #10 × 1½-inch flathead wood screws in each joint will suffice. Screw the drawer box unit in place, then plug the counterbores. Trim the plugs flush.

10 **Construct the drawer.** The drawer is of very simple construction; the sides completely cover the end grain of the drawer front, eliminating the need for rabbets. First sand the drawer parts. Glue and nail the drawer sides to the ends of the drawer front and back as shown in the *Drawer Detail*. The top edges should be flush. Turn the drawer upside down on your workbench and nail the drawer bottom to the back and front, then nail through the sides into the bottom.

The end grain of the drawer sides and bottom are now visible from the front. Hide these edges with the ¼-inch × ⅝-inch molding strip. You can buy this strip from a hardware or building-supply store, or you can make the molding with an ogee bit in a table-mounted router. Miter the ends of the molding to fit the drawer, then glue and nail it around the front edges of the assembled drawer as shown in the *Drawer Detail*. Nail into the sides and bottom, not the oak front, with ¾-inch brads.

11 **Attach the drawer knob and stop.** Drill a screw shank hole in the center of the drawer front for the drawer knob. Screw the knob to the drawer front.

Place the drawer stop in the drawer compartment as shown in the *Side View* and insert the drawer. You can adjust the position of the closed drawer by planing the drawer stop or substituting a wider stop. Glue the stop in place to keep it from rattling or getting lost.

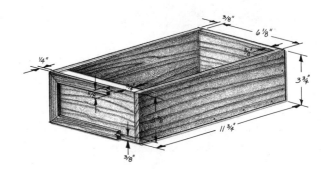

DRAWER DETAIL

12 **Finish the bucket bench.** Your choice of finish will likely depend on your choice of wood and the intended use for the bucket bench. If you want the bench to serve as a plant stand, you may want to paint it with an exterior enamel to help protect it from water damage. If you want to show the wood, use a hard finish like polyurethane.

BENCH

R. C. Pitt is an antique dealer in Kennett Square, Pennsylvania. He found this bench in Vermont, but we must look to the bench itself to learn more about its history. The back rails are made of ¾-inch-thick stock while the seat rails are somewhat thicker, a clue that the seat portion of the bench was made before ¾-inch stock became standard and the back was added at a later date. (Our plans call for ¾-inch stock in both places.) The back may have been added to improve comfort, or to add a touch of formality.

The history of old country furniture is part of its fun, but it's also fun to reproduce it. The bench uses simple exposed joinery. The stretchers join the legs with through mortises and tenons. These joints, some notches, and well-placed nails make a very sturdy bench that will last for generations, as shown by the original.

1 **Select the stock and cut the parts to size.** The bench that Pitt found in Vermont is made of pine. Any good furniture wood will do well. Select a wood to suit your preferences and local availability. Cut all of the parts except the legs to the sizes specified by the Cutting List. Leave the legs a bit longer, say 20 inches overall. You'll probably

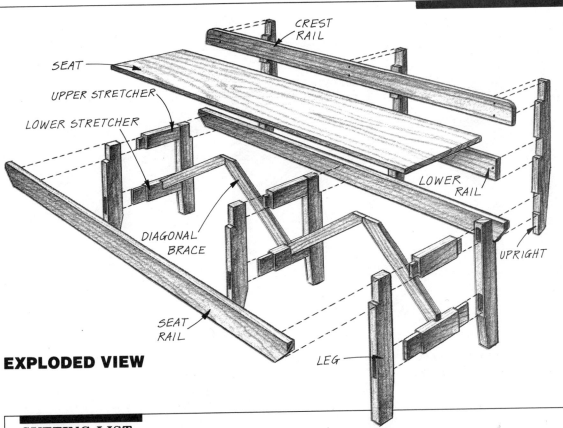

CREST RAIL

SEAT

UPPER STRETCHER

LOWER STRETCHER

LOWER RAIL

DIAGONAL BRACE

UPRIGHT

SEAT RAIL

LEG

EXPLODED VIEW

CUTTING LIST

Part	Dimensions
Legs (6)	$1\frac{1}{2}" \times 2\frac{3}{4}" \times 19\frac{1}{4}"$
Upper stretchers (3)	$1\frac{1}{2}" \times 2\frac{3}{4}" \times 9\frac{3}{4}"$
Lower stretchers (3)	$1\frac{1}{2}" \times 2\frac{3}{4}" \times 13\frac{1}{4}"$
Seat rails (2)	$\frac{3}{4}" \times 3\frac{3}{16}" \times 71"$
Seat	$\frac{3}{4}" \times 14\frac{1}{2}" \times 72"$
Diagonal braces (4)	$\frac{3}{4}" \times 2" \times 19\frac{5}{8}"$
Uprights (3)	$1\frac{1}{2}" \times 2\frac{1}{2}" \times 24\frac{7}{8}"$
Crest rail	$\frac{3}{4}" \times 4" \times 71\frac{1}{2}"$
Lower rail	$\frac{3}{4}" \times 3" \times 66\frac{3}{4}"$

Hardware

6d common nails
8 flathead wood screws, #8 $\times$ $1\frac{1}{4}"$
9 flathead wood screws, #8 $\times$ $1\frac{1}{2}"$
6 flathead wood screws, #10 $\times$ $2\frac{1}{2}"$
6 wood plugs, $\frac{1}{2}"$ dia.

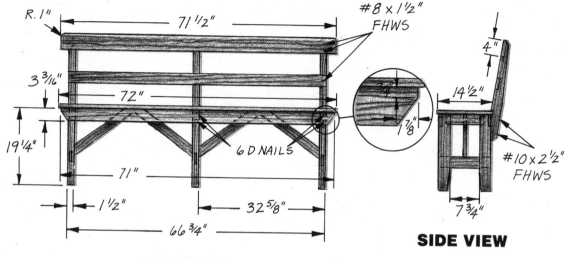

FRONT VIEW

SIDE VIEW

have to glue up several narrower boards to make up the wide plank for the seat. See page 6 for more on edge-gluing. If you look closely at the photo, you may be able to see the joints in the boards that make up the original seat.

2 Mortise the legs. Lay out the mortises on the legs as shown in the *Leg Joinery Detail,* measuring from the bottom of the legs. Since you left the legs a bit long when you cut the parts to size, measuring from the bottom will leave the extra at the top. The extra length will help prevent splitting out the end of the mortise as you're cutting it. The upper mortise should be laid out on the inner edge of each leg. The lower mortise should be laid out on both edges.

Cut the mortises by drilling a series of overlapping holes within the layout marks. Drill as much of the waste away as possible, then clean out the mortise with a chisel. For the through mortises,

drill halfway into the leg from one edge, then turn the piece over and drill the remainder from the opposite edge. If you're drilling with a fence on the drill press, be sure to position the stock with the same face against the fence. You can also cut mortises with a plunge router as explained in "Plunge-Routing Mortises" on page 18.

3 Cut the tenons. Set up a ¾-inch-wide dado cutter on the table saw. Set the depth of cut to just under ½ inch.

For the upper stretchers, set the rip fence 1 inch from the left (or outside) of the cutter. Guide the stretchers over the cutter with the miter gauge. Start at one end of each board and make two or three passes until the end of the board stops against the fence. Turn the board over and repeat the operation on the other side. Check the fit of the tenon in the mortise. Raise the cutter as necessary to make the tenon thinner. Keep in

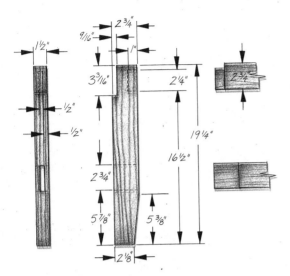

LEG JOINERY DETAIL

View. Cut the notches with the dado cutter on the table saw the same way you cut the tenons. Set the depth of cut to $\frac{9}{16}$ inches and position the fence $3\frac{3}{16}$ inches from the outside of the cutter.

5 **Cut the seat rails to shape.** Lay out the angled cuts on the ends of the seat rails as shown in the *Front View*. Since these pieces are quite long, you may find it easiest to saw these angles with a handsaw. Smooth the sawn edges with a sharp block plane.

6 **Assemble the legs and seat rails.** Sand the legs, stretchers, and seat rails. Glue the stretcher tenons into their respective mortises, checking the assemblies with a framing square before laying them on a flat surface for the glue to dry. Then nail the seat rails to the legs as shown in the *Front View*.

7 **Attach the seat.** Sand the seat and place it on the legs. Center it from front to back and from side to side. Nail it to the seat rails and upper stretchers with 6d common nails.

8 **Make and install the diagonal braces.** Cut the diagonal braces to the shape shown in the *Brace Detail* with a fine-tooth backsaw like a tenon or dovetail saw. Sand the braces, then screw them in place under the bench with #8 × 1¼-inch wood screws. They should be centered from front to back.

9 **Make the uprights.** Lay out the uprights on the blanks as shown in the *Upright Detail.* Cut the notches with the dado cutter on the table saw. Use a handsaw to make the angled cuts. Clean up the sawn edges with a block plane.

mind that raising the cutter $\frac{1}{32}$ inch will reduce the tenon thickness by $\frac{1}{16}$ inch because stock is removed from both faces. Make the adjustments a tiny amount at a time until you get a nice snug fit. Then cut the opposite end the same way. Cut the third shoulder on each end by standing the boards on edge and running them over the cutter.

The procedure for the lower stretchers is the same except this time the fence is set $2\frac{3}{4}$ inches from the outside of the cutter and the tenons have only two shoulders. When the mortise-and-tenon joints fit to your liking, cut the legs to length by sawing the extra off of the top ends.

You can also cut tenons with a circular saw blade. See "Cutting Tenons" on page 60 for a complete discussion.

4 **Notch the legs.** The legs have notches to accept the seat rails as shown in the *Leg Joinery Detail* and *Side*

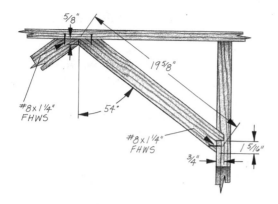

BRACE DETAIL

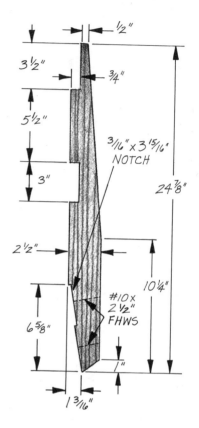

UPRIGHT DETAIL

10 **Attach the uprights.** Notch the seat plank slightly so the uprights fit against the legs. These notches should be 1½ inches wide and centered over the legs. The bottoms of the notches should be flush with the face of the seat rail. Make the end cuts with a dovetail saw and clean out the waste with a chisel.

Sand the uprights, then position them against the legs. Drill and counterbore for #10 screws as shown in the *Upright Detail*. Screw the uprights to the legs with #10 × 2½-inch wood screws. Plug the holes with ½-inch plugs.

11 **Shape and attach the rails.** Round the corners of the crest

rail as shown in the *Front View*. A coping saw works well for this. Sand both the crest rail and the lower rail. Screw them in their respective notches in the uprights with #8 × 1½-inch wood screws.

12 **Finish the bench.** Select a finish to suit your use for the bench. Consider one of the combination stain/urethane finishes if the bench is apt to see hard use. Paint is also appropriate for the bench.

SHOP TIP: The easiest way to do an accurate job of drilling mortises is to hold the stock against a fence clamped to a drill press table.

BIRDHOUSE

Birdhouses replace some of the natural nesting sites that we destroy with our "improvements." Attracting birds adds life, song, and interest to our yards and has other immediate rewards. The average bird will eat many times its own weight in insects, wild seeds, and even rodents. Building birdhouses is fun, too, despite the jokes about woodworkers with a fortune in tools whose sole project was a birdhouse. And building this one will put you in an elite group. How many of your neighbors have reproductions of antique birdhouses?

This birdhouse will accommodate a bluebird, a tree swallow, or even a downy woodpecker. With modifications it could house a number of other species.

You can build the house with common materials and a few basic hand tools. Cedar is an ideal choice of wood since it's naturally weather resistant. Even pine, if it's well finished and sealed against the elements, will last for many years and will make a fine birdhouse. Pressure-treated wood is toxic to birds and should not be used.

1 **Cut the parts to size.** Saw all the parts except the ledges to the sizes specified by the Cutting List. Leave the ledges about ¼ inch longer than the Cutting List calls for. If you're unable to buy ½-inch-thick stock, you still have several options. You can plane ¾-inch stock to ½ inch. You can resaw thicker stock to ½-inch thick on the band saw. Or you can resaw thicker stock on the table saw, sawing as deeply as possible into

each edge and finishing up as necessary with a handsaw.

2 **Cut the front and back to shape.** Lay out and saw the 45-degree roof pitch on the front and back as shown in the *Front View*. The peak is centered on the width of the pieces.

3 **Drill the front and back.** Lay out the locations of the holes on the

EXPLODED VIEW

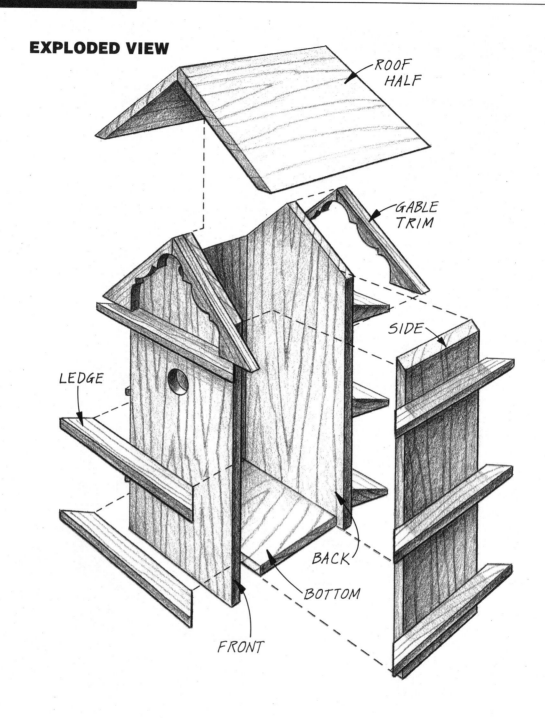

ROOF
HALF

GABLE
TRIM

SIDE

LEDGE

BACK

BOTTOM

FRONT

front and back as shown in the *Front View*. The front gets two holes—a large entrance hole and a ¼-inch-diameter hanger hole. The back gets only the hanger hole. You can hand-drill the large entrance hole with an expansion bit or a hole saw in a brace.

4 Assemble the walls. Glue and nail the sides in place between the front and back. Start 1-inch brads along the edges of the front and back and apply a waterproof glue such as Titebond II to the mating surfaces. Align the sides between the front and back so they are flush at the bottom and fall short of the angled cut at the top, then drive the brads home.

5 Bevel the roof halves. Tilt the blade on the table saw to 45 degrees. Bevel the two long edges of both roof halves as shown in the *Front View*.

SHOP TIP: When using brads, you can avoid splitting the wood by predrilling a pilot hole. Clip the head off one of the brads and chuck it in the drill in place of a drill bit. The brad will make a perfect pilot hole.

6 Attach the roof. Check the fit of the roof halves on the house. Center the roof from front to back as shown in the *Side View*. If necessary, trim the roof pieces with a block plane to get a perfect fit at the peak, then glue the roof halves in place. Be sure to apply glue to the mating beveled surfaces and reinforce the joints with brads as before. The gap between the sides and the roof allows for ventilation inside the house.

CUTTING LIST

Part	Dimensions
Front	½" × 6½" × 14"
Back	½" × 6½" × 14"
Sides (2)	½" × 5½" × 10"
Roof halves (2)	½" × 6½" × 10"
Gable trim (4)	½" × ⅞" × 5¹¹⁄₁₆"
Ledges (12)	¾" × 1⅛" × 8¾"
Bottom	½" × 5½" × 5½"

Hardware

#18 × 1" wire brads
#18 × 1½" wire brads
4 brass flathead wood screws, #6 × 1¼"
6' nylon rope, ¼" dia.

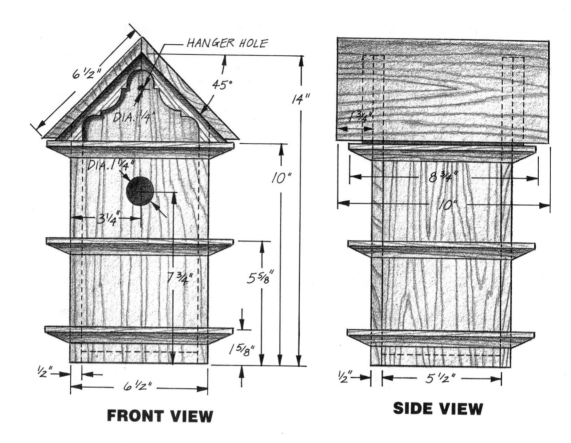

FRONT VIEW

SIDE VIEW

7 **Make and attach the gable trim.** Cut the gable trim pieces to the shape shown in the *Trim Detail.* You'll find that a coping saw with a fairly fine-tooth blade does a nice job on soft, ½-inch stock. Glue and brad the trim in place as shown in the *Front View.*

8 **Cut the ledges to shape.** Tilt the blade on the table saw to 24 degrees from vertical and bevel the edges of the ledges as shown in the *Ledge Cross Section.* To avoid trapping the

stock during the cut, set up the saw so the blade tilts away from the fence. Use push sticks to protect your fingers.

9 **Attach the ledges to the house.** Draw lines around all four sides of the house to locate the ledges as shown in the *Front View.* Set the miter gauge on the table saw to 45 degrees. Miter one end of a ledge. Hold it up to the birdhouse, mark it for length, and cut the second miter. Glue and brad each ledge in place after cutting it. Miter an

80

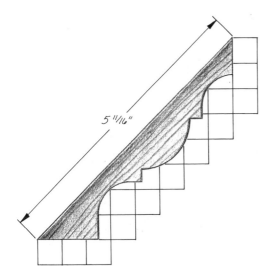

5 ¹¹/₁₆"

TRIM DETAIL

1 ¹/₈"

³/₄"

24°

LEDGE CROSS SECTION

end of the next piece, hold it in place against the previous piece to mark it for length, and cut the second miter. Attach all 12 ledges in this way. You'll need 1½-inch brads to hold the ledges and you may need to predrill for them.

10 **Install the bottom.** Trim the bottom as necessary with a block plane to fit it into the underside of the house. Drill and countersink for #6 × 1¼-inch wood screws through each of the sides into the bottom, then screw the bottom in place. Don't glue it or you won't be able to remove the bottom each spring to remove the old nest.

11 **Finish the house.** You can hang the house out to weather natu-

rally but it will last longer if you paint it. The antique that we measured for this project was originally painted, and paint still offers the best protection. Remove the bottom before painting and paint only the exterior. Birds prefer natural wood on the inside.

Use a good exterior trim paint. If you plan to hang the house in the sun, paint it with light colors to keep it cooler. If you plan to hang it in the shade, dark colors will help camouflage it, making it more attractive to birds.

12 **Hang the house.** Thread the nylon rope through the hanger holes in the front and back. Tie the house up in a tree about 8 to 10 feet above the ground. Most birds prefer seclusion so take this into account when you choose the location. Check the house early each spring. Make any necessary repairs and clean out any debris left from the previous tenants.

PLANT SHELVES

Designs for shelving for plants are not easy to find. If you want the shelving to be suitable for outdoors, they are even more difficult to find. This one fills the bill. It's rugged, it will hold quite a few potted plants, and it will hold them so they don't shade each other from the sun. The stepped shelves also make the plants accessible for watering, put them on display, and take up so little room the unit can easily fit on a porch or patio.

You can build the project out of pine or poplar and.paint it to provide protection from the elements and from water-

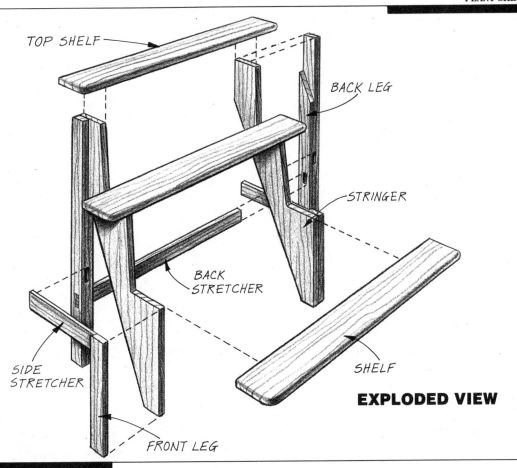

TOP SHELF

BACK LEG

STRINGER

BACK STRETCHER

SHELF

EXPLODED VIEW

SIDE STRETCHER

FRONT LEG

CUTTING LIST

Part	Dimensions
Back legs (2)	$2\frac{1}{8}'' \times 2\frac{1}{8}'' \times 34\frac{5}{8}''$
Side stretchers (2)	$\frac{1}{2}'' \times 2\frac{3}{8}'' \times 13\frac{1}{4}''$
Front legs (2)	$1\frac{1}{4}'' \times 2\frac{1}{8}'' \times 14''$
Stringers (2)	$\frac{7}{8}'' \times 9'' \times 38\frac{3}{4}''$
Shelves (2)	$\frac{7}{8}'' \times 6'' \times 40\frac{3}{4}''$
Top shelf	$\frac{7}{8}'' \times 6\frac{1}{2}'' \times 40\frac{3}{4}''$
Dowels*	$\frac{7}{16}''$ dia. $\times 24''$
Back stretcher	$\frac{1}{2}'' \times 2\frac{3}{8}'' \times 34\frac{3}{4}''$

Hardware

2″ galvanized nails *or* deck screws

*Cut to required lengths.

ing the plants. A better solution to the problem of preservation, however, is to use a naturally rot-resistant wood like redwood or cedar. Then you can paint it, apply a natural finish, or leave it to weather.

1 **Select the stock and cut the parts.** The original that we measured for these plans uses stock thicknesses that are not commonly available today. See what your dealer does have, then adjust the joinery to suit. If you substitute a different thickness for the shelves, choose a thicker rather than a thinner board in order to preserve the weight-carrying capacity of the project; potted plants are not light. You could use ¾-inch-thick stock for the stretchers without weakening the rear legs too much, provided you don't at the same time make the legs any smaller. Having made any necessary adjustments, cut all

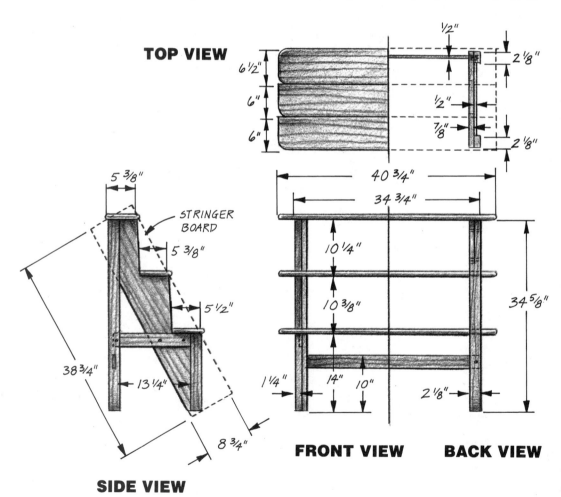

TOP VIEW

SIDE VIEW

FRONT VIEW   **BACK VIEW**

the pieces to the dimensions given in the Cutting List. It may be necessary to edge-glue boards to get sufficient width for the stringers. If so, see "Edge-Gluing" on page 6 for step-by-step instructions.

2 **Mortise the back legs for the stretchers.** The back legs are mortised to receive the full thickness and width of the stretchers. On the original, the side-stretcher mortises are blind while the back-stretcher mortises are through. You could just as well make them both blind or both through and adjust the stretcher lengths accordingly. Lay out these mortises as shown in the *Leg Mortise Detail,* or as you have decided to alter them.

Drill out the mortises with a brad point bit in your drill press. Clamp a fence to the drill-press table to keep the holes properly aligned. If you're cutting through mortises, be sure to put a piece of scrap under the legs to protect the bit and table and to prevent tear-out. Clean up the sides of the mortises and square the ends with a sharp chisel.

3 **Lay out and cut the ends of the stringers.** The stringer ends are best laid out directly from the assembled legs. Begin by clamping together a rear leg, side stretcher, and front leg as shown in the *Side View.* The front leg just butts against the front end of the side stretcher; hold it with a bar clamp. Make certain the pieces are 90 degrees to each other. Measure 26¾ inches up from the bottom of the back leg and mark where the stringer will come.

Lay the clamped leg assembly in position on a stringer board as shown in the *Side View.* Clamp the stringer to the legs and trace the legs and stretcher onto the stringer. Also trace the bottom edge of the stringer onto the back leg. Repeat the process for the other two legs and the other stringer.

Saw along the lines representing the back edge of the back leg and the front edge of the front leg. A hand- or portable saw will be most convenient for these cuts. Plane off the saw marks.

4 **Cut the steps in the stringer boards.** Lay out the steps for the top and bottom shelves perpendicular to the angled cuts that you just made. A carpenter's framing square is handy for this. Since the bottom shelf coincides with the top of the stretcher, you have already laid out most of the bottom-shelf step. Lay out the middle-shelf step by

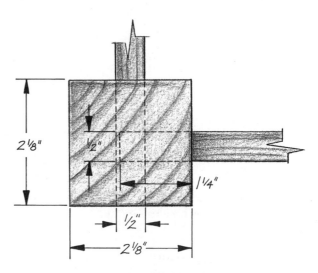

LEG MORTISE DETAIL

setting an adjustable bevel to the angle of the bottom step and drawing the middle step 10⅜ inches away. Lay out the vertical lines by connecting the back of one step with the front of the step above. These are not truly vertical lines as you may notice by looking closely at the *Side View*.

Saw out the steps with a handsaw and smooth the cuts with a fine rasp. Only the vertical cuts will show.

5 Notch the back legs for the stringers. The stringers rest in notches in the back legs as shown in the *Back View*. With the material thicknesses used in the original, these notches are ⅞ inch deep. Lay out the depth of the notches. (You have already laid out the ends of the notches.) Clamp each leg in turn in your vise and saw out its notch with a handsaw.

6 Assemble the side units. Sand the legs, side stretchers, and stringers. Glue and clamp the side stretchers into the back leg mortises, making sure they are square. Be sure to use a glue suitable for outdoor exposure, like Titebond II. Glue and clamp the front legs to the stringers.

When the glue in these joints is dry, apply glue to the notches in the back legs, to the front ends of the stretchers, and to the stringers where the stretchers will join. Clamp the two subassemblies for each side together.

7 Reinforce the side assemblies with dowels. Pin the tenons in the mortises, and the side stretchers to the stringers, with dowels. The original uses ⁷⁄₁₆-inch-diameter dowels but ⅜-inch or ½-inch dowels will do nicely and may be easier to find. The dowel holes in the back legs should go through the tenons and into the far surface of the mortises but to preserve strength they should not pass all the way through the legs. The dowels pinning the stretchers to the stringers can go all the way through. Glue the dowels with weather-resistant glue and saw them off flush when it is dry.

8 Round the corners and edges of the shelves. All four corners of the top shelf and the two front corners of the lower two shelves are rounded to a 2-inch radius. Lay out these corners and cut them with a coping saw. Smooth the corners with a fine rasp and sandpaper. Round-over all of the shelf edges except the back edges of the bottom two shelves with a ⅜-inch-radius piloted roundover bit in your router. Sand the shelves.

9 Glue the back stretcher to the back leg units. If you're building the shelves just like the original, with no shoulders where the back stretcher joins the back legs and with through mortises, you now face a joint that is not common in woodworking today. The assembly cannot be clamped from side to side because the clamp would simply push the legs further onto the stretcher. To assemble the joints, begin by balancing a side assembly on the back surface of the rear leg. Apply glue to the end of the back stretcher and insert it into the mortise in the leg until the end is flush with the outer surface of the leg. Check that the stretcher is square to the leg, then dowel it the same way you doweled the side stretchers. Now put the second side assembly on its back edge, apply glue to the remaining end of the stretcher, and slide the side assembly on. Pin it in place with a dowel as you did the other. Measure to make sure the two sides are parallel, then let the glue dry.

10 Attach the steps to the plant stand. Stand the assembled framework up on its feet on a flat surface and put the shelves in place. Check that all the shelves overhang the same amount on both ends.

Fasten them in place with galvanized nails or deck screws twice as long as the thickness of the shelves. Use two nails or screws at each end of each shelf.

11 Apply a finish. Actually, a finish is optional if you used wood that is rot-resistant for the shelf unit. If you want or need a finish, use materials recommended for the exterior of a house.

APPLE-DRYING TRAY

Every once in a while a design comes along that is pure delight. This tray, which was probably used for drying apples and other fruit, is a good example. The original red stain lends it so much warmth and character you could hang it on your wall. But its generous size and light weight make it so useful that you won't leave it on the wall.

Don't let the angles on the corners of the tray intimidate you. If you haven't made this kind of joint before, just follow the step-by-step instructions and make test cuts on scrap before cutting your tray parts. The tray pieces are joined with glue and nails.

1 **Select the stock and cut the parts.** Choose a light and easily worked wood like pine or poplar for this project and plane it, or have your lumberyard plane it, to ⅝ inch thickness. Edge-glue boards as necessary to obtain the required width for the bottom. (See page 6 for more on edge-gluing.) Rip the parts to width and crosscut them to a couple of inches over the lengths given in the Cutting List.

2 **Bevel the bottom edges of the sides and ends.** The bottom edges of the sides and ends are beveled to join

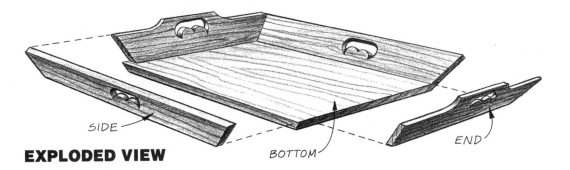

EXPLODED VIEW

SIDE

BOTTOM

END

the bottom. Ripping this bevel before cutting the angled ends makes it easier to cut the ends. Tilt the saw blade 45 degrees and adjust the fence to cut the bevel without narrowing the parts. Rip the bevels, then plane off the saw marks.

3 Cut the angles on the sides and ends. The ends of the tray sides and ends require a compound angle. The simplest way to cut these angles is to make a beveled auxiliary fence for your miter gauge as shown in the *Mitering Jig Detail*. This allows you to cut the joints with only one angle setting: the standard 45-degree blade tilt.

To make the jig, bevel a piece of 8/4 (eight-quarter) stock so the width on the wide surface is no less than the height of your miter-gauge fence. A dry piece of construction lumber will do for this fence. Make the length of the fence twice the distance from your miter-gauge slot to your saw blade. Center the beveled fence on your miter-gauge fence and screw it in place through the holes provided in most miter gauges.

Lay out the bottom edge width on the sides and ends as shown in the *Side View* and *End View.* Tilt the saw blade to 45 degrees, raise the blade to maximum height, and check that the miter-gauge fence is perpendicular to the bar. Hold each part in turn against the beveled

CUTTING LIST

Part	Dimensions
Sides (2)	$\frac{5}{8}'' \times 3\frac{3}{4}'' \times 27\frac{1}{4}''$
Ends (2)	$\frac{5}{8}'' \times 5\frac{1}{16}'' \times 18\frac{1}{16}''$
Bottom	$\frac{5}{8}'' \times 14\frac{1}{2}'' \times 21\frac{15}{16}''$
Hardware	
4d finishing nails	

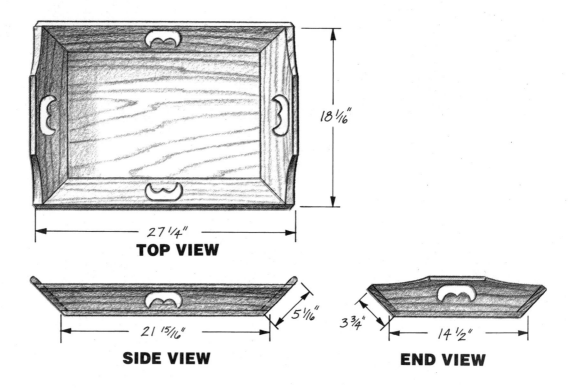

18 ¹/₁₆″

27 ¹/₄″
TOP VIEW

21 ¹⁵/₁₆″

5 ¹/₁₆″

SIDE VIEW

3 ³/₄″

14 ¹/₂″

END VIEW

fence, align the blade with the mark on the bottom edge of the part, and cut the angle on one end of the part. With a 10-inch-diameter saw blade you'll find that the cut is about 1 inch shy of completion on the sides, more on the ends. Finish the cuts with a fine-tooth handsaw.

To cut the second compound angle on each part, turn the miter gauge around and slide it backward into the slot on the saw table. Line up the cut, then screw the part to the beveled fence through the waste area where the handle will be cut out. Make the second cut in each part in this way.

4 Cut out the end piece shapes.
Round-over the top edges of the end pieces with a ¼-inch-radius, ball-bearing roundover bit in your router.

Assemble the sides to the ends on a flat surface, holding them together with masking tape. Mark the top edges of the sides on the ends of the end parts. Since the sides meet the ends at an angle, these marks will angle across the ends. You need only mark the high points at the outside surfaces of the ends.

Make a stiff paper pattern of the end shape as shown in the *End Shape Detail.* Trace the pattern on the outside

SHOP TIP: If two adjoining parts are difficult to hold in position during assembly, drive two small brads into one of them and snip the brads off so they protrude about ¹⁄₁₆ inch. Press the adjoining parts together embedding the brad tips in the second part.

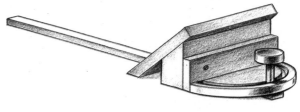

MITERING JIG DETAIL

surface of the ends aligning the bottom of the curve with the marks you made on the ends. Saw to the lines with a coping saw. You'll finish shaping the ends later.

5 **Cut out the handles.** Make a stiff paper pattern of the handle design as shown in the *Handle Detail*. Trace the pattern onto the sides and ends, centering it from end to end. Drill starting holes within the handle layouts, insert the coping saw blade, and cut out the handles. Clean up the sawn edges with sandpaper wrapped around dowels and/or small sticks. While you're at it, soften the edges of the handles for a more comfortable grip.

6 **Assemble the tray frame.** Sand the tray sides and ends. Assemble the sides to the ends on a flat surface, holding them together with masking tape. Make sure the bottom edges are flush. Drill three pilot holes for 4d finish nails to hold each joint together. Drill right through the tape if necessary. Remove the tape, clamp an end piece in your vise, and glue and nail an adjoining side to it. Repeat for all four joints.

Check that the diagonals of the assembly are equal, ensuring that the assembly is square. When the glue is dry, set the nails and fill the nail holes.

7 **Bevel the edges of the bottom.** Tilt the table-saw blade 45 degrees and bevel one edge and one end of the bottom board. Set the assembled sides and ends on the bottom board, align the assembly with the beveled edges of the bottom, and trace the other two edges onto the bottom. Bevel the last two edges of the bottom allowing a little extra for cleaning up the saw marks.

8 **Attach the tray bottom.** Sand the bottom, then tape it to the assembled sides and ends. Drill shank holes for

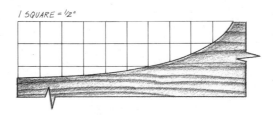

1 SQUARE = ¹⁄₂"

END SHAPE DETAIL

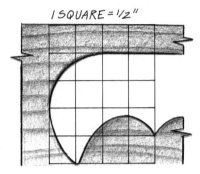

I SQUARE = 1/2"

HANDLE DETAIL

4d finishing nails about every 3 inches to hold the bottom to the sides and ends. Be sure to angle the holes at 45 degrees. Nail the bottom in place, then set the nails and fill the holes. Plane and sand the beveled bottom edges flush with the sides and ends.

9 Bevel the curved ends. The inner surfaces of the ends still protrude above the sides. The curves in the ends must have gradually changing bevels to eliminate this protrusion. The bevels will be 45 degrees at the sides but 90 degrees at the other ends of the curves. Shape the bevels by hand with a round-bottom spokeshave or rasp, then sand them smooth. Clean up any remaining saw marks on the tray.

10 Complete the apple-drying tray. Give the entire tray a final sanding and soften any sharp edges. The original tray has a mellow red-brown stain that you can reproduce if you like, then apply several coats of tung oil or Danish oil, following the manufacturer's instructions.

PART THREE

CABINETS AND CHESTS

ONE-DOOR MILK PAINT CABINET

Antique country furniture is defined by its time and place of origin rather than by its style. Nevertheless, some common designs are classics and this is one of them. Front stiles a quarter of the width of the cabinet, cut out at the bottom to form feet, flanking a single door, characterize a design familiar to everybody.

The original red milk paint on our example holds plenty of scars from heavy use, but it has worn well. The wood is all pine, and the country woodworker worked right through the knots he encountered. Evidence of hand tools is abundant, giving the cabinet plenty of character. The construction, except for the door, is all nailing and gluing. Rather than setting and filling all the nail holes, use cut nails and let the square heads show. You don't need to make the cabinet out of pine but if you substitute a hardwood and want to retain the feel of the original, choose one of the less dense hardwoods like poplar or sycamore.

1 Select the stock and cut the parts. Edge-glue narrower boards to get sufficient width for the top, side, and shelf boards. See "Edge-Gluing" on page 6 if you need help with this. Saw all of the parts to the dimensions specified by the Cutting List. Three boards make up the back on the original, but you can use as many random-width boards as you need. Prepare one board 1 inch × 2 inches × 38 inches for the moldings. You can then mold both edges before sawing it into the front molding and both side moldings. Make the top case rail slightly longer than the given length for now.

One of the appealing features of our original cabinet is the barely perceptible traces of the hand plane that surfaced

EXPLODED VIEW

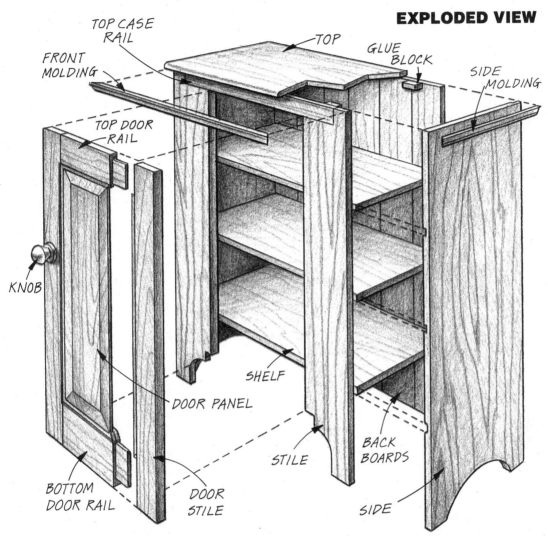

TOP CASE RAIL

FRONT MOLDING

TOP

GLUE BLOCK

SIDE MOLDING

TOP DOOR RAIL

KNOB

DOOR PANEL

SHELF

BOTTOM DOOR RAIL

DOOR STILE

STILE

BACK BOARDS

SIDE

the boards. You can easily achieve that same subtle appearance. Instead of sanding out the machine-planer marks as you normally would just before applying the finish, hand plane them out at this stage of the project. Hone your plane iron to a razor's edge, set it to cut tissue-thin shavings, and systematically remove the machine planer-marks from the outside surfaces of all the parts. You'll notice

from the *Exploded View* that none of the joinery will be affected by this very minor change in thickness.

2 Cut shelf dadoes in the cabinet sides. The cabinet's three shelves are all nailed into dadoes in the sides. Lay out the centerline of the dadoes and clamp a straightedge across the sides

CUTTING LIST

Part	Dimensions
Sides (2)	¾″ × 17¼″ × 44½″
Stiles (2)	¾″ × 7¾″ × 44½″
Shelves (3)	¾″ × 16¾″ × 32″
Top case rail	1″ × 1¾″ × 29¼″
Top	¾″ × 19″ × 34¾″
Glue blocks (6)	¾″ × ¾″ × 2″
Back boards*	½″ × 32⅜″ × 44½″
Front molding	⅝″ × 1″ × 34¼″
Side moldings (2)	⅝″ × 1″ × 18⅝″
Top door rail	¾″ × 3¾″ × 17⅜″
Bottom door rail	¾″ × 5¾″ × 17⅜″
Door stiles (2)	¾″ × 3½″ × 36⅝″
Door panel	¾″ × 11″ × 27⅞″
Knob	1⅞″ dia. × 3¼″
Turn button	½″ × 1¼″ × 3¾″

Hardware

5d cut nails, either common *or* fine finish. Available from many building-supply stores and from
Tremont Nail Company, P.O. Box 111, Wareham, MA 02571; (508) 295–0038.
10d casing nails
2d finish nails
1 pair steel butt hinges, 2″ × 1½″, open
1 dowel, ⅛″ dia. × 1¼″

*The width is made up of several tongue-and-grooved boards, not an edge-glued board. See Step 8.

half the width of your router base from the centerline. The *Side View* gives the shelf locations to the centerlines. Rout the dadoes ¼ inch deep in two or three passes with a ¾-inch straight bit.

3 Rabbet the sides for the back boards. The back boards fit into ½-inch × ½-inch rabbets in the back edges of each side. Use the ¾-inch straight bit already in your router and guide the rou-

ter with its fence attachment. You may need to cut the rabbet in two passes to reduce strain on the router. If you prefer to cut rabbets with a dado cutter, see "Cutting Rabbets with a Dado Cutter" on page 43.

4 Make the foot cutouts. Lay out and saw the foot cutouts shown in the *Front View* and *Side View*. Don't overlook the step in the stile cutouts.

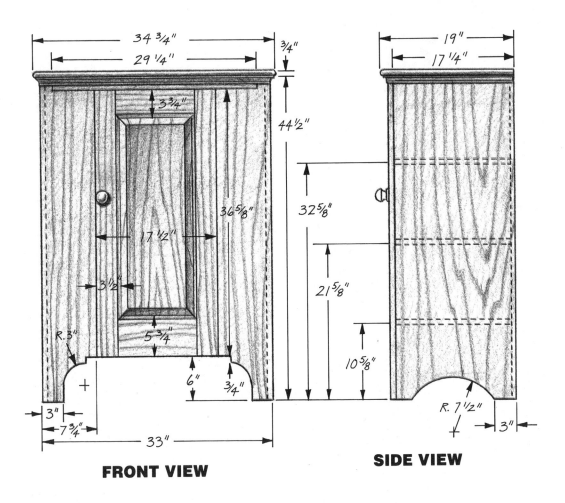

FRONT VIEW

SIDE VIEW

Make the curved cuts with a coping saw and the steps with a backsaw. Clean the sawn edges with a rasp and sandpaper.

5 **Notch the stiles for the top case rail.** The top case rail provides support for the front molding. Lay out the notch in the stiles as shown in the *Front View* with a square and marking gauge and cut it with a handsaw. Clean up the saw cut if necessary with a file. Test the

case rail in the notches to make certain it sits flat.

6 **Assemble the cabinet parts.** Sand the cabinet shelves, and the sides and face boards if you haven't hand planed them. Fit the shelves into their dadoes in the cabinet sides, aligning the back edges of the shelves with the bottom of the back rabbet. If the shelves are not flush with the sides at the front

SHOP TIP: If you know you must fit cabinet parts into dadoes, take one extra step to ensure a proper fit. Set up your router or table saw with the bit or dado cutter you plan to use when you cut the dadoes. Cut a couple of dadoes in scrap wood to use as a test gauge. The depth of the cut is not critical; ¼ inch is fine. Now as you plane your shelf boards to thickness, keep testing them with the gauge. When they slip snugly into the dado without having to be forced, stop planing. If the lumberyard is surfacing your wood for you, take your test gauge along. Ask them to surface it to fit the gauge.

fence attachment gives a straighter, smoother cut. Round-over the end grain first, then the front edge. Sand the edges and the top surface if you haven't hand-planed it.

Glue and nail the top to the cabinet case with 5d cut nails. Drill pilots for the nails and nail the top to the sides and stiles. Clamp the case rail to the top while the glue dries.

Reinforce the joints with glue blocks between the cabinet top and case. To install the glue blocks, turn the cabinet upside down. Apply glue to the blocks, put them in position, and rub them back and forth a few times. They will then stick in place; just don't bump them or move the cabinet for an hour or so.

edges, hand plane them as necessary, then glue and clamp them in place.

Make sure the assembly is lying flat on a flat surface, and check that it's square by measuring diagonally across the corners. Then glue and clamp the cabinet stiles to the sides and shelf boards. Reinforce the joints with 5d cut nails.

Trim the top case rail to fit snugly in its notches in the stiles, then glue and nail it in place. Use a couple of 10d casing nails at each end and predrill for them.

7 **Round the edges of the top and attach it to the cabinet.** Round-over the top and bottom of the front and side edges of the cabinet top with a ¼-inch-radius roundover bit in your router. You can guide the cut with a ball-bearing pilot if your bit is so equipped but you may find that guiding the cut with the

8 **Cut the tongue-and-groove joints on the back boards.** Lay out the back boards across the back opening with the widest boards at the sides. They should more than cover the opening since you'll lose about ³⁄₁₆ inch of width to each joint. Allow an extra ¼ inch or so to trim to fit. Rip the boards as necessary so that their combined width covers the back with allowance for joints and trimming.

Mark each edge at each joint for either a tongue or a groove. Router bits are available for cutting tongues and grooves but they aren't suitable for ½-inch-thick stock so you'll have to cut the joints in multiple passes on the table saw or router table. The *Back Board Detail* gives the dimensions of the joint.

A simple and safe approach to this joint uses a ³⁄₁₆-inch slotting cutter in a table-mounted router. Adjust the router-table fence so that ¼ inch of the cutter

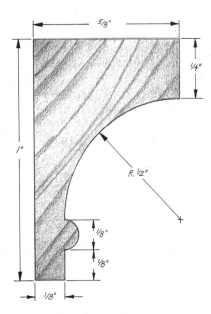

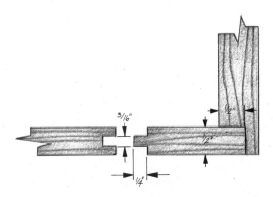

BACK BOARD DETAIL

MOLDING DETAIL

projects beyond the surface of the fence. Adjust the cutter height to center the slot (groove) in the edge of the back boards and cut all of the grooves. Without moving the fence, lower the cutter to cut one side of the tongues, then raise it to cut the other side.

Lay out the back boards across the back opening again, this time assembling the joints. Set pennies on edge between the boards as spacers. This allows the boards to expand in humid weather. The last board should be a bit too wide to fit into the rabbet. Mark it for width from the inside of the cabinet, then rip it on the table saw.

9 **Nail the back boards to the cabinet.** With the last back board fitting nicely in the rabbet and your penny collection spacing the joints, check that all of the boards butt up against the top. Nail the boards in place with two 5d cut nails through each board into each shelf and four more through each end board into the sides. You can have your pennies back now.

Lay out a foot cutout on the back boards similar to the cutout at the front. Saw it with a coping saw.

10 **Rout the front and side molding.** The original molding as shown in the *Molding Detail* was made with a hand-molding plane designed to cut this particular shape. You can come pretty close to the shape with Freud's #99-PK2 Multi-Profile bit (available through dealers that handle the Freud line) or you can substitute a shape produced by one of the many molding bits available today. For safety, cut the molding on a wider piece of wood and then rip the molding from the stock on the table saw.

(continued on page 102)

MILK PAINT

Milk paint has been around at least as long as the Egyptian pyramids. Until the mid-1800s it was the most common form of paint. If you've ever tried to strip off old milk paint, you'll understand why. It sticks with a tenacity that puts modern finishes to shame.

Milk paint is made from skim milk, lime, and whiting or earth pigments. The ready availability of these ingredients contributed to milk paint's popularity.

During the comparatively brief history of modern paints, we've found that the lead in early paints killed our children. Now we are finding that the volatile organic compounds

(VOCs) in paint are equally hazardous to the environment. Milk paint has no lead, petrochemicals, alcohol, or other organic solvents. With the exception of the lime, the ingredients are harmless. Once the paint has fully cured, the lime is also harmless.

Milk paint does have a few drawbacks for some applications. It sticks best to porous surfaces like wood and masonry, it doesn't easily produce the monotonously even color and texture of modern paints, and it watermarks if it isn't sealed.

Cured milk paint consists of a resin, calcium caseinate, that binds particles of colored minerals to each other and to the underlying surface. The calcium caseinate forms when lime, a source of calcium, interacts with milk, a source of casein. Mix milk with lime and colored (or white) minerals and you have milk paint. Follow these specifics:

• Use skim milk, or buttermilk, since butter fat is not good in the paint.

• Use hydrated (slaked) lime, not quick-lime (caustic lime) or ground agricultural limestone. Hydrated lime is available from garden stores and from masonry-supply companies.

• Use alkali-proof earth pigments for the colored minerals. These are readily available for coloring mortar and concrete. Whiting (calcium carbonate or chalk) adds opacity. Zinc oxide makes a white paint and renders a deep earth pigment more pastel.

You can measure the ingredients by either weight or volume since milk and lime have nearly the same density. Use about 12 parts milk to 1 part lime. This is the same as a quart of milk to ⅓ cup of lime. The amount of color to use will vary with the depth of color and consistency that you want. As a starting point for experimentation, use about the same quantity of earth pigment as the amount of lime used. Mix up only as much as you can use in a day and discard any leftovers at the end of the day.

If you want the advantages of genuine milk paint but have no desire to traipse all over gathering ingredients, or don't want to experiment to get the color and consistency that you want, you can buy milk paint in the form of powder. Powdered milk paint is prepared by The Old-Fashioned Milk Paint Company and is available in many paint stores or direct from

the company at Box 222, Groton, MA 01450-0222; (508) 448–6336. Simply mix the powder with water and use it just like milk paint that you made yourself. It comes in sixteen historic colors.

Apply milk paint with a synthetic or foam brush or roller to bare wood or other absorbent surface, or over previous coats of milk paint. Allow it to dry between coats.

Beyond this straightforward application technique, there is room for a variety of special techniques to achieve specific effects.

• You can give your project a mere wash that adds color without hiding the wood by applying a single, thinly pigmented coat.

• You can apply a single, fully pigmented coat and then buff through to the wood in selected wear areas with a Scotch-Brite pad.

• You can apply two or more coats, with or without buffing.

• You can apply coats of different colors, then buff through the top coat in selected wear areas.

• You can overcoat milk paint with linseed or Danish oil or with a modern, clear, acrylic, or polyurethane finish.

Finally, a word of caution. Use only fresh milk and don't use a powdered product that smells spoiled. Try out your paint on disposable materials before using it on a project. If all you want is historically accurate color, you can use Stulbs Old Village Buttermilk Paints. These 100-percent-acrylic paints in Sturbridge Village and Williamsburg colors are available in paint stores. The textures and colors are as close to the original milk paints as modern industry can make them.

11 **Attach the molding to the cabinet.** Tilt the table-saw blade to 45 degrees and check that the miter-gauge fence is square to the bar. Miter the left end of one side molding, the right end of the other side molding, and one end of the front molding. Turn the cabinet upside down. Hold the front molding piece in place and adjust it from left to right so the mitered end joins tightly with the adjoining side molding piece. Holding the front molding in this position, mark the uncut end by scribing along the mitered end of the second side molding. Make the final miter cut right on the scribe line.

Glue and nail the front molding in place with 2d finish nails. Glue the front 3 or 4 inches of the side molding pieces and nail them to the cabinet sides. Set the nails and fill the nail holes. If the side moldings project beyond the back, saw them flush with a fine-tooth backsaw.

12 **Rout the molded edge on the door rails and stiles.** Cut the roundover and fillet on the inside edges of the rails and stiles with a ⅝-inch-radius roundover bit in a table-mounted router. The *Door Joint Detail* gives the critical dimensions.

Next, cut the panel groove in each of the door stiles and rails with a ¼-inch slotting cutter on the router table. You could also cut this groove with a dado cutter by feeding the stock on edge against the saw fence.

13 **Cut the door stile mortises.** The rails join the stiles with ¼-inch through tenons as shown in the

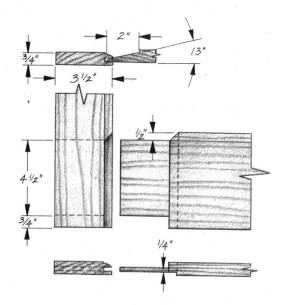

DOOR JOINT DETAIL

drawing. Lay out and cut the mortises first. Remove most of the waste with a ¼-inch brad-point drill bit on the drill press. Clamp a fence to the drill-press table to keep the holes accurately aligned. Keep a piece of scrap wood under the stile to protect the bit and prevent tear-out. Clean up the mortises and square their ends with chisels.

14 **Cut the tenons on the door rails.** "Cutting Tenons" on page 60 provides step-by-step instructions for cutting tenons. For this project, just remember that the shoulders on the tenons have to be offset ½ inch as shown in the *Door Joint Detail.*

15 **Miter the door frame moldings.** The molding on the stiles must be mitered and portions of it removed. The molding on the rails must be mitered to match.

Assemble the door frame as far as it goes. Mark the stile moldings where the rail moldings meet them. With a fine-tooth handsaw, cut from these marks at a 45-degree angle down to the fillet. Then chisel away the molding, down to the fillet, from the end of the stile to the miter cut. Miter the end of the molded edge on the rails with the saw.

16 **Raise the door panel.** There are dozens of panel-raising router bits on the market and while they are not cheap, they do a pretty good job. You can buy one to approximate the shape shown in the *Door Joint Detail*, you can use one that you already own, or you can raise the panel on the table saw.

If you use a panel-raising bit, use it in a table-mounted router. Shape the end grain first, then the side grain.

To raise a panel on the table saw, first attach a tall auxiliary fence to the table-saw fence. Most saws tilt the blade to the right so you'll need to put the fence to the left of the blade and attach the auxiliary fence to the right side of the fence. Tilt the blade to the angle specified in the drawing and adjust the height as specified. Then adjust the fence to produce a tapered edge that will just fit nicely in the frame grooves.

Exercise great care when making the cuts. Hold the boards firmly against the fence and firmly down on the table but be especially careful that your hands don't slip. Since few if any conventional blade guards can be used during this op-

eration, you would be well advised to clamp a 2 × 6 on edge an inch or so to the side of the blade. The 2 × 6 could help prevent a slipping hand from plunging into the blade. The greatest danger is at the end of the cuts when the blade is emerging from the stock.

Saw the ends of the panel first, then the sides. Sand out the saw marks and you're done.

17 **Assemble the door.** Apply glue to the mortises, tenons, and shoulders of the rails and stiles and assemble the frame around the panel. Clamp the joints. Check that the door is

SHOP TIP: A door is built with a framed panel so that its dimensions won't change significantly with changes in humidity. The technique works because wood does not expand and contract in the direction of the grain, even though it may change quite a bit across the grain. The outside dimensions of the door remain constant while the wide panel shrinks and expands.

If the panel is glued into the grooves in the stiles and rails, it will still shrink in dry weather but instead of sliding in the grooves it will split. Most woodworkers are aware of this and don't intentionally glue the panel into the grooves. Many, however, glue the panel by accident; they apply too much glue when assembling the frame joints. The glue squeezes out into the grooves and bonds the panel to the frame. To avoid this, apply only a *very* thin film of glue to the tenons and shoulders and less than normal to the mortises.

square by checking that its diagonals are of equal length. If necessary, place a clamp on the longer diagonal and tighten it until the diagonals are equal. Check that the door is flat by sighting down the plane of the door; the near edge should appear parallel to the far edge. If it isn't, prop or weight corners as necessary.

18 **Make the door knob and turn button.** The turn button in this design is attached to the inside end of the knob stem. Turning the knob latches and unlatches the door.

If you have a lathe, turn the knob as shown in the *Knob Detail*. If you don't have a lathe, you can buy a large wooden knob, drill a ¾-inch hole in the back, and glue in a length of dowel.

Drill a ¾-inch hole in the door stile, then sand the hole larger until the stem on the knob turns easily in the hole. A piece of sandpaper wrapped around a smaller dowel works well for this. Mark

the knob stem where it comes through the inside of the stile.

Make the turn button from a scrap of hardwood. The chamfered ends are not important. Drill the ¾-inch hole in the center. Push the turn button onto the stem up to but not covering the mark on the stem, then drill the pin hole shown in the drawing.

19 **Hang the cabinet door.** Mortise the hinges into the cabinet stile. With the cabinet on its back, lay the door in place with a penny's thickness of clearance at the top. Transfer the location of the hinge mortises onto the door stile and mortise the hinges into the door. Screw the hinges into their mortises, then plane the opposite door stile so the clearance between stiles is the same as the clearance at the top. When you're satisfied with the fit, remove the hinges for finishing.

20 **Finish the cabinet.** Ease the sharp edges on the cabinet with sandpaper to give it a softer, more friendly feel. The milk paint on our cabinet is a tough and time-tested finish. If your local paint dealer doesn't handle it, you can order from The Old-Fashioned Milk Paint Company, Box 222, Groton, MA 01450-0222; (508) 448–6336. You can also make your own as explained on page 100. When your finish is thoroughly dry, rehang the door and install the knob and turn button. Pin the turn button to the knob stem with a short length of ⅛-inch dowel. If you also glue the turn button on, be sure you don't accidentally glue the knob stem into the hole in the door stile.

KNOB DETAIL

DRY SINK

Once common in country homes, dry sinks became obsolete with the spread of indoor plumbing. Still, dry sinks have a charm about them, and they are ideal as a place for houseplants. The example shown here has both shelving and drawers below the sink itself, with doors in front of the shelving. The gallery above the sink provides additional space for display.

Although the design is elaborate for a country dry sink, the construction is simple. The through mortises in the door frames can be made on the drill press. The drawers are rabbeted and nailed together. The carcase is essentially a box with two ends, a partition, and three shelves, all dadoed together. The facing is nailed to this carcase.

The original is made of white pine with poplar drawer sides. Most of the parts are ¾ inch thick; have your supplier plane stock for all of the thinner parts. You can replace the solid wood back, shelves, door panels, and drawer bottoms with plywood if you prefer.

EXPLODED VIEW

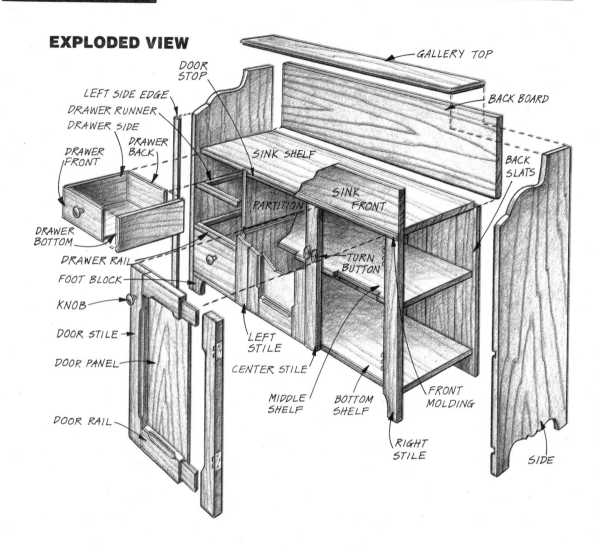

GALLERY TOP

DOOR STOP

LEFT SIDE EDGE

DRAWER RUNNER

DRAWER SIDE

DRAWER FRONT

DRAWER BACK

BACK BOARD

SINK SHELF

DRAWER BOTTOM

PARTITION

SINK FRONT

BACK SLATS

DRAWER RAIL

FOOT BLOCK

TURN BUTTON

KNOB

DOOR STILE

DOOR PANEL

LEFT STILE

CENTER STILE

DOOR RAIL

MIDDLE SHELF

BOTTOM SHELF

RIGHT STILE

FRONT MOLDING

SIDE

1 **Select the stock and cut the parts.** Cut the carcase parts to the dimensions given in the Cutting List. Don't cut the door or drawer parts until after the carcase is assembled. Then if necessary you can adjust the dimensions to fit the openings. Edge-glue stock as necessary to get sufficient width. See page 6 for more on edge-gluing.

2 **Rout shelf dadoes in the sides and partition.** Lay out the shelf dadoes on the inside of each side, and on the right side of the partition. The dimensions are given in the *Side View.* Note in the *Front View* that three shelves join the right side but only two join the left side. The partition requires a dado only for the middle shelf as shown

CUTTING LIST

Part	Dimensions
Sides (2)	$\frac{3}{4}'' \times 18\frac{5}{8}'' \times 38\frac{3}{4}''$
Partition	$\frac{3}{4}'' \times 18\frac{5}{8}'' \times 22\frac{1}{8}''$
Sink shelf	$\frac{3}{4}'' \times 18\frac{5}{8}'' \times 48\frac{3}{8}''$
Bottom shelf	$\frac{3}{4}'' \times 18\frac{5}{8}'' \times 48\frac{3}{8}''$
Middle shelf	$\frac{3}{4}'' \times 18\frac{5}{8}'' \times 37''$
Door stop	$\frac{3}{8}'' \times \frac{3}{4}'' \times 36\frac{3}{8}''$
Sink front	$\frac{3}{4}'' \times 6\frac{7}{8}'' \times 49\frac{1}{4}''$
Drawer rails (2)	$\frac{3}{4}'' \times \frac{13}{16}'' \times 11\frac{5}{8}''$
Drawer rail	$\frac{3}{4}'' \times 1'' \times 10\frac{5}{8}''$
Left stile	$\frac{3}{4}'' \times 2\frac{7}{8}'' \times 22\frac{1}{2}''$
Left side edge	$\frac{3}{4}'' \times \frac{13}{16}'' \times 25\frac{1}{2}''$
Right stile	$\frac{3}{4}'' \times 2\frac{7}{8}'' \times 25\frac{1}{2}''$
Center stile	$\frac{3}{4}'' \times 2\frac{7}{8}'' \times 22\frac{3}{4}''$
Back board	$\frac{3}{4}'' \times 13'' \times 49\frac{1}{4}''$
Back slats*	$\frac{1}{2}'' \times$ random width $\times 25\frac{3}{4}''$
Gallery top	$\frac{3}{4}'' \times 6\frac{3}{4}'' \times 50\frac{3}{4}''$
Drawer runners (4)	$\frac{13}{16}'' \times \frac{3}{4}'' \times 18''$
Foot block	$1\frac{1}{8}'' \times 1\frac{3}{4}'' \times 3''$
Front molding	$\frac{3}{8}'' \times \frac{7}{8}'' \times 49\frac{1}{4}''$
Door stiles (4)	$\frac{3}{4}'' \times 2\frac{7}{8}'' \times 22\frac{7}{16}''$
Door rails (4)	$\frac{3}{4}'' \times 2\frac{7}{8}'' \times 14\frac{1}{2}''$
Door panels (2)	$\frac{3}{8}'' \times 10'' \times 18''$
Turn buttons (2)	$\frac{1}{2}'' \times \frac{7}{8}'' \times 2\frac{1}{4}''$
Drawer front	$\frac{3}{4}'' \times 5\frac{3}{8}'' \times 10\frac{1}{2}''$
Drawer sides (2)	$\frac{1}{2}'' \times 5\frac{3}{8}'' \times 19\frac{1}{8}''$
Drawer back	$\frac{1}{2}'' \times 4\frac{3}{4}'' \times 10''$
Drawer front	$\frac{3}{4}'' \times 6\frac{5}{8}'' \times 10\frac{1}{2}''$
Drawer sides (2)	$\frac{1}{2}'' \times 6\frac{5}{8}'' \times 19\frac{1}{8}''$
Drawer back	$\frac{1}{2}'' \times 6'' \times 10''$
Drawer front	$\frac{3}{4}'' \times 7\frac{1}{2}'' \times 10\frac{1}{2}''$
Drawer sides (2)	$\frac{1}{2}'' \times 7\frac{1}{2}'' \times 19\frac{1}{8}''$
Drawer back	$\frac{1}{2}'' \times 6\frac{7}{8}'' \times 10''$
Drawer bottoms (3)	$\frac{7}{16}'' \times 18\frac{7}{8}'' \times 9\frac{15}{16}''$
Knobs (5)	$1\frac{1}{2}''$ dia. $\times \frac{3}{4}''$

Hardware

6d cut finish nails. Available from many building-supply stores and from Tremont Nail Company, P.O. Box 111, Wareham, MA 02571; (508) 295–0038. Item #CE-6.
16 flathead wood screws, #8 $\times \frac{3}{4}''$
2 pair butt hinges with screws, $2'' \times 1\frac{1}{2}''$, open
2 roundhead wood screws with washers, #8 $\times 1\frac{1}{2}''$
1" brads

*Cut to length during assembly.

in the *Front View.* Rout the dadoes ⁵⁄₁₆ inch deep with a ¾-inch-diameter straight bit. Guide the router with a straightedge clamped across the stock. A simple shop-made T-square is handy for this kind of job.

3 **Rout the partition dadoes in the sink shelf and bottom shelf.** Lay out and rout these two dadoes the same way you did the shelf dadoes. These, too, are ¾ inch wide × ⁵⁄₁₆ inch deep.

4 **Cut out the shaped ends of the sides.** Draw the shapes shown in the *Side View* onto one of the sides. Since the shape at the foot is symmetrical about its centerline, you may find it easier to draw half of it on paper and trace it onto the stock. Clamp the two sides together and saw them both at once with a coping saw or portable jigsaw. Clean up the sawn edges with files and sandpaper. A drum sander in a portable drill can help remove saw marks quickly.

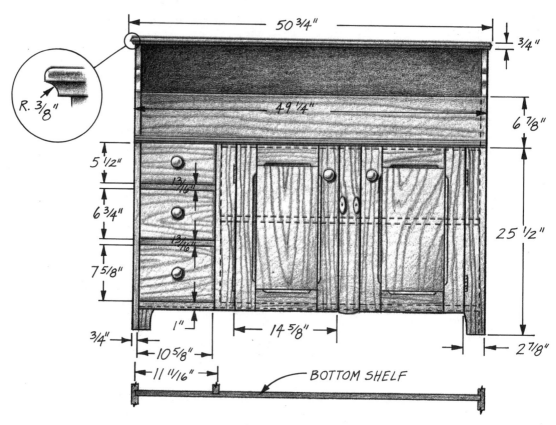

FRONT VIEW

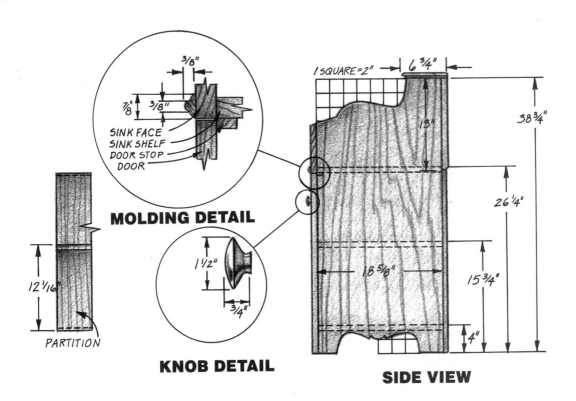

MOLDING DETAIL

3/8"

7/8" 3/8"

SINK FACE
SINK SHELF
DOOR STOP
DOOR

12 1/16"

PARTITION

1 1/2"

3/4"

KNOB DETAIL

1 SQUARE=2"

6 3/4"

13"

38 3/4"

26 1/4"

18 5/8"

15 3/4"

4"

SIDE VIEW

5 **Notch the middle shelf for the door panels.** Unlike most door panels, these are simply screwed to the backs of the frames. Since this makes them proud of the frame surface, the middle shelf must be notched to make space for them. Saw out the notches with a coping saw and clean up the sawn edge with files and sandpaper. The necessary dimensions are given in the *Middle Shelf Detail.*

6 **Glue the carcase together.** Sand the sides and shelves. Test each shelf in its dadoes to make certain they slide in easily. Glue and nail the partition into the sink and bottom shelves. Glue and nail the middle shelf into the parti-

tion. Finally, glue and nail the sides in place. Make certain the front edges of all the pieces are flush with each other. Use 6d cut finish nails about every 8 inches and drive them flush with the wood surface.

Measure diagonally from corner to corner across the face of the carcase. If the two diagonals are not of equal length, reposition the clamps or put a clamp across the long diagonal and tighten it until the diagonals measure the same. Sight across the face of the carcase to make certain it isn't twisted.

7 **Attach the door stop and sink front.** Glue and nail the door stop under the sink shelf in the door compart-

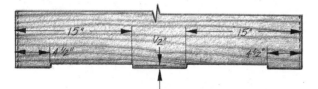

MIDDLE SHELF DETAIL

ment. Make it flush with the front edge of the shelf as shown in the *Molding Detail*. Glue and nail the sink front across the front of the carcase with 6d cut nails. Use three nails at each end and a nail every 6 to 8 inches along the shelf.

8 **Cut the drawer rail joints.** The top two drawer rails join the left stile and left side edge with mortise-and-tenon joints. The bottom drawer rail is simply glued and nailed to the bottom shelf. Lay out the mortises as shown in the *Drawer Detail*. Rout the mortises as explained in "Plunge-Routing Mortises" on page 18 and square the ends. Cut the tenons to match the mortises as explained in "Cutting Tenons" on page 60.

9 **Attach the stiles to the carcase.** Saw the foot curve on the bottom of the right stile with a coping saw. Radius the bottom of the center stile with a rasp. Sand the stiles, the left side edge, and the drawer rails. Glue and nail the stiles to the carcase with 6d nails. They should butt against the sink face. Nail them to the door stop at the top.

Glue the drawer rail tenons into their mortises in the left stile and then into the mortises in the left side edge.

Butt the left side edge against the bottom of the sink face, then nail and glue it to the left side.

10 **Attach the back board.** The back of the dry sink is covered with one wide horizontal board at the top and vertical shiplapped slats at the bottom. Plane a ¼-inch bevel on the lower edge of the horizontal back board as shown in the *Side View*. This leaves a ½-inch-thick edge that matches the

SHOP TIP: Cut nails, even cut finish nails, have enough of a wedge shape to split the wood if they aren't correctly oriented. Turn the nails so their widest dimension is in the direction of the wood grain, not across it.

SHOP TIP: Always thoroughly clean up excess glue. Smeared glue should be wiped up immediately with a wet rag since it dries quickly.

Cleaning up beads of squeezed-out glue is different. If you wipe them up immediately, they smear along the joint. Wait 20 to 30 minutes for the glue to begin to set. Then scrape off the glue with an old chisel. The beads of glue will still be soft but will come off more cleanly. After scraping away the beads with the chisel, wipe the glue joint well with a wet rag to remove any remaining smears, then clean the chisel with the rag.

Keep one old chisel just for glue. It should be at least ¾ inch wide.

DRAWER DETAIL

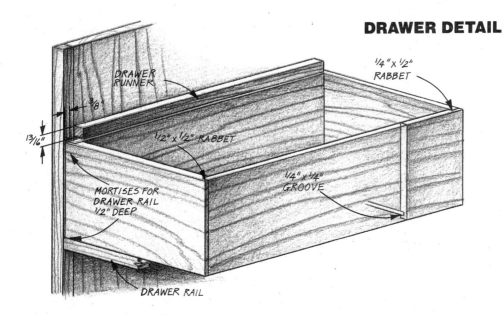

DRAWER RUNNER

3/8"

13/16"

1/4" x 1/2" RABBET

1/2" x 1/2" RABBET

1/4" x 1/4" GROOVE

MORTISES FOR DRAWER RAIL 1/2" DEEP

DRAWER RAIL

thickness of the back slats. Sand the inside surface of the back board, then nail it to the back of the dry sink with 6d nails. Make it flush with the top of the sides. Don't glue this board; it must be able to move with seasonal moisture changes.

11 **Attach the back slats.** Cut the shiplap joints between the random-width back slats with the router. Use the two widest slats at the sides. They get a rabbet (half a shiplap joint) on one edge only as shown in the *Shiplap Detail*. Make sure you cut the rabbets in the rest of the slats on opposite surfaces as shown in the drawing. Cut and fit the slats for the entire back before nailing any in place.

Lay the sink on its front, then position the slats on the back. Leave 1/8 inch between adjoining slats. Trim the outside slats to adjust the overall fit.

Trace along the bottom of the bottom shelf to mark the length of the slats. Crosscut the middle slats to this length. Lay out feet on the two outer slats similar to the front feet shown in the *Front View* and saw them with a coping saw. When you're sure they all fit well, nail them in place.

12 **Install the gallery top.** Rout a 3/8-inch-radius cove on the edges of the gallery top as shown in the *Front View*, using a piloted coving bit. Rout the cove on the side edges, then the front

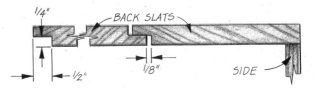

1/4"

BACK SLATS

1/2"

1/8"

SIDE

SHIPLAP DETAIL

edges, but not the back edge. Round-over the top of these edges with a ⅜-inch-radius roundover bit.

Sand the gallery top, then glue and nail it to the sides and back board with 6d nails.

13 **Attach the drawer runners and foot block.** Nail the drawer runners to the side and partition as shown in the *Drawer Detail*. Predrill the nail holes in the runners to minimize the hammering and glue the center 3 inches of each runner.

Saw the foot curve in the inside edge of the foot block with a coping saw, then glue and clamp the foot block to the left side edge as shown in the *Front View*.

14 **Make and attach the front molding strip.** This strip adds a bit of decoration and hides the nails across the sink front. A point-cutting roundover bit with a ³⁄₁₆-inch radius will closely approximate the shape of the original molding as shown in the *Molding Detail*.

Shape the molding on the edge of a larger piece of wood, then saw it free. Mount the router in a router table to make the cuts. Glue and clamp it to the bottom edge of the sink face. A suggestion for clamping it is shown on this page.

15 **Make the door frames.** Lay out the mortises and tenons as shown in the *Door Detail*. These through mortises are too deep to cut with a plunge

SHOP TIP: Use ordinary C-clamps and scraps of stiff wood as shown to obtain greater reach than possible with the C-clamps alone.

router the way you mortised for the drawer rails. Instead, cut them by drilling a series of overlapping holes with a brad-point bit in the drill press, then cleaning up the mortise with a chisel. Cut the tenons as you cut the drawer rail tenons.

Rout the decorative cove cuts on the rails and stiles with the same cove bit you used for the gallery top. Sand the door frame parts and the panels. Glue and clamp the rails and stiles together on a flat surface, and check that the diagonals are of equal length.

16 **Attach the panels.** Sand the door panels. Drill and countersink shank holes for #8 screws in the door panels, three along each side and one centered top and bottom. Drill corresponding pilot holes in the door frames and screw the panels in place with #8 × ¾-inch screws.

17 **Hang the doors.** Set the dry sink on its back to make it easier to fit the doors. Lay out the positions of the hinges on the cabinet and door stiles. Cut the hinge mortises with a sharp knife and chisel to a depth equal to the thickness of the hinge leaves. You can mark the depth of the mortises with a marking gauge. Drill pilot holes for the hinge screws and install the hinges.

The turn buttons, which hold the doors closed, are roughly made and are more attractive for it. Whittle or sand the buttons to a shape that pleases you. Drill screw shank holes in the centers and screw them to the center stile with #8 × 1½-inch roundhead wood screws. Use washers between the stile and turn buttons for easier operation.

18 **Cut the drawer joinery.** In the original, the drawer sides are nailed into rabbets in the drawer fronts and the backs are nailed into rabbets in the drawer sides as shown in the *Drawer Detail*. Rout the rabbets with a table-mounted router.

Rout the drawer bottom grooves in the drawer fronts and sides. If you're using solid wood for the drawer bottoms, hand plane a bevel on the edges of the bottoms so they will fit the grooves.

19 **Assemble the drawers.** Sand the inside surfaces of the drawer parts. Glue and nail the sides to the fronts and backs. Check that the assemblies are square, then slide the drawer bottoms into the grooves. Nail the drawer bottoms to the backs with a couple of 1-inch brads.

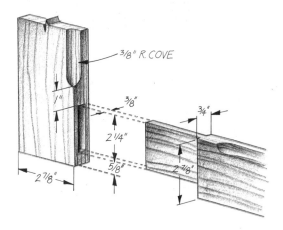

DOOR DETAIL

You can turn the drawer and door knobs on a lathe if you have one, or buy them at most hardware stores. The knobs on the original are shown in the *Knob Detail*. Assuming that you buy or turn knobs that attach with a screw, drill screw shank holes in the center of each drawer front and in the door stiles as shown in the *Front View*. Install the knobs on the drawers and doors.

20 **Complete the dry sink.** Soften any hard edges on the dry sink with sandpaper. Round-over the top edge of the sink face board with a block plane and sand it smooth.

Remove the doors and drawers to apply the finish. Dust the dry sink, first with a brush and then with a tack cloth. Stain the dry sink if you wish. When the stain has thoroughly dried, apply a penetrating oil (such as tung oil), varnish, or polyurethane.

CHIMNEY CABINET

Chimney cabinets got their name from their appearance, not from their function. They were tall and slender, like a chimney, and held anything from plates and dishes to jams and jellies. They were quite common in a variety of styles and sizes and range from the fairly sophisticated, with crown moldings and brass hardware, to simpler examples nailed together from a few wide boards.

While few people today would fill a chimney cabinet with dishes or jellies, the size and proportions make these cabinets convenient for storing sweaters or towels. We've fitted this one with closely spaced hardboard shelves to keep the contents easily accessible. A chimney cabinet takes up very little floor space, will hold an enviable collection of sweaters, and will make each one easy to remove.

This particular design features raised panel doors, shaped top and bottom pieces, and a bead along the face frame. The details are easy to produce and add considerable interest to the cabinet. Inside, there are 2 fixed shelves and provisions for 12 removable shelves. If you like, you can have a separate shelf for each sweater.

The cabinet in the photo was made from poplar and has an antiqued, painted finish. You can reproduce it as shown, or choose a wood and finish to suit your own taste. The back is ¼-inch plywood and the adjustable shelves are ¼-inch tempered hardboard.

1 Cut the pieces to size. Cut all the pieces except the back and the adjustable shelves to the sizes specified by the Cutting List. If you have to edge-glue narrow boards to make the wide pieces, see "Edge-Gluing" on page 6.

2 Dado and rabbet the sides. On each side, lay out the locations of the two fixed shelves as shown in the

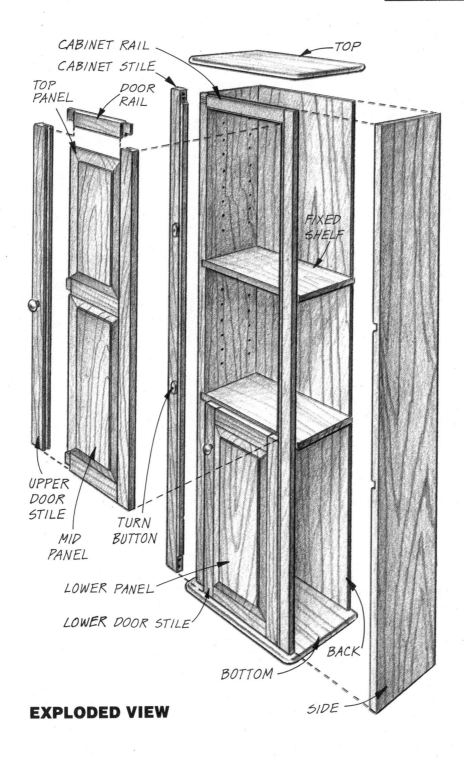

CABINET RAIL

CABINET STILE

TOP PANEL

DOOR RAIL

TOP

FIXED SHELF

UPPER DOOR STILE

TURN BUTTON

MID PANEL

LOWER PANEL

LOWER DOOR STILE

BOTTOM

BACK

SIDE

EXPLODED VIEW

Side View. Set up a ¾-inch-wide dado blade to cut ⅜ inch deep. Make a test cut in a piece of scrap and check the fit of the shelves in the dado. Adjust the setup if necessary to achieve a snug fit. Cut the dadoes in the sides by guiding the pieces past the blade with the miter gauge. An extension fence on the miter gauge will help you get straight cuts, square across the boards.

Next, cut the rabbets in the sides for the back. Position the rip fence so that it's 11 inches from the blade. Guide the sides along the fence to cut the rabbets in the back. Be sure to make a left and a right side.

CUTTING LIST

Part	Dimensions
Sides (2)	¾″ × 11¼″ × 64½″
Cabinet stiles (2)	¾″ × 2″ × 64½″
Cabinet rail	¾″ × 2″ × 12¾″
Top/bottom (2)	¾″ × 12½″ × 17″
Fixed shelves (2)	¾″ × 11″ × 15¼″
Back*	¼″ × 15¼″ × 65¼″
Upper door stiles (2)	¾″ × 2″ × 37½″
Lower door stiles (2)	¾″ × 2″ × 25″
Door rails (5)	¾″ × 2″ × 9″
Top panel	¾″ × 8⅞″ × 14¼″
Mid panel	¾″ × 8⅞″ × 19″
Lower panel	¾″ × 8⅞″ × 22″
Turn buttons (2)	½″ × ¾″ × 1½″
Adjustable shelves†	¼″ × 10⅞″ × 14⅜″

Hardware

4 dowels, ¼″ dia. × 1½″
6d finish nails
#18 × 1″ brads
4 plastic floor glides
2 pairs butt hinges with screws, 1½″ × 1½″, open
2 roundhead wood screws with washers, #8 × 1¼″
2 wooden knobs, 1⅛″ dia.
As many as 48 adjustable shelf brackets. Available from The Woodworker's Store, 21801 Industrial Blvd., Rogers, MN 55374-9514; (612) 428–3200. Part #33894.

*Make from plywood.
†Make from plywood or hardboard; as many as a dozen can be accommodated.

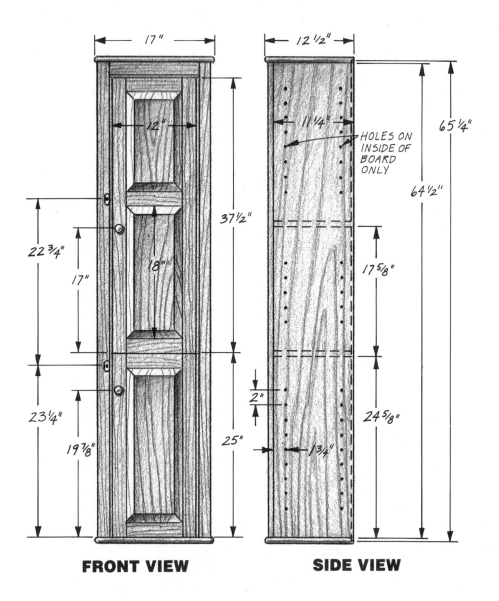

FRONT VIEW

SIDE VIEW

When cross-
cutting a number of pieces to the same
length, use a stop to help ensure accuracy. Screw an extension fence to the
miter gauge, then clamp a stop block to
the fence at the required distance from
the blade. Hold the pieces against the
stop block as you cut them and they will
all be the same length.

3 **Cut the face-frame bead.** Rout a
bead along one edge of the cabinet
stiles and rail as shown in the *Face
Frame Detail*. Some manufacturers call
the bit for this cut a bullnose bit rather
than a beading bit. Mounting the router
in a router table will give you more control than hand-holding the router in this
situation.

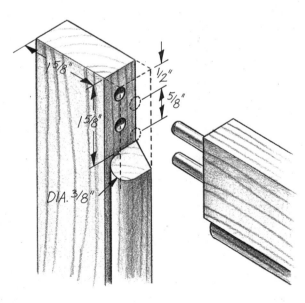

FACE FRAME DETAIL

4 **Bore the face-frame dowel
holes.** Bore the dowel holes in the
ends of the rail first. Lay them out to
the dimensions given in the *Face Frame
Detail*. Use a doweling jig to help align
the drill bit and drill the holes ¾ inch
deep. Transfer the dowel locations to
the stiles with dowel centers. Be sure to
make a right and a left stile; the two are
mirror images of each other. Drill the
holes in the stiles 1³⁄₁₆ inches deep. After cutting away the bead on the stiles
as shown in the drawing, the holes
should be not less than ¾ inch deep.
Use the doweling jig to help keep the
drill bit cutting straight.

5 **Miter the face frame.** In order
for the bead to appear as if it wraps
around the corner, it must be mitered as
shown in the *Face Frame Detail*. Lay out
the cuts on the backs of the stiles. Tilt
the blade on the table saw to a 45-
degree angle. Adjust the height of the
blade so it doesn't cut past the flat next
to the bead. Saw the miters with the
stock on edge against the miter-gauge
fence.

Miter the ends of the bead on the
rail while the saw is still set up for a 45-
degree cut. This is a simple cut that just
removes the corner of the rail. The
Front View shows how the rail meets the
stiles.

To remove the waste portion of the
bead on the stiles, tilt the blade on the
table saw back to 90 degrees and raise it
all the way up. In this position the leading edge of the blade will be as nearly
vertical as possible. Set the rip fence to
remove the bead and the groove (called
a quirk) next to it, but no more. Guide a

stile along the fence into the blade, sawing down the quirk. Stop the cut about ¼ inch before you get to the miter cut. Remember that the blade is cutting slightly farther on the side of the stile that you can't see. You'll be able to cut one of the stiles with the bead up but to cut the other stile you'll either have to cut with the bead down or move the fence to the other side of the blade. Once you've cut both stiles on the table saw, finish with a handsaw. Then clean up with a chisel.

6 **Assemble the frame.** Sand the face-frame parts. Apply glue to the dowel holes, insert the dowels, and clamp the frame together. Check to make sure the rails are square to the stiles and parallel to each other. Set the frame aside to dry.

7 **Shape the top and bottom.** The edges of the top and bottom have a bullnose (half-circle) profile. You can shape the bullnose with a ⅜-inch roundover bit if you don't have a ¾-inch bullnose bit. Do the shaping on the router table if you have one. Rout the ends first, then one side.

SHOP TIP: If you cut dowel pins from longer dowel rod, plane a flat on one side of the dowel with a block plane. This provides an escape route for the air and glue that would otherwise be trapped in the joint.

The back edge of the top and bottom require a rabbet for the back. Chuck a ⅜-inch or larger straight bit in the router and adjust the router and fence to cut a rabbet to match the rabbets in the sides. Rout the rabbet 15¼ inches long, centered in the back edges of the top and bottom. Square up the ends of the rabbets with a chisel.

8 **Assemble the cabinet.** Sand all the pieces. Spread glue in the dadoes and insert the fixed shelves into the sides. Make sure the front edges are flush and the shelves are square to the sides. Drive 6d finish nails through the sides into the shelves to reinforce the joints.

Turn the cabinet upside down and put the bottom in place. It should be flush along the back and centered from side to side. Attach it to the sides with glue and 6d finish nails, then turn the cabinet over and attach the top. Lay the cabinet down on its back and check that the cabinet is square by measuring the diagonals. If the diagonals are equal, the assembly is square. Spread glue on the edges of the sides and put the face frame in place. Make sure the frame is flush along both sides and nail it in place with 6d finish nails.

9 **Install the back and glides.** Measure the back of the cabinet from rabbet to rabbet and cut the plywood back to fit. Apply a bead of glue to the rabbets and tack the back in place with 1-inch brads. While the cabinet is still lying down, screw the plastic floor glides to the underside of the bottom.

10 **Groove the door frame parts.** Adjust a ¼-inch-wide dado blade on the table saw to cut ½ inch deep. Adjust the fence to center the ¼-inch cut in the edge of the ¾-inch-thick door stock as shown in the *Door Detail*. Groove an edge of the door stiles and rails, then groove the second edge of one of the rails.

11 **Cut tongues on the ends of the rails.** Cut the tongues on the ends of the rails as described in "Cutting Tenons" on page 60. The dimensions are given in the *Door Detail*.

12 **Make the door panels.** The panels on this cabinet are raised on both sides. To make them on the table saw, stand the panels on edge and saw them with a tilted blade.

Lay out the panel profile as shown in the *Door Detail* on the edge of one of the panels. Tilt the blade on the table saw to 82 degrees. Position the fence so that the blade angles away from it. On many saws this means that the fence will have to be placed to the left of the blade. Adjust the fence to align the blade with the layout on the panel edge. Hold the panel on edge against the fence to make the cut. Cut all four edges on both sides of the panels.

13 **Assemble the doors.** Sand all the door parts. Fit the panels and rails into the grooves in the stiles. Make sure everything fits together. The panels should have a slight amount of play from side to side. This will allow them to expand with changes in the weather without forcing the door frames apart. When everything fits, apply glue to the tongues on the rails and glue the frames together. Be careful not to get any glue on the panels.

14 **Hang the doors.** Check the fit of the doors in the cabinet. There should be a slight gap all the way around. For appearance, the size of this gap is not as important as its uniformity. An even gap of from ⅟₁₆ to ⅛ inch is fine. You can make adjustments to the doors by planing the edges with a hand plane.

Hang the doors with butt hinges. Depending on the size of the gap around the doors, you may or may not need to cut mortises for the hinges. If mortises are needed, lay them out by tracing around the hinges with a sharp knife.

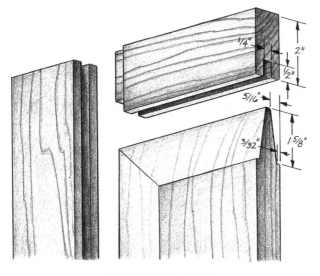

DOOR DETAIL

Cut away the waste with a chisel. Install the hinges with the screws that came with them.

15 **Attach the knobs and turn buttons.** Drill screw shank holes through the door stiles and screw the knobs to the doors as shown in the *Front View.* Round the corners on the turn buttons with sandpaper and screw them in place with #8 × 1¼-inch round-head wood screws. Include a washer between the turn button and the cabinet.

16 **Add the adjustable shelves.** Saw an adjustable shelf to the dimensions given in the Cutting List. Check it for fit up and down the inside of the cabinet and trim it if necessary, then cut the rest of the shelves to match.

17 **Finish the cabinet.** To duplicate the finish shown in the photo, first prime the cabinet with interior latex primer. When the primer is dry, apply a coat of black, semi-gloss latex enamel. When this is dry, apply a coat of red semi-gloss enamel. When the red is dry, rub through it with 00 steel wool as you see fit. Concentrate on outside corners that would be subject to abuse, the handles, and the areas around the turn buttons. You may even want to rub through to the raw wood in these areas to simulate years of use.

18 **Install the shelf brackets.** With the finish applied, the danger of filling the shelf bracket holes with paint is over. Use a template to accurately drill the holes in the inside of the cabinet. Cut a 2¼-inch × 21-inch template out of ¼-inch plywood or hardboard. Lay out the shelf bracket holes on the template starting 4 inches from one end, 1¾ inches from one edge. Lay out and drill ¼-inch holes every 2 inches as shown in the *Side View.* Use the template to position and guide the drill bit. Drill both rows of bracket holes ½ inch deep in both sides of the top and bottom sections of the cabinet. Then saw off the template to 14 inches long and drill the holes in the middle section. Use a drill stop to avoid drilling the holes too deep.

SLANT-FRONT CABINET

Built-in kitchen cabinets are a relatively recent innovation. Before their widespread use, dinnerware and other utensils were stored and displayed in open-front, freestanding cabinets. Today, the open-front cabinet is more likely to hold and display collectibles, whether

commemorative plates, antique teacups, old photos, or even dolls or books.

This cabinet is unusual because the upper, open part slopes back. While most of the construction is straightforward, the front stiles are kerfed and bent where the slanted top portion meets the vertical bottom portion. A simple crown molding decorates the top. Identical or at least very similar moldings are available at lumberyards, though probably not in a choice of wood species. The cabinet in the photo is made of poplar.

1 Cut the parts to size. Cut all the parts except the stiles, the crown molding, and the back to the sizes specified by the Cutting List. If you need to edge-glue narrow boards to make up the wider widths, see "Edge-Gluing" on page 6. Cut the stiles about ¼ inch longer than called for and the crown molding about 2 inches longer than called for. Leave the stock for the back until later.

2 Rabbet and dado the sides. The sides require dados for the shelves, and rabbets for the back and top. Set up a dado cutter for ¾-inch width and ⅜-inch depth of cut. Test the setup on scrap and check the fit of the shelves in the dado. They should fit snugly.

With a long extension fence on the miter gauge, cut the dadoes for the shelves as shown in the *Side View.* Then cut a ¾-inch-wide rabbet at the top of

EXPLODED VIEW

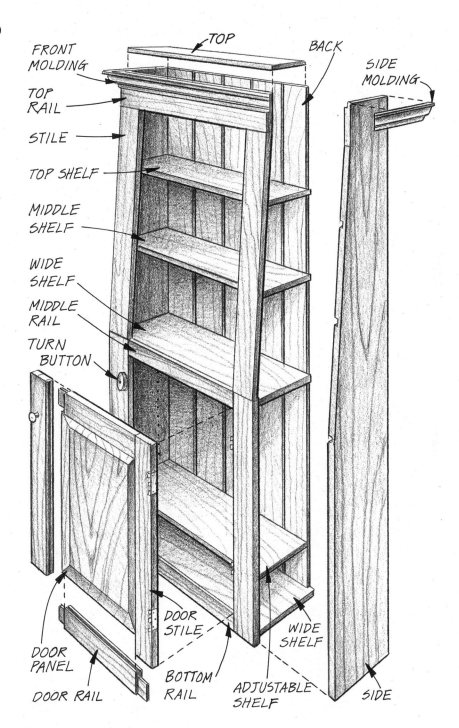

FRONT MOLDING

TOP

BACK

SIDE MOLDING

TOP RAIL

STILE

TOP SHELF

MIDDLE SHELF

WIDE SHELF

MIDDLE RAIL

TURN BUTTON

DOOR STILE

WIDE SHELF

DOOR PANEL

DOOR RAIL

BOTTOM RAIL

ADJUSTABLE SHELF

SIDE

CUTTING LIST

Part	Dimensions
Sides (2)	$\frac{3}{4}'' \times 11\frac{1}{4}'' \times 72''$
Top	$\frac{3}{4}'' \times 9\frac{1}{8}'' \times 29''$
Wide shelves (2)	$\frac{3}{4}'' \times 10\frac{7}{8}'' \times 29''$
Middle shelf	$\frac{3}{4}'' \times 10\frac{1}{4}'' \times 29''$
Top shelf	$\frac{3}{4}'' \times 9\frac{5}{8}'' \times 29''$
Top rail	$\frac{3}{4}'' \times 5'' \times 29\frac{3}{4}''$
Stiles (2)	$\frac{3}{4}'' \times 4'' \times 37\frac{1}{16}''$
Middle rail	$\frac{3}{4}'' \times 2'' \times 21\frac{3}{4}''$
Bottom rail	$\frac{3}{4}'' \times 2\frac{1}{2}'' \times 21\frac{3}{4}''$
Back*	$\frac{3}{8}'' \times 29'' \times 70\frac{1}{4}''$
Side moldings (2)	$\frac{3}{4}'' \times 2\frac{1}{4}'' \times 12''$
Front molding	$\frac{3}{4}'' \times 2\frac{1}{4}'' \times 32\frac{3}{4}''$
Door stiles (2)	$\frac{3}{4}'' \times 2\frac{7}{8}'' \times 27\frac{1}{2}''$
Door rails (2)	$\frac{3}{4}'' \times 3'' \times 17''$
Door panel	$\frac{3}{4}'' \times 16\frac{7}{8}'' \times 21\frac{1}{2}''$
Adjustable shelf	$\frac{3}{4}'' \times 10\frac{3}{4}'' \times 28\frac{1}{8}''$
Turn button	$\frac{3}{4}'' \times \frac{1}{2}'' \times 2''$

Hardware

3d and 5d fine cut finish nails. Available from many building-supply stores and from Tremont Nail Company, P.O. Box 111, Wareham, MA 02571; (508) 295–0038. Items #CE-3 and #CE-5.

1 pair brass butt hinges with screws, $1\frac{1}{2}'' \times 2''$, open

1 wooden knob with screw, $1\frac{1}{2}''$ dia.

1 roundhead wood screw, #6 × 1″

4 shelf supports, $\frac{1}{4}''$ dia. Available from The Woodworker's Store, 21801 Industrial Blvd., Rogers, MN 55374-9514; (612) 428–3200. Item #33894.

*Made up of random-width boards.

the sides for the top. Use the rip fence to guide the stock while cutting the ⅜-inch-wide rabbets for the back. See page 43 for more on cutting rabbets with a dado cutter. These rabbets can run the full length of the sides.

3 **Drill the sides for the adjustable shelf.** Drill a series of ¼-inch holes in the sides for the shelf brackets as shown in the *Side View.*

4 **Cut the sides to shape.** Lay out the angled cuts on the sides from the dimensions shown in the *Side View.* Note that the slant does not go all the way to the top; the last 5 inches is vertical. One way to produce this somewhat unusual shape is to cut the angled part all the way to the top and then glue on a wedge to restore the vertical part. Make the angled cuts with a portable circular or saber saw, then plane the sawed edges of the sides and the scraps. Cut 5-

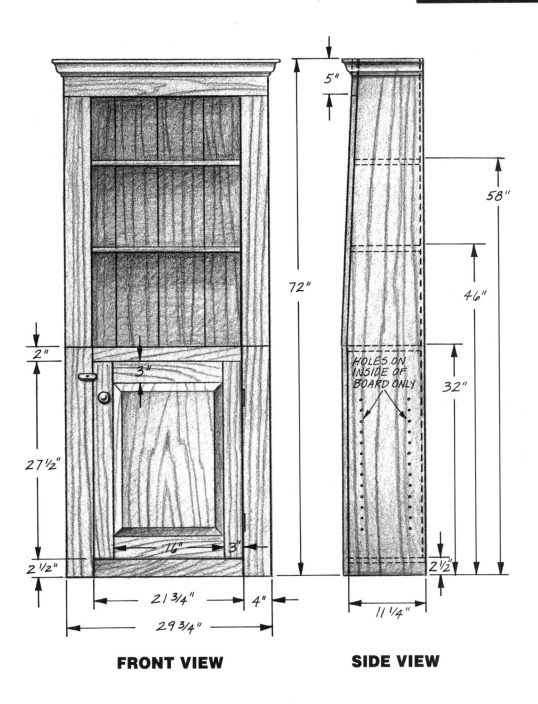

FRONT VIEW   **SIDE VIEW**

72"

5"

58"

46"

32"

2"

27½"

2½"

3"

16"   3"

21¾"   4"

29¾"

HOLES ON
INSIDE OF
BOARD ONLY

2½"

11¼"

125

inch-long wedges from the pointed ends of the scraps and glue them in place on the sides as shown in the *Cross Section at Top.*

When the glue is dry, notch the wedges with a backsaw to restore the rabbets at the tops of the sides.

5 **Assemble the cabinet.** Sand the top, the sides, and all the shelves. Assemble the cabinet without glue to check the fit of all the parts. When

everything fits right, apply glue to the dadoes and top rabbet, then reassemble the cabinet. Make sure the shelves and the top are flush with the front of the cabinet. Reinforce the joints with 5d cut nails, three nails per shelf. Check that the diagonals at the back are equal, assuring that the cabinet is square.

6 **Attach the top rail.** Glue the top rail in place across the front of the cabinet. Reinforce the glue joint with 5d fine cut finish nails.

7 **Bend and attach the stiles.** The stiles on the front of the cabinet are kerfed and bent to the shape of the sides. With a regular blade on the table saw, set the depth of cut to ⅝ inch. Kerf each stile 32 inches from one end. The ⅝-inch depth of cut should leave ⅛ inch of wood uncut. Hold a stile in place along one side of the cabinet with its top end against the top rail. The kerf should fall right at the vertex of the side angle. If it doesn't (remember, you left the stiles ¼ inch longer than the Cutting List called for), trim the top end to adjust where the kerf falls. Repeat with the other stile.

When both stiles fit, bend the lower ends into position. If the wood seems reluctant to bend, place a wet cloth over the area that needs to bend and heat it with a steam iron until it bends easily. Glue the stiles to the cabinet, and nail them with 5d finish nails.

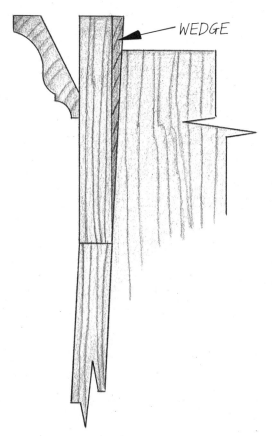

WEDGE

CROSS SECTION AT TOP

8 **Attach the lower two rails.** Sand the middle and bottom rails. Glue and nail them flush with the shelves, between the stiles.

9 **Make and attach the back.** The back of the cabinet is made up of shiplapped, random-width boards. Shiplapping allows the boards to expand and contract without opening any gaps at the back of the cabinet. The joints are disguised and the back is decorated with a bead along each joint. The back boards should run from the top of the cabinet to the bottom of the lowest shelf.

Plane or resaw the stock to ⅜ inch thick. Make sure you have enough boards to cover the width of the cabinet plus ⁹⁄₁₆ inch per board. Rabbet the edges of the boards as shown in the *Beaded Back Detail*. Cut the rabbets with a dado cutter as explained on page 43. Rabbet the two outside boards on one edge only.

The easiest way to cut the beads along the edges of the rabbets is with a molding head on the table saw. The cutters that produce this size bead produce several parallel beads. Set up the saw so the corner to be beaded passes over one edge of the cutters, cutting a single bead. If you prefer, you can bead the edges with a scratch stock or hand-

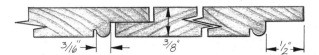

BEADED BACK DETAIL

molding plane. When you're done, sand all the boards.

Start at one side of the cabinet and nail the boards to the shelves one at a time. Nail the boards only along the side of the board that's beaded, about 1 inch from the edge, in order to miss both the rabbet and the bead. The unbeaded edge is held in place by the beaded edge of the adjoining board. Leave a ¹⁄₁₆-inch expansion gap between the boards as shown in the drawing.

10 **Install the crown molding.** The crown molding wraps around the top of the cabinet with miter joints at the corners. Mitering crown molding is not as difficult as it looks. The secret is to hold it against the miter gauge as shown in *Mitering Crown Molding*.

Put the miter gauge in the left hand slot and adjust it counterclockwise to 45 degrees. At this setting, holding the stock as shown in the drawing, miter the right end of the left side molding and the right end of the front molding. Don't worry about length at this time; remember that you have about 2 extra inches on each piece. Now put the miter gauge in the right hand slot and adjust it clockwise to 45 degrees. Miter the left end of the right side molding.

Keep the right side molding in place against the miter-gauge fence. Without

SHOP TIP: Use coins as spacers when installing parts with a gap between them. Pennies, nickels, dimes, and quarters all have useful and different thicknesses. Insert the coins on edge between the boards to keep the spacing consistent.

moving it along the fence, pull the miter gauge and molding back toward you to the front side of the blade. Put a small piece of masking tape on the saw table and mark, on the masking tape, the location of the miter cut that you just made.

Now hold the front and right side moldings in place on the cabinet. Adjust them so the miter joint closes tightly. With the molding in this position, mark the right side molding for length at the back of the cabinet and mark the front molding for length at the left front corner of the cabinet.

Put the front molding in place against the miter gauge fence, align the mark on the left end of the molding with the mark on the masking tape, and miter the left end of the front molding.

To attach the molding to the cabinet, apply glue to the bottom back edge of the front molding and center it on the top rail. Nail it in place with 3d finish nails along its bottom edge. Attach the side moldings in a similar way, gluing the

miter joints and first 2 inches of the back edge but leaving the remainder of the back edge without glue. Fit the miter joints as tightly as you can, even if that means that one piece of molding projects slightly beyond the adjoining piece. When the glue is dry, sand off any small projection while preserving a crisp corner at the joint.

11 **Make and assemble the cabinet door.** The door for this cabinet is a straightforward, country-style, frame-and-raised-panel door. Dimensions are given in the *Door Detail*. Begin by cutting a ¼-inch-wide by ½-inch-deep groove centered in an edge of each stile and rail piece. Then cut tenons on the ends of the rails to fit the groove. See page 60 for how to cut tenons on the table saw.

Raise the panel for the door by bevel-cutting all four edges of the panel on both sides. Use a high auxiliary fence fastened to the table-saw fence to keep the panel stable during the cut. After sanding the parts, glue the frame together around the panel but make sure the panel itself is not glued to the frame.

12 **Hang the door.** Ideally, the assembled door is too tight in the door opening. This allows you to plane a uniform clearance all the way around. The amount of clearance is largely a matter of personal taste but should be great enough that even in humid weather the door opens and closes freely. If you're fitting the door at a humid time of year, ¹⁄₁₆ inch of clearance is plenty. A more sophisticated design might call for

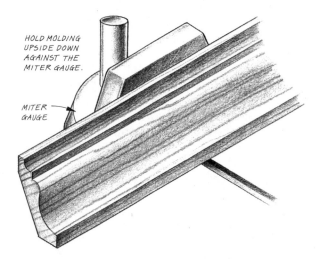

HOLD MOLDING
UPSIDE DOWN
AGAINST THE
MITER GAUGE.

MITER
GAUGE

MITERING CROWN MOLDING

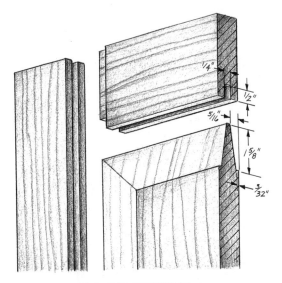

DOOR DETAIL

the waste with a chisel. Screw the hinges to the cabinet and the door with flathead wood screws.

13 **Attach the hardware.** Drill a shank hole and screw the knob to the door at a convenient height as shown in the *Front View.* Round the corners on the turn button with sandpaper and attach it to the cabinet stile with a #6 × 1-inch roundhead wood screw. Place a washer between the turn button and the cabinet.

14 **Finish the cabinet.** Choose a finish that's appropriate for the room where you intend to use the cabinet. You can give it a front room appearance by finishing it with walnut stain and polyurethane as shown in the photo, or you can make it more at home in a kitchen or family room by painting it. Milk paint, as described on page 100, would be appropriate.

less. If you're fitting the door late in a relatively dry season, allow more clearance; ⅛ inch could prove to be too little in some parts of the country. Plane the edges of the door to achieve the clearance that you want.

Hang the door with brass butt hinges as shown in the *Front View.* Depending on the size of the gap around the doors, you may or may not need to cut mortises for the hinges. If you do need to cut mortises, mark the hinge locations with a sharp knife and cut away

15 **Install the adjustable shelf.** When your finish has thoroughly dried, insert the shelf supports in holes in the sides at an appropriate height for your needs and place the adjustable shelf on them.

PIE SAFE

The pie safe was once a common furnishing in American homes. It kept baked goods and other foodstuffs safe from pests. This miniature version is not an antique but does capture the flavor of early pie safes. It was designed and built by Butch Roller of Richmond, Virginia, for his apartment. He puts his TV set on top and his VCR on the shelf.

1 Select the stock. Butch made the side and back panels of ¼-inch plywood and framed them with solid wood of the same species. Most original pie safes were constructed of softwoods such as pine or poplar, but examples in cherry and other hardwoods are also common. Choose a wood and finish to suit your own taste, then select the

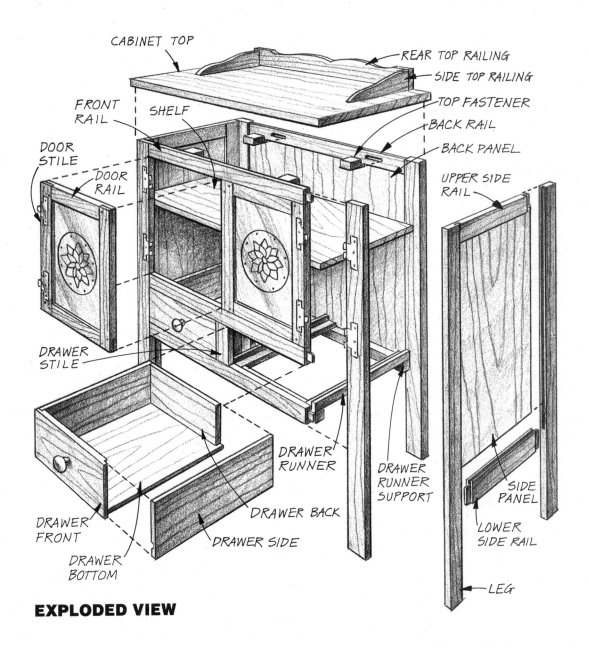

CABINET TOP

REAR TOP RAILING

SIDE TOP RAILING

TOP FASTENER

FRONT RAIL

SHELF

BACK RAIL

BACK PANEL

DOOR STILE

DOOR RAIL

UPPER SIDE RAIL

DRAWER STILE

DRAWER RUNNER

DRAWER RUNNER SUPPORT

SIDE PANEL

DRAWER FRONT

DRAWER BACK

DRAWER SIDE

LOWER SIDE RAIL

DRAWER BOTTOM

LEG

EXPLODED VIEW

131

CUTTING LIST

Part	Dimensions
Legs (8)	$\frac{3}{4}'' \times 2'' \times 31''$
Front rails (3)	$\frac{3}{4}'' \times 1\frac{1}{2}'' \times 23\frac{1}{2}''$
Drawer stile	$\frac{3}{4}'' \times 1\frac{1}{2}'' \times 5''$
Lower side rails (2)	$\frac{3}{4}'' \times 3'' \times 10\frac{3}{4}''$
Upper side rails (2)	$\frac{3}{4}'' \times 1\frac{1}{2}'' \times 10\frac{3}{4}''$
Back rails (2)	$\frac{3}{4}'' \times 1\frac{1}{2}'' \times 23''$
Top fasteners (4)	$\frac{3}{4}'' \times 1\frac{1}{4}'' \times 2''$
Side panels* (2)	$\frac{1}{4}'' \times 10\frac{3}{4}'' \times 18''$
Back panel*	$\frac{1}{4}'' \times 23'' \times 19\frac{1}{2}''$
Drawer runner supports (2)	$\frac{3}{4}'' \times 1'' \times 25''$
Shelves (2)	$\frac{3}{4}'' \times 14\frac{1}{8}'' \times 24\frac{7}{8}''$
Drawer runners (4)	$\frac{3}{4}'' \times \frac{3}{4}'' \times 14\frac{1}{4}''$
Drawer fronts (2)	$\frac{3}{4}'' \times 3\frac{15}{16}'' \times 10\frac{3}{8}''$
Drawer backs (2)	$\frac{3}{4}'' \times 3\frac{7}{16}'' \times 9\frac{7}{8}''$
Drawer sides (4)	$\frac{3}{4}'' \times 3\frac{15}{16}'' \times 14\frac{7}{8}''$
Drawer bottoms* (2)	$\frac{1}{4}'' \times 9\frac{5}{16}'' \times 14\frac{3}{4}''$
Door stiles (4)	$\frac{3}{4}'' \times 1\frac{1}{2}'' \times 13\frac{3}{8}''$
Door rails (4)	$\frac{3}{4}'' \times 1\frac{1}{2}'' \times 11\frac{3}{16}''$
Pane retainers† (8)	$\frac{1}{4}'' \times \frac{1}{4}'' \times 12''$
Side top railings (2)	$\frac{3}{4}'' \times 2\frac{3}{4}'' \times 8\frac{1}{2}''$
Rear top railing	$\frac{3}{4}'' \times 3'' \times 24\frac{1}{2}''$
Cabinet top	$\frac{3}{4}'' \times 16\frac{1}{4}'' \times 27\frac{1}{2}''$

Hardware

6d finish nails
8 flathead wood screws, #6 $\times$ 1¼"
4d box nails
16 dowels, ¼" $\times$ 1"
2 pieces aluminum flashing, 10⅞" $\times$ 8¹¹⁄₁₆"
⅝" brads
2 pair H hinges, 1¾" wide
7 flathead wood screws, #6 $\times$ 1½"
4 porcelain knobs, 1¼" dia.

*Make from plywood.
†Cut to length at assembly.

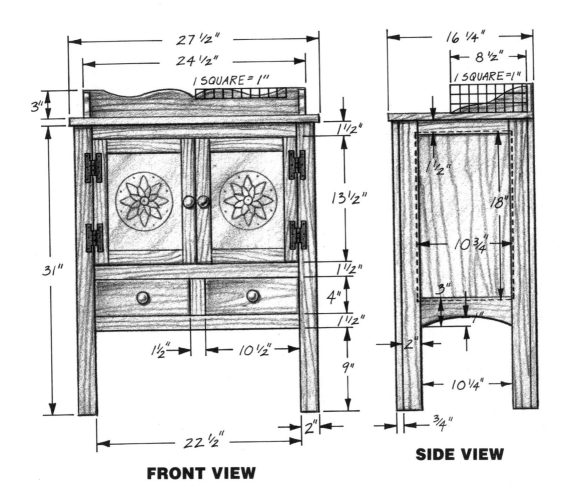

FRONT VIEW

SIDE VIEW

most attractive boards for the visible parts.

2 **Cut the carcase parts to size.** Cut the main carcase parts to size, leaving the plywood panels, shelves, drawer parts, and door parts until later. The top is made up of edge-glued narrow boards. See "Edge-Gluing" on page 6 for step-by-step instructions.

3 **Cut the front-frame mortise- and-tenon joints.** The front frame of the carcase is joined together with mortise-and-tenon joints. These all have ¼-inch shoulders. Since the tenon pieces are all ¾ inch × 1½ inches, the tenons are all ¼ inch thick and 1 inch wide. The tenons are ½ inch long so the mortises should be just a bit deeper, say 9/16 inch. Lay out the position of the front rails on the two legs that you intend to be the front legs. The *Front View* gives the necessary dimensions. Lay out the mortises from the rail layout as shown in the *Mortise-and-Tenon Detail*. Cut the mortises as described in "Plunge-Routing Mortises" on page 18 and square the ends with a chisel. Lay out and cut the mortises for the drawer stile in the same way. Cut the tenons to match the mortises, as described in "Cutting Tenons" on page 60.

4 **Cut the side and back joinery.** The side and back legs and rails form frames around plywood panels. Since plywood does not expand and contract the way solid lumber does, these panels can be glued into grooves in the legs and rails. Gluing the panels gives these assemblies considerable strength allowing smaller tenons on the rails. Hence, the side and back rails have ¼-inch-thick, ¼-inch-long tenons that fit into the same groove as the side and back panels, as shown in the *Panel Detail*.

Chuck a ¼-inch straight bit in a table-mounted router and adjust it to cut

¼ inch deep. Adjust the fence to center the cut in the edge of the ¾-inch-thick legs. Test the setup on a piece of scrap, then cut stopped grooves on the inside edge of the six remaining legs. These grooves are open at the top of the legs and stop 21¾ inches from the top. Square the stopped ends of the grooves with a chisel. With the same setup, rout grooves in the inner edges of the upper and lower side rails and the back rails. These grooves, which hold the plywood panels, are open on both ends.

Cut tenons on the ends of the side and back rails the same way you cut the tenons for the front framework. These tenons are only ¼ inch long. They all have shoulders on both sides but the only edge shoulders are on the bottom edge of the lower side rails.

5 **Rout grooves for attaching the top.** The pie-safe top will swell and shrink as the humidity changes. To accommodate these changes, the top is fastened down with four small tongued blocks that engage grooves in the side rails. Keep the bit and depth adjustment

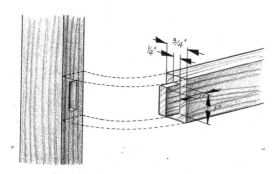

MORTISE-AND-TENON DETAIL

SHOP TIP: When making stopped cuts on the router table, you can't watch the cut being made. To tell where you're cutting, mark the location of the bit onto the fence. Lay out the ends of the cut on the side of the stock opposite where the cut will be. You can now begin and end the cut in the correct places by lining up the layout marks with the bit location marks.

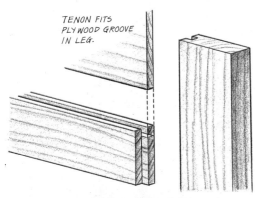

TENON FITS
PLYWOOD GROOVE
IN LEG.

PANEL DETAIL

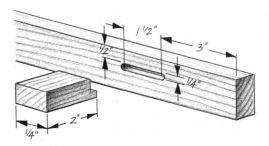

TOP FASTENER DETAIL

that you used for the panel grooves, but move the fence to ½ inch from the bit. Rout two 1½-inch-long grooves in the upper front rail and two in the upper back rail as shown in the *Top Fastener Detail.*

6 **Make the top fastener blocks.** Select a scrap of ¾-inch-thick stock that is 2 inches in the direction of the grain and 5½ inches across the grain. With the ¼-inch straight bit still in the router, cut a rabbet ½ inch high and ¼ inch wide along a 5-inch edge of the stock. Crosscut the piece into four 1¼-inch-wide blocks with ¼-inch tongues on the end. Set these aside until you're ready to install the top.

7 **Cut arches in the lower side rails.** The lower side rails are relieved with a 1-inch-high arc as shown in the *Side View.* (The radius is 13⅝ inches.) Lay out the arc on a piece of paper, cut it out, and trace it onto the rails. Saw to the traced line with a coping saw, then remove the saw marks

with a file and sandpaper. Round the edges slightly.

8 **Saw the plywood side and back panels to size.** Assemble the side and back frames without glue. Measure the insides of the frames and add ½ inch to the length and width. The resulting dimensions should be the same as the dimensions given in the Cutting List for the side and back panels. If they differ slightly, use your own dimensions rather than the Cutting List dimensions. Saw the panels to size making sure you will have the grain running vertically in the assembled project. Double-check that the widths of the panels do not exceed the overall lengths of the corresponding rails and trim the panels if necessary.

9 **Assemble the side and back frames.** Sand all of the parts. Chamfer the edges of the tenons and panels very slightly with a block plane. Starting with one of the sides, apply glue to the grooves in the rails and install them on the panel. Apply glue to the grooves in the legs and to the tenon shoulders, then assemble the legs to the rails and panels. Clamp the assembly and check that it's square by checking that the two diagonals are of equal length. Repeat this procedure for the other side and the back.

10 **Assemble the front frame.** Glue the drawer stile to the two lower rails, then glue this assembly to one of the legs. Glue the top rail to this leg, then glue the second leg in place. Clamp the assembly and check that it's square.

11 **Mount the drawer runner supports.** The drawer runners rest on two supports screwed to the front and back lower frame rails as shown in the *Drawer Runner Detail*. Glue and clamp them to the assembled front and back flush with the bottom edge of the lower rails.

12 **Drill the shelf support pin holes.** Lay out the shelf support pin holes in the side legs as shown in the *Shelf Pin Layout*. Wrap masking tape around the drill bit ½ inch from the tip

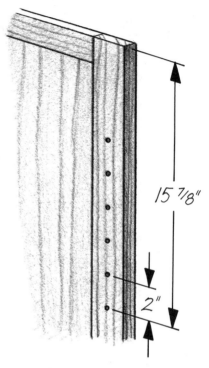

SHELF PIN LAYOUT

to act as a depth gauge, then drill all the holes.

13 **Assemble the carcase.** Assemble the front and back assemblies to the side assemblies without glue, holding them in place with clamps. Make sure the assembly is square, then drill holes for the 6d finish nails that will hold the carcase together. Use a drill bit slightly smaller than the nail diameter. Unclamp one side frame and carefully slip it out of the assembly. A stick of scrap $14\frac{5}{16}$ inches long may be handy to hold the front and back slightly apart for the time being. Apply glue to the edges

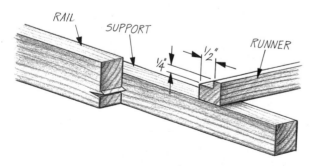

DRAWER RUNNER DETAIL

of the side, then replace the frame in the assembly and nail it. Check again that the assembly is square, then glue and nail the other side frame in the same manner. Reclamp the assembly, check that it is square, and let the glue dry.

14 **Make the shelves.** Measure the inside of the cabinet to check that the shelves will fit with ⅛-inch clearance. Edge-glue boards to create the necessary width if necessary, then saw the shelves to size and plane off the saw marks.

15 **Make the drawer runners.** Saw four drawer runners to the dimensions given in the Cutting List, then rout a ½-inch × ¼-inch rabbet along an edge of each. Position the runners on the supports as shown in the *Drawer Runner Detail* and check that they are flush with the bottom and sides of the drawer openings, parallel, and perpendicular to the front frame. Drill shank and pilot holes for #6 × 1¼-inch flathead wood screws and screw the drawer runners in place.

16 **Make the pie safe drawers.** Measure the drawer openings in the front framework of the pie safe. If your dimensions differ from those shown in the *Front View*, adjust the dimensions of the drawer parts to compensate. The drawers should have ¹⁄₁₆ inch of clearance on both sides and at the top.

The drawer sides fit into ¾-inch × ⅜-inch rabbets in the drawer fronts as shown in the *Drawer Detail*. The drawer

SHOP TIP: When you need to drill several identical sets of holes, shelf support holes for example, tape a piece of poster board to the stock in the area requiring one set of holes. Lay out the holes on the poster board instead of directly on the stock. Drill the holes right through the poster board into the stock. Then tape the poster board to the next piece of stock and drill the new set of holes using the holes in the poster board as a guide. If you require many sets of identical holes, use plywood instead of poster board.

backs simply butt against the sides where they are glued and nailed. The drawer bottom fits in a ¼-inch × ¼-inch groove in the sides and front. Cut the fronts, backs, and sides to length and width, then rabbet the fronts with a ¾-inch straight bit in a table-mounted router. Change to a ¼-inch straight bit and groove the sides and front for the bottom. Saw the bottoms out of ¼-inch plywood. They should slide easily into the grooves in an assembled drawer.

Sand all of the drawer parts, then clamp the drawers together without glue. Check that they're square and drill pilot holes for 6d finish nails to hold the sides to the fronts and backs. Remove the clamps, apply glue to the joints, and nail the sides in place. Slide the bottoms into their grooves, check that the drawers are square, and nail the bottoms to the backs with a couple of 4d box nails. Do not glue the bottoms. Drill a drawer-knob screw hole in the center of each drawer front.

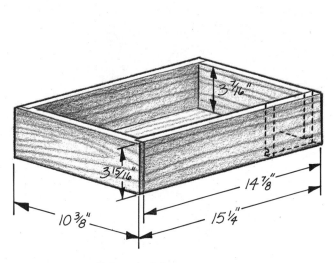

DRAWER DETAIL

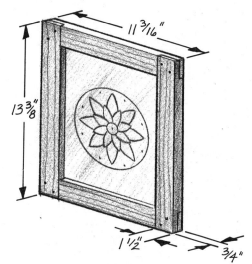

DOOR DETAIL

17 **Make the door frames.** Measure the door openings in the pie safe and adjust the Cutting List dimensions as you did for the drawer parts. The doors should have 1/16-inch clearance on all four sides. Cut the parts to your dimensions.

The corners of the door framework have glued and pinned lap joints as shown in the *Door Detail.* Cut each half of a lap joint as though you were cutting one cheek of a tenon. Refer again to "Cutting Tenons" on page 60 if you need to.

Clamp the door frames together without glue to check the fit of the joints and make sure they are square, then sand the pieces. Glue and clamp the doors together and again check that they are square. Set them aside and let the glue dry.

Drill 1/4-inch-diameter holes for pins as shown in the *Door Detail* and glue in short lengths of dowel. When the glue is

dry, trim the dowels flush with the frame with a sharp chisel and sandpaper.

Rout 1/4-inch-deep by 1/4-inch-wide rabbets for the tin inserts in the inner edges of the door frames. This will be easiest with a piloted rabbeting bit in a table-mounted router. Square up the corners with a sharp chisel.

18 **Make the tin inserts.** Decoratively punched "panels" were traditionally made out of tin-plated sheet steel known as "tinplate." Tinplate is no longer commonly available but easily found aluminum flashing as used in roofing is a very close look-alike. Cut the metal to fit in the back rabbet.

The *Punch Pattern* is printed actual size. Trace or photocopy the pattern. Make a complete circular pattern on paper by pricking through the tracing at each mark, then pivoting the tracing about the center and pricking through at each mark again. Seven repeats make a full circle.

Center the pattern on one of the pieces of metal, tape it in place, and tape the metal to a piece of plywood. Punch through the pattern and the metal at each mark with a nail or awl. Repeat the procedure for the second piece of metal but don't use the same plywood surface; the dimples in the surface will misguide the nail or awl.

To install the metal, place it in the rabbets in a door frame and hold it with ¼-inch-square panel retainers tacked to the frame with ⅝-inch brads. Miter the retainers at the corners for a neat job.

19 **Hang the doors.** Place the hinges on the doors as shown in the *Front View*. Mark the center of each screw hole and drill pilot holes for the screws. Screw the hinges to the doors, then place the doors in the opening. Shim the doors so they have uniform clearance all the way around. If either the doors or the opening are a bit off, you won't be able to shim them to get nice uniform clearances. In this case, carefully plane the door edges as needed. When you have the fit right, drill pilot holes for the hinge screws that go in the cabinet and screw the hinges in place.

20 **Install the top railing.** The railing on the top is decorative but also keeps things from sliding off. Saw the side and rear railings to the shapes shown in the *Front View* and *Side View*. If you don't have a scroll or band saw, a coping saw will do just fine. Re-

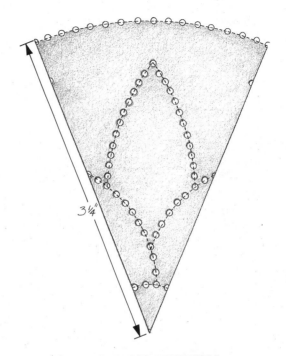

3¼"

PUNCH PATTERN

move the saw marks with a fine rasp and sandpaper and round the edges just a bit with the sandpaper. Position the railings on the top as shown in the drawings and lightly trace their position onto the top. Drill shank holes for #6 × 1½-inch flat-head wood screws through the top, inside the tracings. Drill two evenly spaced holes for each side and three for the back. Countersink the holes on the underside of the top. Clamp the railings in position and drill pilot holes up through the shank holes into the railings. Sand the top, removing the traced lines, then glue and screw the railings in place.

21 **Apply your finish.** Remove the hinges and finish sand the entire pie safe. Ease any sharp edges as you sand.

Both painted and natural finishes are appropriate. Boiled linseed oil and paste wax provide an attractive and economical finish in keeping with the traditional design of the project.

If you choose the oil finish, apply the oil with a rag. Allow it to soak in for a half hour, then wipe off as much as you can. Hang the rags out like laundry on a clothesline to keep them from spontaneously combusting. Allow the oil in the wood to cure for a day, then rub it with 0000 steel wool. Apply a second and third coat in the same manner. Allow the third coat to cure for several days. Apply a paste wax with an ultra-fine Scotch-Brite pad, let the wax dry, then buff it with a soft cloth or lambswool buff.

If you prefer a painted finish, consider milk paint as described on page 100.

22 **Attach the top.** Put a towel or blanket over your workbench as a protective pad, then put the pie-safe top upside down on the bench. Put the pie-safe carcase upside down on the top. Position the carcase as shown in the *Front View* and *Side View.* Put the top blocks in place and drill shank and pilot holes for the top block screws. Be especially careful not to drill through the top. Screw the blocks to the top.

Reinstall the door hinges and install the door and drawer knobs.

BOOKCASE

Brian and Faith Thompson of St. Thomas, Ontario, Canada, designed this oak bookcase to house their expanding collection of books. They included in the design some of the classic country decorative techniques such as wave-form shapes on the top of the back and on the front foot piece, carved foliar shapes, and a carved rosette made from a contrasting wood. It's a design that will fit a great many homes.

The joinery is uncomplicated, consisting of dadoes and rabbets. The carved decoration is not at all difficult and adds a very nice touch to the project.

1 **Cut out the parts.** Choose an attractive hardwood that will go well in your home. The rosette will show off to best advantage if it contrasts with the

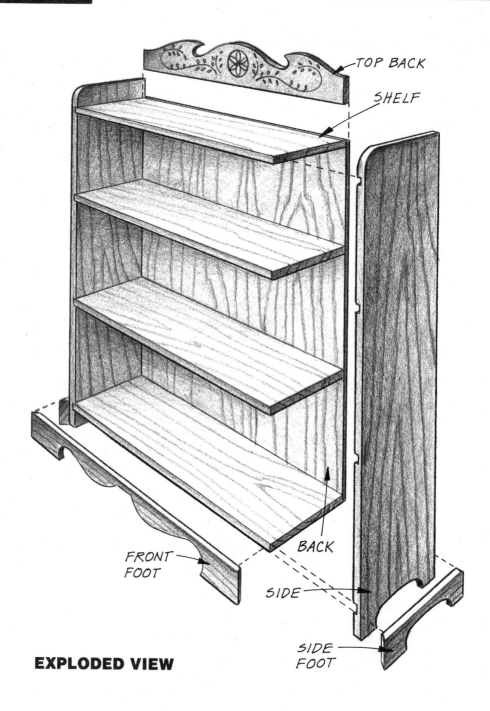

TOP BACK

SHELF

FRONT FOOT

BACK

SIDE

SIDE FOOT

EXPLODED VIEW

primary wood of the bookcase so choose a species for each while keeping the other in mind. The Thompsons used oak as the primary wood and walnut for the rosette. The back panel is ¼-inch plywood with oak surface veneer. Saw and plane the parts to the sizes specified by the Cutting List.

2 **Saw out the scroll work.** Lay out the shapes of the top back, front foot, and side feet as shown in the *Shape Details*. Saw out the top back with a coping saw but leave the feet until later. Lay out and saw the rounded top front corners of the sides. Smooth the sawn edges with rasps and sandpaper.

3 **Rout the dadoes.** The shelves join the side panels in dado joints. The dadoes for the upper three shelves stop ⅜ inch from the front edge. The bottom shelf dadoes go all the way across the sides. All of the dadoes are ⅜ inch deep.

As you lay out the dadoes, make sure you mark where they stop and make sure you lay out a right side and a left side.

To cut the dadoes, chuck a ¾-inch straight bit into your router and set the depth of cut to ⅛ of an inch. Clamp a straightedge to a side of the bookcase to guide the router and cut the first ⅛ inch of depth. Remember the stop marks at the front edge. Repeat the cut twice, lowering the bit ⅛ inch each time for a total depth of ⅜ inch. Then move the straightedge for the next dado and repeat until all eight dadoes are cut. Square the stopped ends with a chisel.

4 **Rabbet the back edges of the sides.** The back and top back fit into rabbets in the back edges of the sides. The rabbet for the plywood back is ¼ inch wide while the rabbet for the top back is ¾ inch wide. Both rabbets are the same depth as the shelf rabbets, ⅜ inch. Rout the back rabbet first, then

---

CUTTING LIST

Part	Dimensions
Top back	¾″ × 5″ × 33¾″
Sides (2)	¾″ × 11″ × 41¾″
Shelves (4)	¾″ × 10¾″ × 33¾″
Back*	¼″ × 33¾″ × 37″
Front foot	¾″ × 3″ × 36″
Side feet (2)	¾″ × 3″ × 11¾″

Hardware

¾″ wire nails

*Make from plywood to match solid wood.

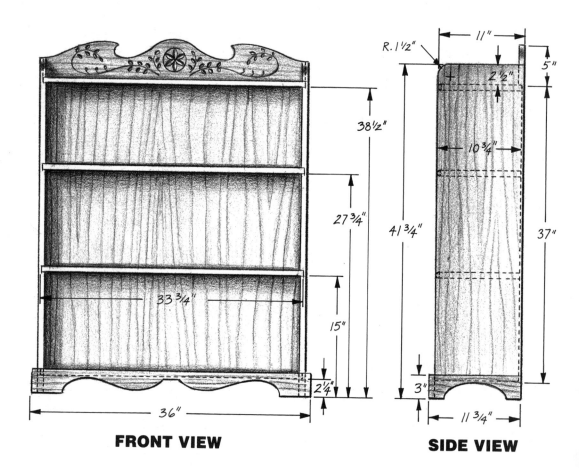

FRONT VIEW

SIDE VIEW

widen it from the top shelf rabbet to the end of the side for the top back.

5 Notch the shelves. Lay out ⅜-inch × ⅜-inch notches at both ends of the front edges of the top three shelves. These notches allow the shelves to fit into the blind dadoes. Saw them out with a fine-tooth backsaw.

6 Carve the leaf pattern. Sand the top back ready for finishing, then lay

out the foliar decoration. Well-marked lines will make the carving job easier. Clamp the top back to your workbench.

Carve the stem lines first. Where the stem goes in the same direction as the grain, you can use a small V-shaped carving chisel. Cut these parts of the pattern in stages, a shaving at a time until you reach the depth that you want. Apply steady even pressure, without forcing the blade. Keep the chisel sharp.

Where the stem crosses the grain you will find it much better to use a straight chisel, cutting down the sides of the stem at the same angle as the previously cut stem parts.

Cut the oval leaves with an 8- to 10-millimeter gouge. Make a leaf in two cuts, one from each end of the leaf.

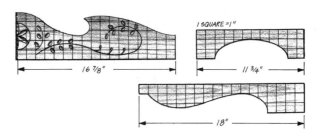

SHAPE DETAILS

7 **Carve and fit the rosette.** The rosette is a contrasting decorative element ¼ inch proud of the surface of the top back. The rosette itself is carved in ¾-inch-thick stock and then recessed ½ inch into the top back.

Cut the recess first by sawing the circle with a hole saw mounted in the drill press, then routing out the waste. The Thompsons then beveled the edges of the recess at 45 degrees, a nice touch that you can follow if you like.

Lay out the rosette pattern on a piece of stock larger than the finished plug. Unlike the leaf pattern where the design elements are carved out, the rosette background is carved out leaving the design elements in relief. Each line shown in the *Shape Details* must therefore be drawn as two parallel lines indicating the outside edges of the parts that will be in relief. These parallel lines can be about ¹⁄₁₆ to ³⁄₃₂ inch apart. Clamp the stock with the layout to your workbench.

Begin the carving by cutting down along the lines with a chisel or carving knife. These outline cuts should angle slightly toward the waste areas. Remove the waste in the background with gouges. Deepen the outline cuts and remove more background waste until the rosette pleases you. The Thompsons even hollowed out the interior of the flower petals. When the carving is complete, saw out the circle, sand the edges, and glue it to the top back.

8 **Assemble the case.** Sand all of the parts, easing the edges that will be exposed as you go. Assemble the bookcase without glue to make sure everything will fit properly.

Apply glue to the shelf dadoes and the rabbet for the top back. Assemble the shelves and top back to the sides. Make sure the shelves are flush with the sides at the front. Clamp the assembly and check that it is square by checking that the diagonals of the case are equal. When the glue is dry, remove the clamps and apply glue sparingly to the rabbet for the plywood back and the back edges of the shelves. Put the back in place and nail it with ¾-inch wire nails. You may find it helpful to drill pilot holes for the nails.

9 **Install the feet.** The front and side feet are mitered together at the front corners. Hold the left side foot in position on the case and mark where the front edge of the side falls. Miter the left foot at the line, then miter the left end of the front foot. Hold these two parts in position with the miter joint closed tightly and mark where the front edge of the right side falls on the front foot. Miter the front foot to this line and miter the left end of the right foot.

Check that everything fits properly, then saw the curved shapes of the feet. Glue and clamp them in place.

10 **Apply a finish.** You can apply a stain but, if you do, make sure the rosette will still contrast nicely with the rest of the bookcase. Choose your final finish carefully. A film finish like polyurethane is very tough, a desirable characteristic for shelving, but will show the scratches that do occur more than an oil finish will. An oil finish, on the other hand, has a tendency to bleed out of some woods like oak and if not thoroughly cured can stain your valuable books.

APOTHECARY CHEST

An apothecary chest is a chest of little drawers. An apothecary used such a chest to store the ground botanicals and earths that he blended to the doctor's prescription. Similar chests were used by seedsmen and spice dealers. Today there are dozens of hobbies and pursuits that could put an apothecary chest to good use. It could help organize seeds for the gardener, "lumber" for the model maker, hardware for the woodworker, feathers and furs, hackles and hooks for the flytier.

Diane Windle of Log Cabin Antiques, Parkesburg, Pennsylvania, bought this chest in New England. It was covered with layers of peeling paint. She asked a local woodworker to remove the paint and make a few repairs. After stripping it down to a stubborn layer of red that wouldn't come off, he brought it back and told her that for an extra $80 he'd try again. Diane decided that she liked the red well enough. It's probably milk paint, which is about as tenacious as paint gets.

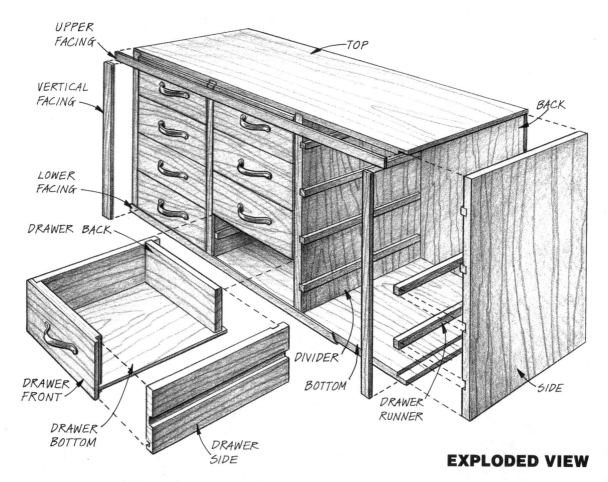

UPPER FACING

TOP

VERTICAL FACING

BACK

LOWER FACING

DRAWER BACK

DRAWER FRONT

DRAWER BOTTOM

DRAWER SIDE

DIVIDER

BOTTOM

DRAWER RUNNER

SIDE

EXPLODED VIEW

The joinery of the chest is simple: rabbets, dadoes, and a handful of nails. The only problem in building an accurate reproduction is finding identical drawer pulls. The originals, shown in the photo, are simple wire bails screwed directly to the drawer fronts. If you can't find similar pulls at a flea market, consider the brass pulls shown in the drawings and listed in the Cutting List.

The chest was made from a relatively soft, easy-to-work wood, probably pine. Either basswood or poplar would make a chest of similar weight, strength,

and appearance. You could also produce a durable and beautiful chest with a harder cabinet wood like cherry, maple, or walnut.

Before you begin building the chest, notice in the drawings and the photo that the edge of the back is exposed at the sides. This construction is quite practical and easy to build but may not be as pleasing in appearance as you want. If you would rather hide the edge of the back, make three changes. First, make the sides the same width as the top and bottom. Second, rabbet the back edge of the sides the same way you rabbet the back edge of the top and bottom. Third, cut the back to fit inside the rabbets all the way around.

1 Prepare the parts. Edge-glue boards as necessary to make up the wider parts specified by the Cutting List. See "Edge-Gluing" on page 6 for detailed step-by-step instructions. With exceptions as follows, plane the parts to the required thickness, then saw and plane them to length and width. Plane the runner stock to ½ inch thick, then rip off ⅜-inch-wide runners. Cut the facing slightly longer than specified so you can trim it to a perfect fit at assembly time.

The back and drawer bottoms can be made from ¼-inch plywood instead of solid wood even if the plywood sold as ¼ inch is actually somewhat less.

2 Rabbet and dado the top and bottom. The sides, dividers, and back fit into rabbets and dadoes cut in the top and bottom. Adjust a ¾-inch-wide dado cutter to cut ¼ inch deep. Make a test cut and check the fit of the dividers in the dado. Shim or adjust the dado cutter as necessary to obtain an easy but snug fit.

Cut the rabbets for the sides and dadoes for the dividers into the top and bottom as shown in the *Front View.* Use

CUTTING LIST

Part	Dimensions
Top	½″ × 13″ × 30¾″
Bottom	½″ × 13″ × 30¾″
Sides (2)	¾″ × 12¾″ × 15¼″
Dividers (2)	¾″ × 12¾″ × 15¼″
Drawer sides (24)	½″ × 3⁹⁄₁₆″ × 12½″
Drawer fronts (12)	¾″ × 3⁹⁄₁₆″ × 9⁵⁄₁₆″
Drawer runners (24)	⅜″ × ½″ × 12½″
Back*	¼″ × 15¼″ × 30¾″
Upper facing	¼″ × ¾″ × 30¾″
Lower facing	¼″ × ½″ × 30¾″
Vertical facing (4)	¼″ × ¾″ × 14½″
Drawer backs (12)	½″ × 3¹⁄₁₆″ × 8⁷⁄₁₆″
Drawer bottoms* (12)	¼″ × 11¾″ × 8¹¹⁄₁₆″

Hardware

4d finish nails

12 drawer pulls. Available from The Woodworker's Store, 21801 Industrial Blvd., Rogers, MN 55374-9514; (612) 428–3200. Item #26682.

*These parts may be made from ¼″ plywood instead of solid wood.

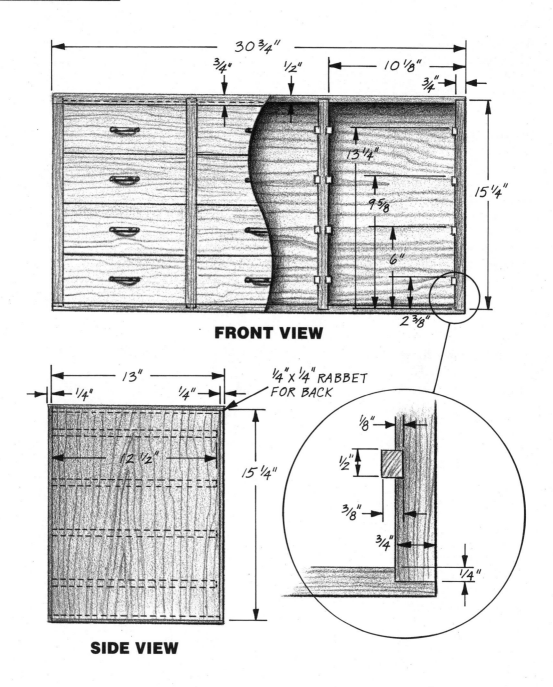

FRONT VIEW

1/4" x 1/4" RABBET FOR BACK

SIDE VIEW

the miter gauge to guide the parts over the blade. Cut the rabbets for the back along the back edges of the top and bottom as shown in the *Side View*. Guide the parts with the rip fence for these cuts.

3 Dado the sides and dividers. The drawer runners fit in dadoes cut in the sides and dividers. Adjust a dado cutter on the table saw to cut a dado that snugly fits the ½-inch dimension of the drawer runners. Adjust the depth of cut to ⅛ inch.

Mark the bottom end of the sides and dividers. Keep this end against the rip fence while cutting all of the drawer-runner dadoes. Cut the dadoes across the width of the sides and dividers as shown in the *Front View*. Cut the dadoes in all the pieces at a given setting before moving the fence for the next cut. Be sure to cut dadoes in both surfaces of the dividers but only the inner surface of the sides.

4 Cut the runner grooves in the drawer sides. With the dado blade still on the saw, reset the depth of cut to ¼ inch. The dado blade is adjusted to a snug fit on the drawer runners but a sliding fit is needed in the drawer sides. The following procedure gives a good sliding fit.

Divide the 24 drawer sides into 12 right-hand sides and 12 left-hand sides. Mark the top edge, inside face, and back end of each side.

Apply two thicknesses of masking tape to the bottom edge of the table-saw fence on the side facing the dado cutter.

Adjust the fence so there is exactly 1½ inches between the masking tape and the dado cutter. Groove all 24 drawer sides with the top edge against the masking tape on the fence and the inside face up. Without moving the fence, remove the masking tape and run all 24 sides over the cutter again, widening the cut by the thickness of the removed tape.

5 Dado the drawer sides. The drawer backs are held in dadoes in the drawer sides. If your drawer backs are exactly the same thickness as the width of the runners, the dado cutter still on the saw should cut a dado that fits the drawer backs perfectly. Set the depth of cut to ⅛ inch, then cut the drawer-back dadoes in the drawer sides as shown in the *Drawer Detail*.

6 Rabbet the drawer fronts. With the ½-inch dado cutter still on the saw, set the depth of cut to ½ inch. Position the rip fence 9/16 inch from the left (outside) of the blade to act as a stop. Making two passes per rabbet, cut a 9/16-inch-wide rabbet on both ends of each drawer front as shown in the *Drawer Detail*. Work with the ½-inch dado cutter is now complete.

7 Glue the runners in place. Apply glue to the front 2 inches of the dadoes in the sides and dividers. Position the runners so that they are flush with the front edges of the dividers and sides, then clamp them in place while the glue dries. By gluing only the front ends of the runners, the sides and dividers can

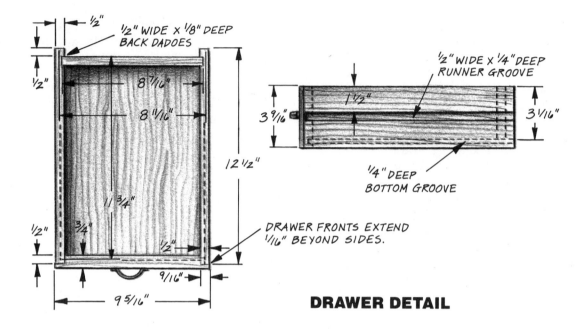

DRAWER DETAIL

expand and contract with the seasons at a different rate than the runners.

8 **Assemble the cabinet.** Glue and nail the top and bottom to the sides and dividers. Make sure the marked bottom ends of the sides and dividers join the bottom. Use four or five 4d finish nails per joint and predrill the nail holes to avoid splitting the stock. Check that the cabinet is square, then glue and nail the back in place.

9 **Attach the facings.** Glue and nail the upper and lower facings to the top and bottom respectively. The lower facing should be flush with both faces of the bottom. The upper facing should be

flush along the top of the cabinet. Sand the ends flush with the sides of the cabinet.

Saw the vertical facing pieces to fit snugly between the upper and lower facings. Glue and nail them in place.

10 **Cut the drawer bottom grooves.** Adjust a dado cutter to the thickness of the drawer bottoms. Set the depth of cut to ¼ inch. Cut grooves for the drawer bottoms in the drawer fronts and sides as shown in the *Drawer Detail*. Adjust the fence to guide the top edge of the drawer parts. Be sure the runner groove is up as you cut the drawer bottom groove in the sides and the end rabbets are down as you groove the drawer fronts.

11 **Assemble the drawers.** Sand all the drawer parts. Glue and nail the sides to the fronts and backs. Slide the bottoms into their grooves and nail them to the backs to hold them in place. Thoroughly clean off any squeezed-out glue with a damp cloth, then slide the drawers into the chest while the glue in the drawer joints dries. This will ensure that the drawers will dry to compensate for any imperceptible misalignment of the runners. Check after 10 or 15 minutes to make sure they aren't sticking to the chest.

When the drawer joints are completely dry, sand down any spots on the runners or runner grooves that tend to rub or stick, then rub a little paraffin on the runners.

12 **Finish the cabinet.** Sand the entire chest and all the drawers. You can apply a natural finish to the chest, a good choice if you chose to build it with one of the better cabinet woods. Or you can give it a coat of red milk paint with the assurance that a hundred years from now it will still be stubbornly red. For more on milk paint, see page 100.

SMALL SPICE CHEST

This small two-drawer chest originally held spices. It can still do an admirable job of that; when we borrowed it from Diane Windle of Log Cabin Antiques in Parkesburg, Pennsylvania, she had the drawers filled with packaged spices. But it could hold a variety of other things just as well, and it would look good on a dresser, a hall table, or a buffet.

While many country antiques are plain and roughly made, spices were precious and chests to hold them were well made and elegant. This example, made of mahogany, has more decorative detail than most country antiques. Identical knobs are no longer available, but you can choose knobs with the general appearance of those shown in the photo. The knob listed in the Cutting List would be appropriate.

The construction of the chest is a bit unusual. The frame is doweled together in all three directions. Solid wood panels fit within the frame, held with a molded liner on the outside and angled brads on the inside.

The top and bottom of the original

EXPLODED VIEW

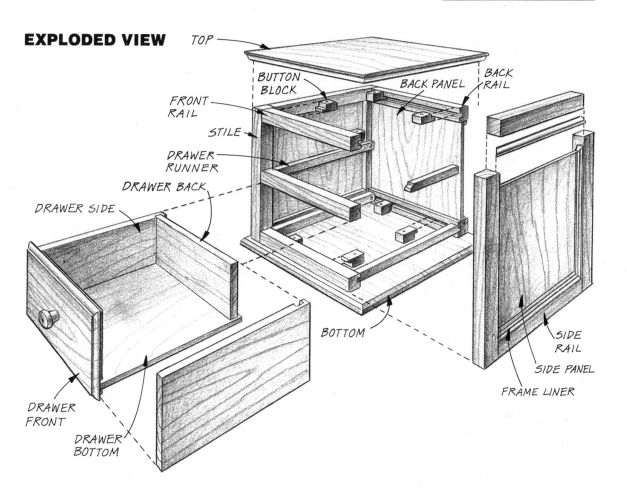

TOP

BUTTON BLOCK

BACK PANEL

BACK RAIL

FRONT RAIL

STILE

DRAWER RUNNER

DRAWER BACK

DRAWER SIDE

DRAWER FRONT

DRAWER BOTTOM

BOTTOM

SIDE RAIL

SIDE PANEL

FRAME LINER

were simply glued to the frame. Seasonal expansion and contraction have broken the glue bond leaving large gaps. The drawings show the top and bottom attached with button blocks. These allow movement of the parts and should save your chest from the fate of the original.

1 **Cut the parts for the frame.** Begin this project with the frame. If you buy your lumber rough, you may be able to plane the ¹⁵⁄₁₆-inch-thick stiles

and rails from 4/4 (four-quarter) stock. If not, begin with 5/4 (five-quarter) stock. When sawing out the stiles and rails, be sure to allow a little extra for planing out the saw marks.

2 **Drill the dowel joints.** The dowel joints in the side and back frames are each made with two dowels. The joints that hold the drawer rails in place are made with just a single dowel. Make sure you bore dowel holes for left and right versions of a part where required. The *Exploded View* will help you keep track of where all the dowel holes must go. It helps to mark each part indicating its position in the chest.

Use a doweling jig to help position the holes as shown in the *Frame Detail*. Drill the holes into the ends of the rails first. Then insert dowel centers into the holes to transfer the locations to the

stiles. Be sure to use a depth stop on the bit when you are drilling into the stiles; you don't want to drill all the way through.

3 **Shape the stiles.** The outside corner on each stile is rounded-over to a ³⁄₁₆-inch radius. Cut this profile with a table-mounted router.

CUTTING LIST

Part	Dimensions
Side rails (4)	¹⁵⁄₁₆″ × 1¼″ × 8¹⁵⁄₁₆″
Back rails (2)	¹⁵⁄₁₆″ × 1¼″ × 8″
Front rails (3)	¹⁵⁄₁₆″ × ¹⁵⁄₁₆″ × 8″
Stiles (4)	¹⁵⁄₁₆″ × 1¼″ × 10³⁄₁₆″
Frame liner* (12)	⅜ × ⅜″ × 10″
Side panels† (2)	¼″ × 7½″ × 8¹⁵⁄₁₆″
Back panel†	¼″ × 7½″ × 8″
Drawer runners (4)	½″ × ⅝″ × 9¾″
Top	½″ × 10¾″ × 12⅝″
Bottom	½″ × 10¾″ × 12⅝″
Button blocks (8)	½″ × ¾″ × 1¼″
Drawer fronts (2)	¾″ × 4″ × 8½″
Drawer sides (4)	⁷⁄₁₆″ × 3⅝″ × 10⅛″
Drawer backs (2)	⁷⁄₁₆″ × 3⅛″ × 7⅜″
Drawer bottoms† (2)	¼″ × 9¹¹⁄₁₆″ × 7⁹⁄₁₆″

Hardware

26 dowels, ¼″ dia. × 1¼″
#18 × 1″ brads
#18 × 1¼″ brads
4 flathead wood screws, #6 × 1″
8 flathead wood screws, #6 × ¾″
2 knobs. Available from The Woodworker's Store, 21801 Industrial Blvd., Rogers, MN 55374-9514; (612) 428–3200. Item #64709 (or similar).

*Trim to final length during assembly.
†Use either plywood or solid lumber.

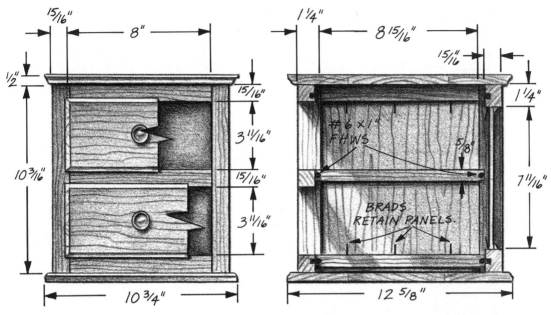

FRONT VIEW   **SIDE CROSS SECTION**

4 **Assemble the side frames.** Sand all the frame parts. Glue and dowel the side frame parts together.

5 **Make the frame liner.** Flat panels fill the spaces between frame members. They're held in place by a molded frame liner on the outside and wire brads on the inside as shown in the *Panel Edge Detail*.

The ⅜-inch × ⅜-inch liner is too small to mold safely on its own so begin with wider boards ⅜ inch thick. Mold an edge of the wider board with a table-mounted router, then rip the molded liner from the board edge. Repeat the process until the board is too narrow to work with safely, then start another wider board. You'll need twelve 10-inch pieces of liner but make a couple of extras in case you ruin one or two.

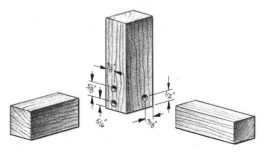

FRAME DETAIL

SHOP TIP: Glue often accumulates in the bottom of dowel holes and prevents the dowels from entering all the way. To allow the excess glue to escape, flatten one side of each dowel with two or three passes from a block plane.

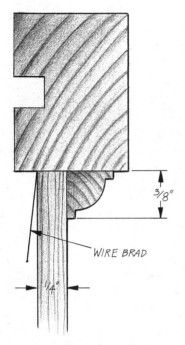

3/8"

WIRE BRAD

1/4"

PANEL EDGE DETAIL

6 **Attach the liner to the frame.**
With the table-saw blade tilted to
cut a 45-degree miter, cut the liner to fit
within the frame openings. Attach the
liner to the frames with glue and 1-inch
brads as shown in the *Side Cross Section*. Predrill the brad holes to avoid
splitting the liner.

7 **Install the side panels.** You can
use either solid wood or cabinet-
grade plywood for the panels. If you use
solid wood, make the panels ⅛ inch narrower (across the grain) than listed in
the Cutting List so they can expand and
contract with the seasons. Hold them in
the frames with 1-inch brads as shown in
the *Side Cross Section*. Three brads per
side should be adequate.

> **SHOP TIP:** Finish
> panels before installing them to prevent
> an unfinished edge from showing when
> the panel shrinks in dry weather.

8 **Attach the drawer runners.** Cut
the runners to the dimensions specified by the Cutting List. Drill and countersink the runners for #6 wood screws
5/32 inches from both ends. Temporarily
assemble the drawer rails to the front
stiles to help align the runners as shown
in the *Side Cross Section*. Drill pilot holes
and screw the runners in place with #6 ×
1-inch wood screws, then unscrew and
remove the runners for the upper
drawer.

9 **Rout the drawer and back rails.**
The *Side Cross Section* shows the
button block grooves in the top and bottom (drawer) front rails and the back
rails. Cut these grooves with a ¼-inch
straight bit in a table-mounted router.

10 **Assemble the cabinet.** Apply
glue, insert the dowels in the
holes, and join the side frames to the
back rails and drawer rails. Tightly clamp
the joints and check that the assembly is
square.

11 **Install the back panel.** Fit the
remaining frame liner to the back
opening the same way you did for the
sides. Cut the back panel to size and fit
it into the frame. Fasten it with brads as

you did the side panels. Reinstall the runners for the upper drawer.

12 **Make the top and bottom.** Cut the top and bottom to the size specified by the Cutting List. Mold the lower edges of the top as shown in the *Front View* with an ogee bit in a table-mounted router. Switch to a chamfering bit and chamfer the upper edges of the bottom as shown.

13 **Make the button blocks.** Cut the button blocks to the size specified by the Cutting List. Cut a tongue on one end of each block as shown in the *Button Block Detail*. Drill and countersink the blocks for #6 screws as shown.

14 **Attach the top and bottom.** Sand the top and bottom. Center the cabinet on the bottom. Fit the button blocks in the grooves in the rails, one block about ¼ inch from each stile. Use the blocks as guides as you drill pilot

holes for the screws that attach the bottom. Before you drive the screws, turn the cabinet over and repeat the process to locate the blocks on the top. Assemble the top and bottom to the cabinet with #6 × ¾-inch wood screws through the button blocks.

15 **Cut the drawer parts to size.** Cut the drawer parts to the sizes listed in the Cutting List. The fronts, sides, and back should be made from solid wood, but the bottoms can be made from ¼-inch plywood. On the original, the drawer bottoms were made from parts of old packing crates. The original destination stamps are still visible on the undersides.

16 **Shape the drawer fronts.** The outside edges of the drawer fronts are shaped with a ¼-inch bead. Cut the beads with a table-mounted router.

17 **Rabbet the drawer fronts.** The drawers require several widths of rabbets, dadoes, and grooves. To avoid constantly readjusting the dado blade, set up a ¼-inch-wide dado blade on the table saw and cut the wider rabbets and dadoes with multiple passes. Set the depth of cut to ⅜ inch.

The drawer fronts are rabbeted on all four sides as shown in the *Drawer Detail*. The rabbets across the ends are ¹¹⁄₁₆ inch wide and the ones along the length are ³⁄₁₆ inch wide. Lay out the rabbets, then cut the end rabbets by guiding the fronts past the blade with the

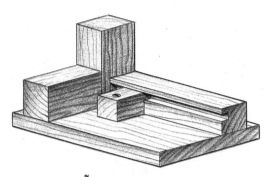

BUTTON BLOCK DETAIL

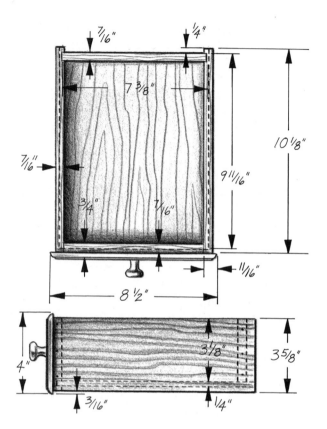

DRAWER DETAIL

a stop to help position the dadoes. Make the cuts in two passes.

19 **Assemble the drawers.** Sand all the drawer parts. Glue and nail the sides to the fronts and backs with 1¼-inch brads. Predrill the holes to prevent the wood from splitting. Slide the bottoms into their grooves and nail the bottoms to the backs to hold them in place. Drill through the drawer fronts and install the knobs, centering them in the drawer fronts as shown in the *Drawer Detail.*

miter gauge. Cut the lengthwise rabbets by guiding the fronts along the fence.

18 **Cut the grooves for the bottom and back.** Reset the dado's depth of cut to ¼ inch. Groove the length of the sides and the fronts for the bottoms as shown in the *Drawer Detail.* Use the fence to position the grooves and don't forget to change the fence setting between cutting the sides and the fronts.

Cut the dadoes that hold the backs using the miter gauge. Use the fence as

20 **Fit the drawers.** Slide the drawers into their openings. If they don't slide in easily, plane the drawer sides with a block plane where they rub the cabinet. When they fit well, rub paraffin on the drawer sides and the runners to help them slide easily.

21 **Finish the cabinet.** The original chest was stained to bring out the color of the mahogany and then finished with several coats of varnish. You can do the same or finish the chest to your own taste. Consider finishing the inside of the drawers with shellac. It dries hard and won't impart an odor to the contents of the drawer.

PART FOUR

CHILDREN'S FURNITURE AND TOYS

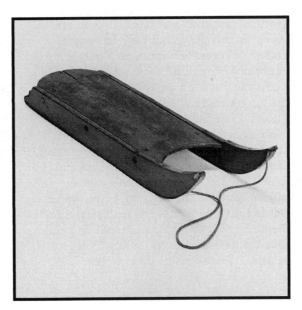

COUNTRY SLED

This sled is a gem. It could easily fit right into a Currier and Ives print or Norman Rockwell painting. It could just as easily fit right into a den, large mudroom, or recreation room as a purely decorative item. But most easily of all, it could race down a snow-covered hill with a couple of screaming kids on board. The cheerful red paint of the original is well worn and the sled shows other signs of hard use, yet it's still serviceable—a testament to its design.

The sled should be made from strong, straight-grained, knot-free wood but not a wood that is too heavy. You want the sled to be light enough that the kids can pull it back up the hill by themselves. The original is pine. Poplar and basswood are also good choices. The runners have bands of steel that reinforce the front ends and eliminate wear on the bottom edges.

1 **Select the stock and cut the parts.** The runners and stretchers are ⅞ inch thick, finished dimension. The seat board is ½ inch thick. Have your supplier plane stock to these thicknesses if you don't have your own planer. Saw the parts to the dimensions specified by the Cutting List. If necessary, edge-glue narrower boards to get the required width of the seat board. (For more information on edge-gluing see page 6.) The stretchers have round

EXPLODED VIEW

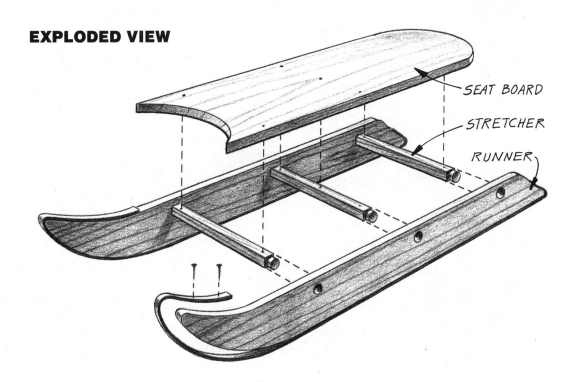

SEAT BOARD

STRETCHER

RUNNER

CUTTING LIST

Part	Dimensions
Runners (2)	$\frac{7}{8}'' \times 6'' \times 41''$
Stretchers (3)	$\frac{7}{8}'' \times \frac{7}{8}'' \times 11\frac{1}{2}''$
Seat board	$\frac{1}{2}'' \times 9\frac{5}{8}'' \times 32\frac{1}{2}''$

Hardware

2 metal bands, $\frac{3}{32}'' \times \frac{7}{8}'' \times 55\frac{1}{2}''$
6 flathead wood screws, #10 × 1¾″ *or* 6 dowels, ³⁄₁₆″ dia. × 2″
Five 5d common nails with ⅜-inch O.D. washers, *or* 5 roundhead machine screws, 10-32 × 1½″,
   with washers
14 flathead wood screws, #8 × 1″
Pull rope to suit user

TOP VIEW

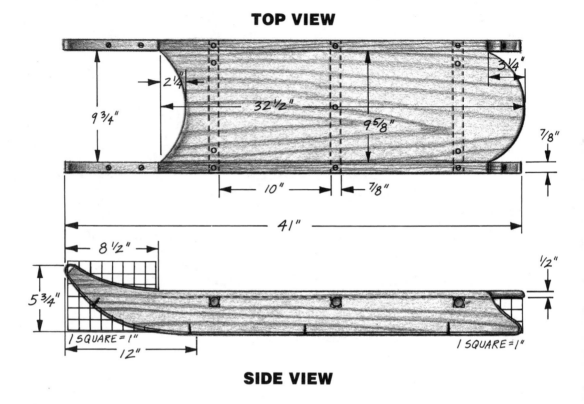

SIDE VIEW

tenons on both ends. If you intend to turn these on a lathe, leave the blanks longer so you can cut off the marks left by the head and tailstock.

2 **Saw out the sled runners.** Lay out the shape of the runner as shown in the *Side View* on one of the runner blanks. At the front of the runner, lay out the full, rounded tip; don't cut it off square to provide a rope hole yet. Saw out the profile with a coping saw, jigsaw, or band saw. If you're using a band saw, cut out both runners together, as one, by taping the two blanks

together. If you're sawing them out separately, trace the first one onto the second blank, then saw out the second one. Remove the saw marks with a plane, spokeshave, and rasp.

3 **Bore stretcher tenon holes in the runners.** Lay out the ⅞-inch-diameter holes in the runners shown in the *Side View*. Back up the runners with scrap where the drill bit will exit and drill the holes completely through the runners. You can clamp the runners together and drill both at the same time if you prefer.

4 **Make the round tenons on the ends of the stretchers.** The stretcher tenons on the original sled were whittled by hand and are not perfect. To whittle your own, begin by laying out ⅞-inch-diameter circles on the ends of each stretcher. Scribe the tenon shoulders ⅞ inch from the stretcher ends with a layout knife and a square. The shoulders can be cut with a fine-tooth saw, a chisel, or a utility knife. The sides can be cut with a knife or chisel. Use whatever combination of tools you're most comfortable with but avoid cutting the shoulders too deep or the tenons too small. One good approach is to saw the shoulders part way, chisel away waste from the end, saw a little further, chisel away more, and so on until the tenon is uniformly ⅞ inch in diameter and fits the holes in the runners snugly. If you have a lathe, you can turn the stretcher tenons quite easily. Either way you make the tenons, check the fit regularly in the drilled stretcher holes.

5 **Fit the metal bands onto the runners.** If you've never before worked with metal, it may be tempting simply to take the runners to your blacksmith the next time your horse needs shoeing. Don't; doing it yourself is not difficult. Mild steel such as you can buy at a good hardware store is easy to work.

Clamp the metal band to the straight bottom surface of the runner. Hold the runner in a vise and bend the band along the bottom edge of the front end of the runner. You can bend it easily with your hands. Continue around the tip. If you have trouble at the tip, tap it

SHOP TIP: If you are turning round tenons on the lathe to fit in a drilled hole, drill a sample hole in a scrap of thin plywood and slip it over the center on the head and/or tailstock of the lathe. When the tenon approaches the desired diameter, turn the lathe off and try the sample hole on the tenon. Turn until you get just the fit you want, all the way up the tenon.

with a hard rubber mallet. Another useful trick for getting a nice, tight fit is to first bend it as tightly as you can around the tip of the runner, then remove the band from the runner and hammer it around a pipe of slightly smaller radius than the runner tip. Continue bending the strip into the inside curve on the top of the runner.

Repeat the process on the back end of the runner, then bend the second strip to fit the other runner. Set the bands aside for now.

6 **Glue the stretcher tenons into the runner holes.** Sand the runners and stretchers. Glue and clamp the stretcher tenons into the drilled holes in the runners. Check with your square to make certain the stretchers are perpendicular to the runners.

The tenons on the original sled are fastened with screws from the top edge of the runners. You can use 1¾-inch #10 wood screws or pin the tenons with ³⁄₁₆-inch-diameter dowels. If you use screws, drill pilot and shank holes for them and countersink them well. If you use dowels, cut the dowels 2 inches long, glue them into 1¾-inch-deep holes, then trim them flush with the top edge of the runners.

7 Cut the seat board to shape. Lay out the curves on the front and back edges of the seat board as shown in the *Top View*. If your sled will see real use, eliminate the sharp corners at the front by reversing the curve in the last ½ inch at each side. Saw the seat ends with a coping saw and smooth the edges.

Round-over both top and bottom edges of the front curve, and the top edge of the back curve with a ¼-inch-radius piloted roundover bit in your router.

8 Install the seat board on the stretchers. The original seat board is fastened to the stretchers with nails that are clinched on the underside of the stretchers. Washers, ⅜-inch outside-diameter (O.D.), under the nail heads distribute the stresses. The washers are recessed so the nail heads are flush with the surface of the seat board. If you copy this construction, predrill all the nail holes and fasten the seat board with 5d common nails, clinched below the stretchers. A good alternative is 1½-inch, 10-32 roundhead machine screws with washers under the heads (use brass for class). Again, counterbore so the screw heads don't project above the surface.

Clamp the seat board in position on the stretchers. There should be ¹⁄₁₆-inch clearance between the seat and the runners on each side. Lay out the fastener locations as shown in the *Top View*, then counterbore and drill shank holes as appropriate. Sand the seat board, then bolt or nail it in place.

9 Attach the metal bands to the runners. Saw off just enough of the front tip of each runner to thread a rope behind the metal band (see the *Side View*.) Fit the prebent bands to the runners and clamp them in place. Mark the screw locations shown in the *Top View* and *Side View* with a center punch. Drill 1-inch-deep pilot holes for #8 screws through the bands and into the runners. Countersink the holes so the screw heads will be flush or very slightly below the surface of the bands. Enlarge the top ¼ inch or less of the pilot holes to shank diameter, then screw the bands in place.

10 Complete the country sled. The final step is the finish. The original has bright red paint. Use an exterior trim paint, or milk paint with an overcoat of polyurethane. See page 100 for more information on milk paint.

When the finish is thoroughly dry, tie a stout pulling rope to the loops formed by the bands at the tips of the runners. If you want the sled to show signs of hard usage, give it to a bunch of kids after the next snowstorm.

CRADLE

Cradles seem to have been displaced by cribs in the last few decades. That's unfortunate because cribs aren't easily moved from room to room. A cradle on the other hand can readily move to where the mother will be for the next few hours. That's not only much easier on the mother but much better for the baby. And as the baby grows older, the cradle becomes an excellent place for dolls or stuffed animals.

This particular cradle, like most country antiques, is simply nailed together. You could add a couple of inches to the length and width to make the cradle usable a few months longer but beware of making it too big to conveniently move about. Long rockers make the cradle quite stable.

1 **Select the stock and cut the parts to size.** The cradle is made of pine and the sides and end boards are

EXPLODED VIEW

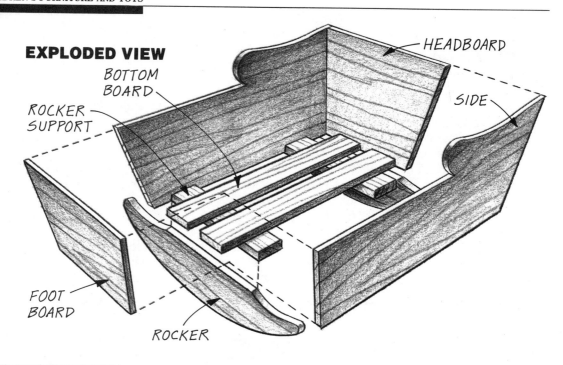

BOTTOM
BOARD

ROCKER
SUPPORT

HEADBOARD

SIDE

FOOT
BOARD

ROCKER

CUTTING LIST

Part	Dimensions
Sides (2)	$\frac{1}{2}'' \times 11\frac{1}{2}'' \times 32\frac{3}{4}''$
Headboard	$\frac{1}{2}'' \times 11\frac{1}{2}'' \times 17''$
Footboard	$\frac{1}{2}'' \times 8\frac{3}{4}'' \times 15\frac{9}{16}''$
Rockers (2)	$\frac{15}{16}'' \times 4\frac{1}{2}'' \times 25''$
Rocker supports (2)	$\frac{3}{4}'' \times 3\frac{1}{4}'' \times 12\frac{1}{8}''$
Bottom boards (2)	$\frac{3}{4}'' \times 3\frac{1}{4}'' \times 27''$

Hardware

4d cut finish nails *or* #6 × 1¼″ flathead wood screws. Cut finish nails are available from many building-supply stores and from Tremont Nail Company, P.O. Box 111, Wareham, MA 02571; (508) 295–0038. Item #CE4.

only ½ inch thick. Together, these two characteristics make the cradle light and easily portable. You can substitute another wood if you like, but be aware that substitution of a heavier wood will make the cradle less convenient. If you cannot thickness your own stock, have your dealer plane clear pine for these parts. Edge-glue as explained on page 6 if necessary to get the required width.

The dimensions specified by the Cutting List are finished dimensions.

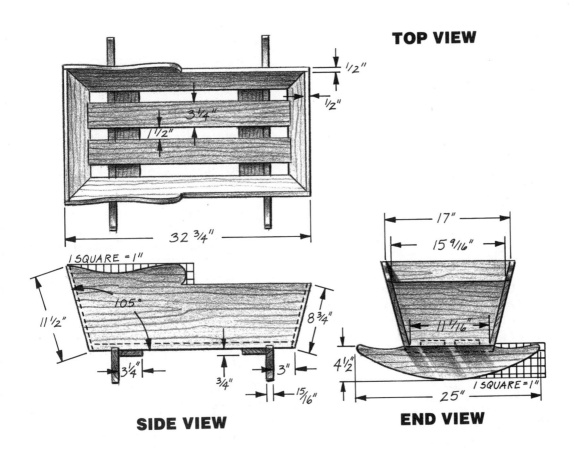

TOP VIEW

1/2"

1/2"

3 1/4"

1 1/2"

32 3/4"

SIDE VIEW

1 SQUARE = 1"

105°

11 1/2"

8 3/4"

3 1/4"

3/4"

3"

15/16"

END VIEW

17"

15 9/16"

11 11/16"

4 1/2"

25"

1 SQUARE = 1"

When selecting and preparing stock, allow an inch or more in length and width to make it easier to cut shapes and angles later on. The rockers on the original are $^{15}/_{16}$ inch thick but you could, if necessary, make them ¾ inch thick like the rocker supports and bottom boards.

2 **Cut the angles on the sides and ends.** This is the only part of making the cradle joinery that is even remotely difficult. Rather than attempting to cut compound angles on the sides and ends, cut the face angles and then bevel the cuts with a block plane to fit, as follows.

Lay out the angled ends of the sides, headboard, and footboard. Set your table-saw gauge at 15 degrees from square. Crosscut the ends.

Now assemble the four parts without glue, holding them together with masking tape. Check that the assembly is square at the bottom edges where it rests on your workbench. Set an adjustable bevel to the inside angle between two of the parts. To be precise in doing this, make sure that the two arms of the adjustable bevel are perpendicular to the joint line when you lock the angle of the bevel.

Carefully remove the footboard and

169

bevel the angled ends to match the adjustable bevel. This will not be difficult if you use a very sharp block plane held slightly askew. Check the fit by taping the board between the sides again and adjust the bevel with the block plane if necessary. When the fit pleases you, leave the footboard taped in place and bevel the headboard in the same way. Later, just before applying your finish, you can plane the ends of the sides.

3 **Bevel the bottom edges.** The angle between the bottom of the cradle and the sides and end boards is just over 105 degrees. Set the adjustable bevel to this angle and plane the bottom edges much as you did the ends. If you have a jointer you can set the fence to the correct angle and joint the bottom edges to the angle.

4 **Cut out the shape of the cradle sides.** Once again, assemble the sides and end boards with tape and mark the top corners of the end boards on the sides. Lay out the side shape as shown in the *Side View* on one of the sides. Make sure that the flat section of the shape comes to the footboard corner mark that you made. Stack the two sides so the end corner marks line up, clamp them together, and saw out the pattern in both pieces at once with a coping saw. Clean up the sawn edges with a spokeshave, files, and sandpaper.

5 **Round-over the top edges of the sides, headboard, and footboard.** The top edges on the original have been rounded-over by hand. You

can do the same, if you wish, with a spokeshave, coarse file, and sandpaper. If you prefer, round-over the edges with a ¼-inch-radius, ball-bearing roundover bit in your router. Whichever method you choose, stop 1 inch short of the ends of the side pieces. You'll finish rounding these edges after the cradle is assembled.

6 **Assemble the cradle.** Sand the cradle parts. The original cradle is nailed together with small nails that are flush with the surface of the wood. You can join the sides to the ends with 4d cut finish nails or 1¼-inch #6 screws. If you nail the cradle together, predrill the nail holes. If you use screws, countersink the heads. You may also want to glue the joints. If so, use a glue with a fairly long assembly time like liquid hide glue. Assembling the angled parts is time-consuming, and ordinary white or yellow glues don't allow enough time.

Apply glue to the ends of the end boards if you like, then tape the cradle together. Lay the taped assembly on its side on your workbench and drill for your fasteners. Drill right through the tape if it's in your way. Nail or screw the side in place, then turn the cradle over and fasten the other side in the same way.

7 **Cut out the rockers.** Lay out the pattern of the rockers on the rocker blanks as shown in the *End View*. You may be able to cut both rockers at once as you did for the cradle sides but the two together are a bit much for a coping saw. The alternative is to cut out one rocker and let it be the template for laying out the second. Clamp the rockers together to clean up the sawn edges. This ensures that both are exactly the same for smooth rocking.

8 **Attach the rocker supports to the rockers.** The ends of the rocker supports should be flush with the sides of the cradle. Crosscut one end of each rocker support at 15 degrees on the table saw. Hold the rocker supports to the bottom of the cradle to mark the length, then cut the second end of each at 15 degrees.

Clamp a rocker support flush with the top edge of a rocker. Center it along the length of the rocker. Check to make certain the surfaces of the rocker and rocker support are 90 degrees to each other and make any necessary corrections, then glue and clamp them together. Repeat for the other rocker and rocker support.

9 **Fit the bottom boards.** If you fit these boards snugly, they will reinforce the rockers. But you can't hold them in their final position to mark them for length because they won't fit between the end boards yet. So, to mark them, lay them upside down on your bench and put the cradle right side up on top of them. Now, from inside the cradle, mark the length of the bottom surface of the bottom boards, that is, the side that is up at the moment. Keeping in mind that these marks are the *short* length of the bottom boards, crosscut them at the marks with the table-saw blade tilted 15 degrees. Try them out inside the cradle and trim them if necessary.

10 **Attach the rockers to the cradle.** Sand the rocker assemblies. Turn the cradle upside down on a protective pad on your bench. Lay out the positions of the rockers on the bottom edges of the cradle. The rocker supports on the original are nailed to the cradle. You can use screws if you prefer.

Position the rocker assemblies on the cradle, predrill for your fasteners, then glue and nail or screw the rocker supports to the bottom edges of the cradle.

11 **Glue the bottom boards to the rocker units.** Sand the bottom boards, then glue and clamp them to the rocker units as shown in the *Top View.* You can further reinforce the cradle by nailing or screwing through the cradle end pieces into the ends of the bottom boards.

12 **Complete the cradle.** Plane the ends of the sides flush with the outside surfaces of the headboard and footboard. Finish rounding the ends of the top edges of the sides.

The walnut stain on the pine of the original has worn well. If you stain your cradle or leave it natural, finish with several coats of polyurethane or shellac. If you prefer paint, see "Milk Paint" on page 100.

The original cradle had hand-sewn mattress ticking for the bedding to go over. Today, you will probably want to sew a covering around a piece of 2-inch-thick foam of the sort available at fabric stores.

CHILD'S HUTCH

Miniatures of furniture can be toys but they don't need to be. For example, valuable antique pocket watches are sometimes displayed in miniature grandfather clock cases. The little hutch in the photo was probably intended as a child's toy when it was first built, but it now houses an assortment of collectibles at Log Cabin Antiques in Parkesburg, Pennsylvania. You can make it for a child, or for an adult, or just because it's fun to make. Use pine to accurately reproduce the original, or use your choice of hardwoods. The drawings reflect a few minor changes from the original to make it an easier and more durable project to build.

1 **Cut the pieces to size.** Cut the parts to the sizes in the Cutting List. All the parts on the original are made of solid wood but you may find it easier and more practical to use plywood for the back and drawer bottoms. If you intend to finish the hutch natural, be sure the back matches the rest of the hutch. Any good ¼-inch plywood will make good drawer bottoms.

2 **Dado and shape the sides.** The shelves join the sides with dadoes and rabbets as shown in the *Front View.* Set up a ⁷⁄₁₆-inch-wide dado cutter on the table saw and make a test cut. Check the fit of the shelves in the test dado and adjust the cutter as necessary. Cut the dadoes and rabbets.

Lay out the semi-circular foot cutouts at the bottom of the sides, then cut them out with a coping saw. Smooth the sawn edges with sandpaper.

3 **Attach the shelves.** Sand the sides and shelves. Apply glue to the dadoes and rabbets and fit the shelves into the sides. Reinforce the joints with 1½-inch brads. Measure across the diagonals to make sure the cabinet is square.

EXPLODED VIEW

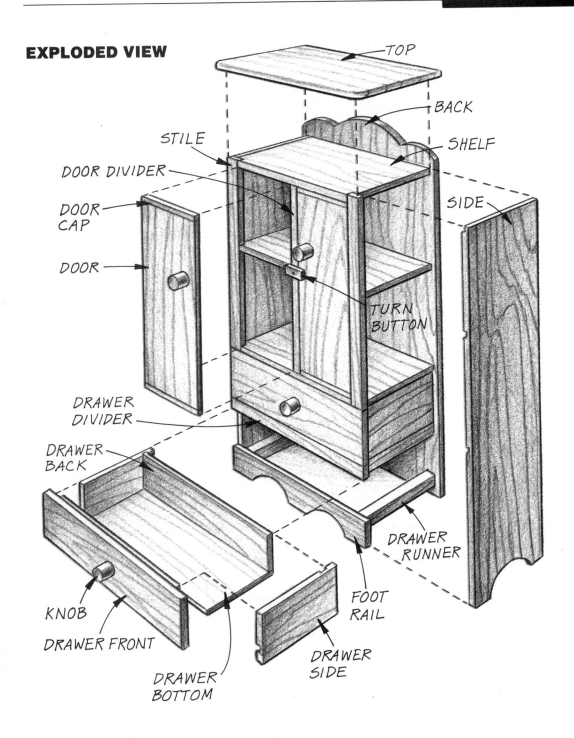

TOP

BACK

STILE

SHELF

DOOR DIVIDER

DOOR
CAP

SIDE

DOOR

TURN
BUTTON

DRAWER
DIVIDER

DRAWER
BACK

KNOB

DRAWER FRONT

DRAWER
BOTTOM

DRAWER
SIDE

FOOT
RAIL

DRAWER
RUNNER

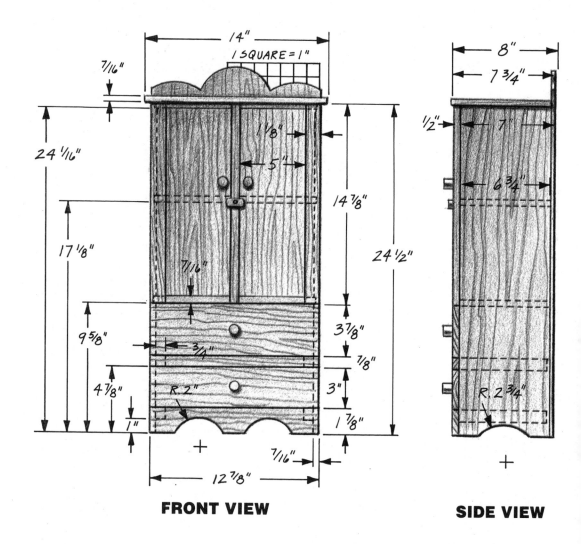

FRONT VIEW

SIDE VIEW

4 **Shape and attach the top.** Slightly round the ends and the front edge of the top with a file and sandpaper and sand the entire top. Place the top on the cabinet. It should be centered from side to side and flush with the top shelf along the back. Drill and countersink pilot holes for #6 screws through the top shelf and into the top.

One screw near each corner of the shelf is appropriate. Secure the top with #6 × ¾-inch flathead wood screws.

5 **Shape and attach the back.** Lay out the curves at the top of the back as shown in the *Front View*. Cut along the layout with a coping saw and

CUTTING LIST

Part	Dimensions
Sides (2)	$\frac{7}{16}'' \times 7'' \times 24\frac{1}{2}''$
Shelves (3)	$\frac{7}{16}'' \times 7'' \times 12\frac{1}{4}''$
Top	$\frac{7}{16}'' \times 7\frac{3}{4}'' \times 14''$
Back*	$\frac{1}{4}'' \times 12\frac{7}{8}'' \times 27\frac{1}{4}''$
Drawer runners (4)	$\frac{3}{4}'' \times \frac{7}{8}'' \times 6\frac{3}{4}''$
Door divider	$\frac{1}{2}'' \times \frac{5}{8}'' \times 14\frac{7}{8}''$
Drawer divider	$\frac{1}{2}'' \times \frac{7}{8}'' \times 12\frac{7}{8}''$
Stiles (2)	$\frac{1}{2}'' \times 1\frac{1}{8}'' \times 14\frac{7}{8}''$
Foot rail	$\frac{1}{2}'' \times 1\frac{7}{8}'' \times 12\frac{7}{8}''$
Door caps (4)	$\frac{1}{2}'' \times \frac{1}{2}'' \times 5''$
Doors (2)	$\frac{1}{2}'' \times 5'' \times 13\frac{5}{8}''$
Top drawer sides (2)	$\frac{3}{8}'' \times 3\frac{7}{8}'' \times 6\frac{3}{4}''$
Bottom drawer sides (2)	$\frac{3}{8}'' \times 3'' \times 6\frac{3}{4}''$
Top drawer front	$\frac{3}{4}'' \times 3\frac{7}{8}'' \times 12\frac{7}{8}''$
Bottom drawer front	$\frac{3}{4}'' \times 3'' \times 12\frac{7}{8}''$
Top drawer back	$\frac{3}{8}'' \times 3\frac{3}{8}'' \times 11\frac{1}{2}''$
Bottom drawer back	$\frac{3}{8}'' \times 2\frac{1}{2}'' \times 11\frac{7}{16}''$
Drawer bottoms* (2)	$\frac{1}{4}'' \times 6\frac{1}{4}'' \times 11\frac{7}{16}''$
Knobs (4)	$\frac{3}{4}''$ dia. $\times \frac{3}{4}''$
Turn button	$\frac{3}{8}'' \times \frac{5}{8}'' \times 1\frac{3}{8}''$

Hardware

#16 $\times$ 1½" wire brads
4 flathead wood screws, #6 $\times$ ¾"
12 flathead wood screws, #6 $\times$ 1"
2 pair butt hinges with screws, 1" $\times$ ¾", open
1 roundhead wood screw, #6 $\times$ ¾"

*May be plywood or solid lumber.

smooth the edge with sandpaper. Attach the back with glue and 1½-inch wire brads.

6 **Attach the drawer runners.** Drill and countersink #6 shank holes near the ends of the drawer runners.

Screw the runners to the sides as shown in the *Front View.*

7 **Attach the dividers and stiles.** Sand the dividers and stiles. Glue them in place on the front of the cabinet as shown in the *Front View.* Hold them in place with brads while the glue dries if you find that more convenient than clamps.

8 **Shape and attach the foot rail.** Lay out the semi-circular cutouts on the foot rail as shown in the *Front View*. Saw to the line with a coping saw, then sand the entire foot rail and glue it to the front of the cabinet.

9 **Make and hang the doors.** Attach the caps to the ends of the doors with both glue and brads. Sand the doors. Install the hinges, mortising both the doors and the stiles to accept the hinge leaves.

10 **Make the drawers.** Make the two drawers at the same time; the only difference between them is their heights. Set up a ⅜-inch-wide dado blade on the table saw. Test the width of the cut and adjust it as necessary to get a snug fit on the drawer backs. Adjust the depth of cut to ⅛ inch and cut the drawer-back dadoes in the sides as shown in the *Drawer Details*. Raise the depth of cut to ¼ inch and cut the rab-

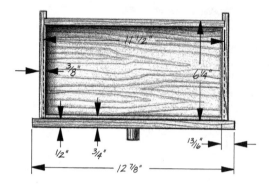

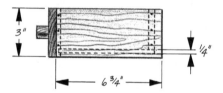

DRAWER DETAILS

bets across the ends of the drawer fronts. Each rabbet will require three passes but making three passes for each of four rabbets is easier than changing the cutter. Rout the groove for the bottom with a ¼-inch straight bit.

Sand all the drawer parts. Attach the sides to the fronts and backs with glue and brads. Slide the bottoms into their grooves and nail them to the backs with a couple of brads.

Try the drawers in their openings. If they bind, sand or plane the offending high spots until the drawers run smoothly. A little paraffin on the runners and sides of the cabinets will improve the smoothness of their operation.

11 **Attach the knobs and catch.** Cut the knobs from ¾-inch dowel

SHOP TIP: You can improve the strength of a glue joint that involves end grain by priming the end grain. Apply glue to the end grain first. Let it soak in for a couple of minutes, then scrape off the excess. Apply fresh glue to both surfaces and screw, nail, or clamp the joint.

and the turn button from scrap. Gently round the hard edges with sandpaper. Drill and countersink shank holes for #6 screws through the doors and drawers. Drill pilot holes in the knobs and screw the knobs in place with #6 × 1½-inch screws. Drill a slightly larger shank hole through the turn button and screw it to the front of the cabinet with a #6 × ¾-inch roundhead wood screw.

12 **Finish the cabinet.** Examine the entire cabinet carefully, touching up with sandpaper as necessary. Keep in mind that small projects are often examined more closely than large ones. Finish the cabinet to suit the wood you chose and its intended use. If it's for a child, be sure to use a finish that it's safe to chew on, like shellac.

ROCKING HORSE

Yee-Haw! Every young cowpoke needs a horse, and it's been that way since before Detroit made horses obsolete. Diane Windle of Log Cabin Antiques in Parkesburg, Pennsylvania, put this particular one out to pasture. Made of pine, with the grain running lengthwise, it broke parallel to the grain at the neck and front foot. Diane keeps it in her kitchen just for its nostalgia.

You can duplicate the original by gluing up pine to 16 inches wide for the horse and then attaching pine runners with dowels. The instructions that follow, however, suggest using plywood to overcome the weakness across the grain inherent in solid lumber. Plywood also allows you to make the horse and runners all in one piece. Use a plywood with no voids so you won't have to fill and patch edges. Lauan plywood and so-called "Baltic-birch" plywood are both good choices. Your dealer should be able to tell you what he has in stock that has no voids.

1 Cut the parts to size. Cut all of the rocking horse parts to the sizes specified by the Cutting List. Use plywood for all of the parts except the handle. Use hardwood dowel or recycle an old broom for the handle. Not every dealer has 1-inch-diameter dowel and not every old broom has a 1-inch-diameter handle so be prepared to make a substitution.

EXPLODED VIEW

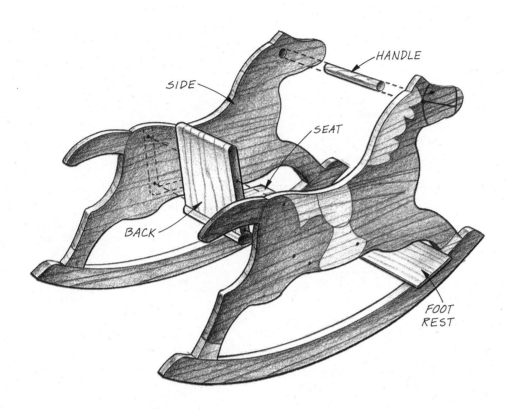

HANDLE

SIDE

SEAT

BACK

FOOT REST

CUTTING LIST

Part	Dimensions
Sides (2)	$\frac{3}{4}'' \times 19'' \times 33''$
Seat	$\frac{3}{4}'' \times 8\frac{1}{2}'' \times 10\frac{1}{2}''$
Back	$\frac{3}{4}'' \times 7\frac{3}{4}'' \times 10\frac{1}{2}''$
Foot rest	$\frac{1}{4}'' \times 5\frac{1}{2}'' \times 13\frac{3}{4}''$
Handle	$1''$ dia. $\times 10\frac{1}{2}''$

Hardware

10 flathead wood screws, #8 $\times$ 1½"
4 flathead wood screws, #6 $\times$ 1"

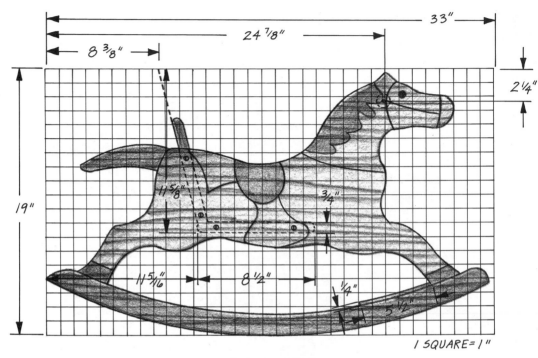

SIDE VIEW

2 **Lay out the seat and back dadoes.** Lay out the seat and back dadoes on the sides as shown in the *Side View*. Mark the center of the handle hole as shown. Be sure you make the sides mirror images of one another. The drawing shows the inside of the left side.

3 **Rout the dadoes for the seat and back.** You want these dadoes to fit the plywood snugly to help prevent the screws from splitting the seat and back, but ¾-inch plywood is seldom ¾ inch thick. Three ways to get a good fit, depending on your plywood, are:

- Find a bit that fits. Eagle America (P.O. Box 1099, Chardon, OH

44024; (800) 872-2511) lists straight bits with ¹¹⁄₁₆-inch and ²³⁄₃₂-inch diameters.

- Rout with a readily available ⅝-inch-diameter bit and then widen the dado by taping a shim to the edge of the router base and making a second pass.

- Rout with a ⅝-inch bit as above, then move the guiding straight-edge over and make a second pass.

Whichever method you choose, make test cuts to be sure the dadoes will fit properly. Then cut the dadoes ¼ inch deep in the stock. Drill ¼-inch-deep holes to fit your handle.

4 **Cut out the sides.** Lay out a 1-inch square grid on the outside of one of the sides, then lay out the shape of the horse as shown in the *Side View.* Tape the two sides together, inside to inside, and saw out the horses with a saber saw. (If your saber saw hasn't had enough oats to saw 1½ inches of plywood, saw out one side at a time. Saw out the side you've laid out, than trace the outline onto the second part.) Smooth the sawn edges with scrapers, files, and sandpaper.

5 **Attach the back, seat, and handle.** Adjust the table-saw blade to 15 degrees from vertical. Bevel the bottom edge of the back at this angle. Chuck a ⅜-inch-radius roundover bit in a table-mounted router. Round-over the front and back sides of the top edge of the back, the top and bottom of the front edge of the seat, and the bottom of the back edge of the seat.

Drill #8 shank holes through the sides in the five locations shown in the *Side View.* If you drill from the dadoed side you can eyeball the locations. Assemble the horse without glue and use the shank holes to position pilot holes in the seat, back, and handle. Countersink the shank holes on the outsides.

Sand all the pieces. Apply glue to the dadoes and handle holes and assemble the horse. Screw the horse together with #8 × 1½-inch wood screws.

6 **Attach the foot rest.** Sand the foot rest, then glue and screw it to the runners just behind the front feet. Let it overhang equal amounts at both ends. The ¼-inch plywood should be flexible enough to conform to the curvature of the runners.

7 **Finish the horse.** Look over the horse carefully and sand off any smeared glue. Make sure that all the edges are gently rounded and that there are no splinters.

Give the whole horse a coat of latex primer, then a finish coat of enamel. Paint in the details with an enamel or trim paint as shown in the *Side View* and photo. A little consultation at this stage may save you from creating a pinto for an aficionado of Arabians or Morgans.

GAME BOARD

This country-crafted game board offers a chess and checkers board on one surface and a carom board on the reverse surface. The octagonal board has the advantage of being easily portable yet offering room on the sides for captured pieces or a cup of coffee. The game board is sturdily constructed of poplar, but the design allows the use of plywood for the playing surface. You can even make your own game pieces by sawing discs from ¾-inch or 1-inch dowel.

1 **Select the stock and cut the parts.** The stock for the game board is relatively thin; the frame pieces are only ½ inch thick and the playing circle is only ⅜ inch thick.

First decide whether you want to substitute plywood for the playing circle. A good hardwood plywood with no voids will make an excellent, stable playing surface but will not be an accurate reproduction of the antique original. If you stick to the construction of the original, you will need to edge-glue ⅜-inch-thick stock to a width of 26 inches. (For more information on edge-gluing, see page 6.)

Cut the frame pieces to the dimensions given in the Cutting List. Cut the border pieces to thickness and width but leave them longer than specified for the time being.

2 **Cut the bridle joints in the frame pieces.** The frame pieces

EXPLODED VIEW

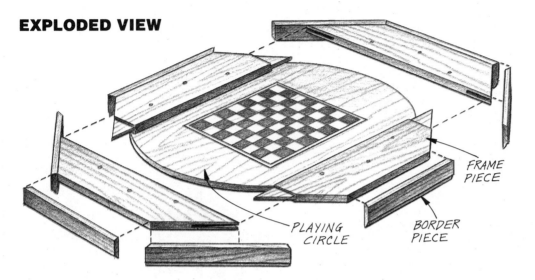

FRAME
PIECE

PLAYING
CIRCLE

BORDER
PIECE

are joined with bridle joints as shown in the *Frame Joint Detail*. When first assembled, only the inside corners join and the outside of the joint is open. When the frame is cut into an octagon, the open parts are cut off.

Both halves of the joint are best made with a tenoning jig as described on page 60. Cut the mortises in several

side-by-side cuts and the tenons in the conventional manner.

3 Glue the frame together. Glue and clamp the four frame pieces together on a flat surface. Make sure the joints are tight at the shoulders and the bottom of the mortises. Bridle joints also

CUTTING LIST

Part	Dimensions
Frame pieces (4)	½″ × 5½″ × 23¼″
Border pieces (8)	½″ × 1¾″ × 12⁷⁄₁₆″
Playing circle	⅜″ × 26″ dia.
Carom pins (8)	⁷⁄₁₆″ dia. × ½″

Hardware

4d finish nails
20 brass flathead wood screws, #6 × ¾″

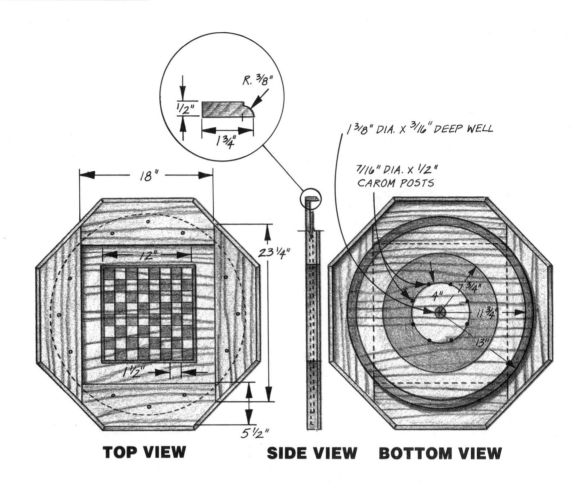

R. ⅜"

½"

1¾"

18"

12"

1½"

23¼"

5½"

1⅜" DIA. X 3/16" DEEP WELL

7/16" DIA. X ½" CAROM POSTS

4"

¾"

11¾"

13"

TOP VIEW   **SIDE VIEW**   **BOTTOM VIEW**

require that the cheeks be clamped. Check that the diagonals of the assembly are equal, indicating that the assembly is square.

4 **Saw the frame into an octagon.** Lay out the 45-degree cuts on the corners of the frame to create an octagon with 12-inch sides. Saw off the corners with a sharp handsaw or on a table or radial arm saw.

It's difficult to clean up the sawn edges since the grain of the wood

changes direction in the middle of each joint. Plane from each direction toward the middle of the cut and make sure your plane is as sharp as you can get it. Sand the frame.

5 **Shape the border edges.** The border pieces that surround the frame have a stepped roundover along one edge as shown in the *Side View*. Rout the roundover with a ⅜-inch roundover bit in a table-mounted router. Sand the border pieces.

6 Install the border pieces. Adjust
the miter gauge to 22½ degrees
from square. Miter one end of a border
piece, hold it in place on the frame,
aligning the miter with a corner of the
frame, mark it for length at the next corner, and miter the other end at the
mark. Glue and nail it in place with 4d
finish nails. Repeat the procedure for the
remaining seven pieces, butting each
tightly against the previous piece when
marking it for length.

**7 Saw out the circular playing
surface.** Lay out the circle on the
playing surface blank. If you don't have
trammels or a beam compass, you can
still do a fine job of laying out a large
circle by clamping a pencil and a nail to a
stick of wood with a couple of small

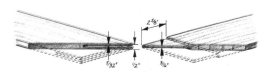

FRAME JOINT DETAIL

spring clamps. The points of the pencil
and nail must be 13 inches apart.

Saw out the circle with a coping
saw, then clean up the sawn edge with a
fine rasp and sandpaper.

**8 Bore the well in the center of
the carom board.** Drilling the 1⅜-
inch-diameter well in the center of the
carom board side of the playing circle
poses a bit of a problem. The ³⁄₁₆-inch-
deep hole should have a nice flat bottom.
The usual bit for a flat-bottom hole is a
Forstner bit but that requires a drill
press and few woodworkers have a drill
press that will drill to the center of a 26-
inch-diameter circle.

A solution to the problem is to saw the 1⅜-inch circle ³⁄₁₆ inch deep with a hole saw, then chisel out the center. Alternatively, bore the hole with an expansion bit and brace, boring only until the spur is ³⁄₁₆ inch deep. Again, chisel out the center. With either method, fill the pilot hole with wood filler and sand smooth.

9 **Stain the frame and border.** Since poplar has a pale color and indistinct grain, stain the frame and border. The original is stained walnut brown, but you are not limited in your choices. Allow the stain to dry overnight.

10 **Paint the playing circle.** The entire playing surface on the checkerboard side of the circle is painted a rich red. When you paint alternate checkerboard squares black, you have a distinctive game surface. Paint the checkerboard side red, then lay out the checkerboard lightly in pencil. Paint alternate squares black using masking tape to shield the red squares if you don't have a steady enough hand to get straight lines freehand.

Two fine yellow-gold painted lines border the checkerboard, and also form the three circular lines marking out the scoring areas on the carom side of the board. Lay out these lines lightly in pencil. Paint them with a wheeled paint striper (available from Woodcraft, P.O. Box 1686, Parkersburg, WV 26102-1686, (800) 225–1153, item #03T27). The striper has an adjustable guide for following a straightedge that is useful for the border lines on the checkerboard side.

You can remove the guide and substitute a long piece of stiff wire to make a painting compass for painting the circular lines on the carom side.

If you're using plywood for the playing circle, paint the circular edge with the same yellow-gold paint.

11 **Screw the playing circle to the frame.** Place the frame over the checkerboard side of the playing surface. Center the checkerboard within the square opening in the frame and clamp it there temporarily. Drill and countersink shank and pilot holes for #6 × ¾-inch screws as shown in the *Top View.* Screw the frame to the playing circle with brass screws.

12 **Screw the carom posts to the playing circle.** To make the carom posts, saw ½-inch lengths of ⁷⁄₁₆-inch-diameter dowel. Drill shank holes for #6 × ¾-inch screws down the center of each post and countersink them on one end. To mark the post locations on the board, lay a straightedge from corner to opposite corner of the octagonal frame and mark where the straightedge crosses the inner circle. Drill ¼-inch-deep pilot holes at each mark, then screw and glue the pins to the playing circle.

13 **Finish the game board.** Apply a clear finish such as shellac, lacquer, or varnish to the areas that are not painted. Two or three light coats with a light, very fine sanding between them will give the finest finish. If you prefer, you could use a Danish oil or tung oil.

PART FIVE

WALL-HUNG PROJECTS

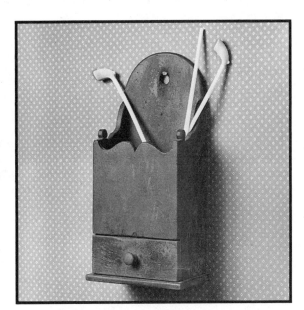

PIPE BOX

Pipe boxes held the long-stemmed clay pipes that were popular during the colonial period. The pipes went in the top compartment, or well, while tobacco was kept in the drawer.

Clay pipes went out of fashion long ago, and smoking of any sort now seems to be following the same road to oblivion. Pipe boxes, however, have never been more popular. They are handy for incoming or outgoing mail and make de-lightful containers for dried-flower arrangements. Pipe boxes, like other clearly antiquated furnishings, give our homes an air of rootedness in our past, even if we no longer indulge in the practices that gave rise to them.

Except for the drawer front, the pipe box is made entirely from ½-inch-thick pine. Hardwoods are equally suitable. The parts are butt-joined and held with cut brads set flush with the surface of the wood. The original red finish has been painted over with dark green paint, much of which has worn off.

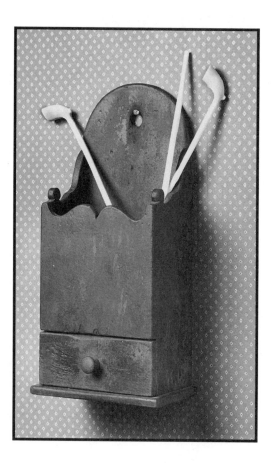

1 **Cut the parts to size.** If you lack a thickness-planing capability, have your lumber supplier plane stock to ½ inch thick. Cut the parts to the dimensions specified by the Cutting List. The drawer front can be made the required thickness by gluing together two ½-inch-thick pieces. If you glue a 5¹⁵/₁₆-inch-long piece centered on an 8-inch-long piece, you won't need to cut rabbets on the ends of the front.

2 **Cut the dadoes for the well bottom.** The bottom of the well in the pipe box fits in ½-inch-wide, ¼-inch-deep dadoes in the front, back, and sides. The dadoes in the front and back must stop short of the edges so they won't show on the sides of the pipe box.

Use a ½-inch straight router bit and the router's fence attachment to cut the dadoes. Note that the dadoes in the sides and back are 3½ inches from the

EXPLODED VIEW

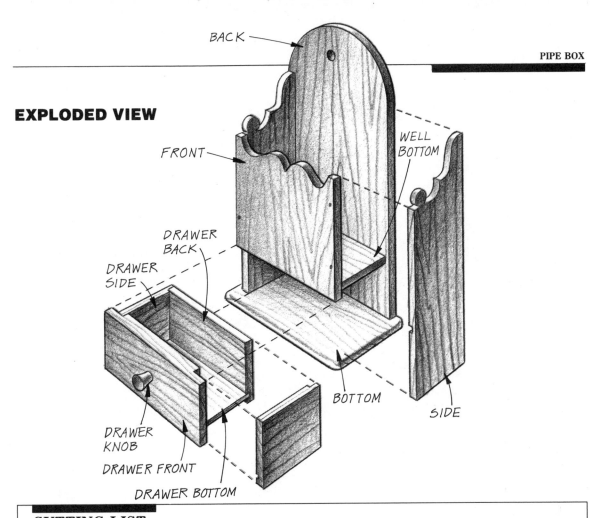

BACK

FRONT

WELL BOTTOM

DRAWER BACK

DRAWER SIDE

BOTTOM

SIDE

DRAWER KNOB

DRAWER FRONT

DRAWER BOTTOM

CUTTING LIST

Part	Dimensions
Front	$\frac{1}{2}'' \times 8'' \times 7\frac{3}{4}''$
Back	$\frac{1}{2}'' \times 8'' \times 18''$
Sides (2)	$\frac{1}{2}'' \times 4\frac{1}{8}'' \times 14''$
Well bottom	$\frac{1}{2}'' \times 7\frac{1}{2}'' \times 4\frac{1}{2}''$
Bottom	$\frac{1}{2}'' \times 5\frac{1}{2}'' \times 9''$
Drawer front	$1'' \times 3\frac{3}{16}'' \times 8''$
Drawer sides (2)	$\frac{1}{2}'' \times 3\frac{3}{16}'' \times 4''$
Drawer back	$\frac{1}{2}'' \times 3'' \times 6\frac{3}{8}''$
Drawer bottom	$\frac{1}{2}'' \times 3\frac{3}{8}'' \times 6\frac{3}{8}''$
Drawer knob	$1''$ dia. $\times 1\frac{3}{4}''$

Hardware

2d cut brads. Available from many building-supply stores and from Tremont Nail Company, P.O. Box 111, Wareham, MA 02571; (508) 295–0038. Item #CRB-2.

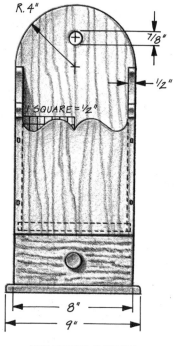

FRONT VIEW

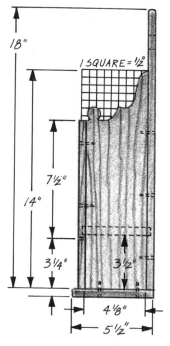

SIDE VIEW

bottom edge but the dado in the front is only ¼ inch from the bottom edge. The dadoes run clear across the width of the sides but stop ¼ inch short of the edges of the front and back. Square the ends of the stopped dadoes with a chisel.

3 **Radius the back piece.** The top of the back piece is a 4-inch-radius semi-circle. Draw the curve with a compass, then saw it with a coping saw. Smooth the curve with a fine rasp and sandpaper. Drill a ⅞-inch-diameter hole in the back piece, centered 2⅛ inches from the top.

4 **Cut out the top shape of the sides.** The top ends of the side pieces are decoratively shaped. Lay out the pattern shown in the *Side View* on one of the sides. Tape or clamp the two sides together and saw to the line with the coping saw. Clean up the sawn edges with files and sandpaper.

5 **Cut out the front scroll design.** The scroll on the top of the front piece is symmetrical as shown in the *Front View*. It will be easiest to make a paper pattern of one half of it and trace the pattern on the stock.

The length of the front piece given in the Cutting List is ¼ inch longer than shown in the drawing to allow you to adjust the curve to match the side. Assemble the front, two sides, and well bottom without glue or nails and mark where the shape of the sides meet the front piece. Align the front scroll pattern with these marks and trace it. Saw to the line and smooth the sawn edges as you did before.

6 **Round the front and side edges of the base.** The edges of the base are not rounded uniformly as they would be if they were rounded-over with a router. Instead, they seem to have been blunted with a plane. The front edge below the drawer has worn down even more. Reproduce these shapes now, before assembling the box.

7 **Assemble the pipe box.** Sand the remaining box parts and assemble the box with glue and cut brads. The well bottom doesn't need to be glued but keep it in position as you assemble the front, back, and sides to make sure the dadoes line up, and to make sure you don't forget it. Let the glue in these joints dry, then glue and nail the bottom of the box in place.

8 **Make the drawer-front rabbets for the drawer sides.** Check that the drawer front fits easily between the front and bottom of the box and trim the drawer parts if necessary. If you're mak-

ing the drawer front out of a single thick piece of wood instead of gluing it up as suggested earlier, saw $1\frac{1}{32}$-inch $\times$ ½-inch rabbets on the ends.

9 **Cut the drawer-back rabbets in the drawer sides.** Saw the ½-inch-wide, ¼-inch-deep rabbets in the back end of both drawer sides as shown in the *Drawer Detail*. If you have a tenoning jig, you can cut the shoulders and then cut out the waste with the stock on end. But don't try to saw the stock on end without a tenoning jig. If you don't have a jig, cut the rabbets with a succession of saw kerfs parallel to the shoulder cut. Since the drawer sides are quite small, you might want to cut the rabbets on both ends of a longer piece, then cut the sides from the ends of the longer piece.

10 **Cut the drawer-bottom groove and assemble the drawer.** The edges of the drawer bottom are beveled to fit a ¼-inch-wide

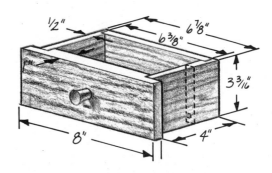

DRAWER DETAIL

groove. Rip the groove in the drawer front, sides, and back with a dado cutter, or in two or three passes with a saw blade. Bevel the edges of the drawer bottom with a hand plane to fit the groove.

Sand the drawer parts, then glue and nail the drawer sides in the drawer-front rabbets. Slide the drawer bottom in place, then glue and nail the drawer back to the drawer sides. Don't glue the drawer bottom, since it's captive on all four sides.

11 **Make and attach the drawer knob.** Turn the drawer knob on the lathe, if you have one. The knob on the original has an integral tenon as

shown in the *Drawer Detail.* Drill a ½-inch hole in the center of the drawer front and glue the knob in place. If you don't have a lathe, buy a small knob at a hardware store. Most manufactured knobs attach with a screw.

12 **Complete the pipe box.** Apply a finish to your own liking. Both paint and natural finishes are appropriate. The box in the photo was originally painted a dark red, then at some point repainted a green that is almost black. The green has worn through revealing the earlier red. You can reproduce this appearance by painting very dark green over red and then sanding through the green at natural wear areas.

CORNER SHELF UNIT

Corner shelves are popular country antiques. This example in pine is made more attractive by the scroll on the front edges of the shelves, as well as on the sides. A beaded shiplap joint between the back boards adds interest on the inside. Although not large, the shelves are roomy and extremely sturdy. If you have dishes to display, rout a plate groove across the back edges of the shelves.

1 Select the stock and cut the parts. You can conveniently make this entire project out of 6-inch-wide boards. Edge-glue three, 6-inch-wide, 4/4 (four-quarter) boards for the shelves. (See page 6 for more on edge-gluing.) Resaw 6-inch-wide, 5/4 (five-quarter) boards for the back. Six-inch-wide stock can be resawn on most table saws by ripping from both edges. Plane the stock

EXPLODED VIEW

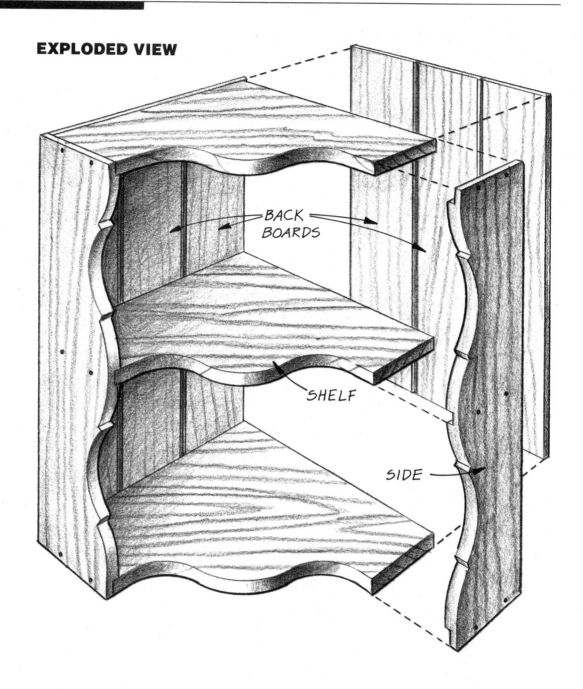

BACK
BOARDS

SHELF

SIDE

TOP VIEW

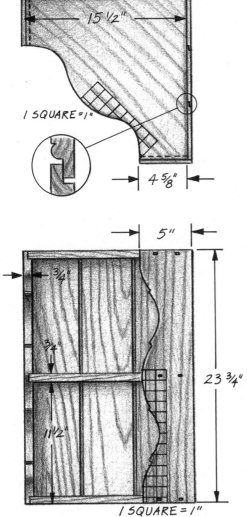

15 1/2"

1 SQUARE = 1"

4 5/8"

SHELF LAYOUT

5"

3/4"

3/4"

23 3/4"

1 1/2"

1 SQUARE = 1"

SIDE VIEW

if you don't buy surfaced stock and cut the parts to length.

2 Dado and rabbet the sides. Lay out the shelf dadoes and rabbets on the inside of the side pieces. You can cut the dadoes and rabbets with the miter gauge and a dado cutter on the table saw or you can rout them. If you choose to rout them, use the router's fence attachment for the rabbets but clamp a straightedge to the stock to cut the dadoes.

Rabbet the sides for the back but

CUTTING LIST

Part	Dimensions
Sides (2)	¾″ × 5″ × 23¾″
Shelves*	¾″ × 14¼″ × 49½″
Back boards (6)	⅜″ × 5½″ × 23¾″

Hardware

3d cut box nails. Available from many building-supply stores and from Tremont Nail Company, P.O. Box 111, Wareham, MA 02571; (508) 295–0038. Item #CX-3.

*See *Shelf Layout* for cutting into three shelves.

note that these rabbets are only ³⁄₁₆ inch deep, not ⅜ inch deep like the shelf rabbets.

3 Shape the edge of the sides. Lay out the curved edge on one of the sides. Stack the two sides face to face and tack them together through the waste portion. Saw them to shape with a coping saw. Clean up the sawn edges with files and sandpaper. A sanding drum on a drill press can help clean up the curves.

4 Cut the shelves to shape. Lay out the 45-degree cuts shown in the *Shelf Layout* on the shelf stock. Adjust the table-saw miter gauge to 45 degrees and cut the shelf boards to size. Stack the shelves to make certain the three shelves are identical and plane the edges with a very sharp hand plane if necessary.

5 Shape the front edges of the shelves. Mark the shelves as top,

middle, and bottom. Before you shape the front edges of the shelves, set them in the side rabbets and dadoes. Mark the front edges of the sides on each shelf. Make a stiff paper template of the shape of the front edge of the shelves. Line up the template with the marks you made on the shelves and trace the shape. Saw out each shelf separately just outside the line, then smooth the edge down to the line. This procedure assures that any variation from the given side shape will not result in shelves that aren't flush.

6 Rabbet the back boards. The *Top View* shows the layout of the back boards and the shiplap joints. You can cut the rabbets that form the shiplap joints with a dado cutter on the table saw or with a straight bit on the router table. Note that the outside boards have only one edge rabbeted. These boards will be trimmed to fit when you assemble the shelves.

7 Cut the bead on the back boards. Ideally the bead would be cut not as shown in the *Top View* but on the shoulder of the adjoining piece. In that location it would be in no danger of weakening an already thin edge. Unfortunately it cannot be cut there with readily available router bits. You *can* cut it there if you have beading cutters for a molding head. To cut the beads on the router table, use a half-round beading bit with a bead radius of no more than 3/32 inch such as the Freud #82-100. Cut the beads with the boards on edge against the router-table fence. Sand the inside of the boards when you're done cutting the beads.

8 **Assemble the shelves.** Glue and nail the project together using 3d cut box nails. Predrill two nail holes per shelf through the sides, and two holes per shelf through each back board.

Sand the shelf and sides. Glue and nail the sides to the shelves first. Make sure the back edges of the shelves line up exactly with the bottom of the backboard rabbets in the sides. Assemble one side to all three shelves, then rotate

the assembly 90 degrees, and assemble the second side.

Glue and nail the back boards to the back edges of the shelves starting at the back corner. Apply glue sparingly to the edges of the shelves and nail the boards only when you are sure the assembly is square. Space the boards a penny's thickness apart to allow for some expansion. Plane the edge of the third back board to just fit into the rabbet in the side. Finish nailing the three boards on one side, then turn the assembly around and complete the other side.

9 **Finish the corner shelves.** Shelves of this sort can be found at antique dealers with a variety of finishes. Some are stained and varnished, some are simply oiled with boiled linseed oil, some are finished with milk paint. (See page 100 for more information on milk paint.) Urethane or lacquer finishes are also appropriate. This project is small enough to finish with an aerosol spray finish. Be sure to clean off all dust with a tack cloth before applying your choice of finish.

SHOP TIP: When assembling a series of shelves into dadoes or rabbets, hold the shelves on edge or on end by screwing a clamp to the bottom of the shelf. Attach the clamp so the body of the clamp functions like a stand. You can still move it around as needed, but it won't tip over so easily.

10 **Hang the shelves.** You can safely hang the shelves by screwing through the back into studs in the wall. Countersink brass flathead wood screws for a workmanlike appearance. Use #10 or larger screws long enough to go through the wall plaster and at least 1¼ inches into the studs. If there are no conveniently located studs, use toggle bolts.

PINE MIRROR

If you've ever been frustrated by not having the right tools for a project, you're not alone. A century ago, when building-your-own was the only choice for many people, woodworkers had the same frustration. The maker of this mirror frame solved the problem with imaginative use of the tools that he had. He made a simple but attractive mirror frame without any tools for molding curved shapes. If you have a table saw, a hammer, and perhaps a hand plane, you're well equipped to reproduce his frame.

The sides of the frame are glued up from pieces with beveled edges. The mitered corners are glued and nailed with cut nails. The original is pine, but there's nothing about the design to prevent the use of other woods.

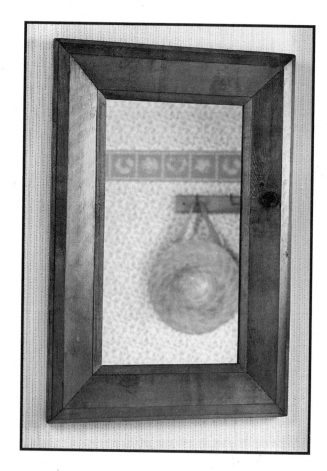

1 **Select the stock and cut the parts.** Select the stock carefully for attractive grain since a mirror frame is routinely viewed from fairly close. The dimensions given in the Cutting List are final sizes. Cut the parts for the frame sides an inch or so longer than listed. You'll cut them to correct length when you miter the ends. Rip the outside edges to the correct thickness and all of the parts to the correct width.

2 **Bevel the edges of the narrow and wide faces.** Tilt the table-saw blade 17 degrees (90 degrees minus 73 degrees) and rip both edges of the faces as shown in the *Cross Section through Frame*. Plane the edges so you'll get a good glue bond.

3 **Cut the rabbet in the inside edges.** A rabbet can be cut in a single pass with a dado cutter or in two passes with a saw blade. On small pieces like the inside edges the dado cutter is probably the safer choice. Adjust the

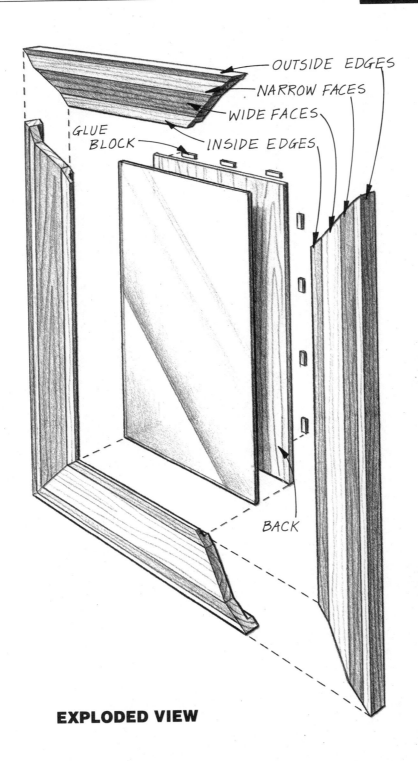

OUTSIDE EDGES
NARROW FACES
WIDE FACES
GLUE BLOCK
INSIDE EDGES
BACK

EXPLODED VIEW

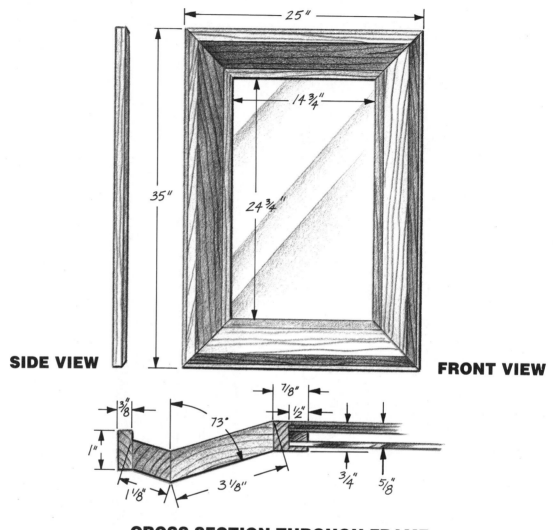

SIDE VIEW

FRONT VIEW

CROSS SECTION THROUGH FRAME

cutter for a ½-inch-wide, ⅝-inch-deep cut as shown in the *Cross Section through Frame* and make the cut with the visible face of the piece up.

4 **Glue the parts of the four frame sides together.** First glue the nar-row faces to the wide faces. The angles make clamping the joint a bit of a puzzler but there's an easy way to do it. First nail a couple of cleats 3⅞ inches apart on a scrap board. Make sure the cleats are parallel. Fit the narrow and wide faces together between the cleats as shown in the *Clamping Detail*. Place another scrap

CUTTING LIST

Part	Dimensions
Short narrow faces (2)	¾" × 1⅛" × 25"
Long narrow faces (2)	¾" × 1⅛" × 35"
Short wide faces (2)	¾" × 3⅛" × 25"
Long wide faces (2)	¾" × 3⅛" × 35"
Short inside edges (2)	¾" × ⅞" × 25"
Long inside edges (2)	¾" × ⅞" × 35"
Short outside edges (2)	⅜" × 1" × 25"
Long outside edges (2)	⅜" × 1" × 35"
Glue blocks (14)	¼" × ½" × 1"
Back*	¼" × 15½" × 25½"

Hardware

Four 8d fine cut finish nails. Available from many building-supply stores and from Tremont Nail Company, P.O. Box 111, Wareham, MA 02571; (508) 295–0038. Item #CE-8.
1 mirror, ⅛" × 15⅜" × 25⅜"
¾" wire brads
Picture-hanging hardware

*Use ¼" plywood for the back.

board over the top and weight it as shown in the drawing. Five pounds or so every 6 inches along the joint should be enough. Check that the full width of the joint closes. (You'll only be able to check at the ends.) If it's open at the top, move the cleats farther apart. If it's open at the bottom, shim the space between the cleats narrower. When the joint closes properly, apply glue to the mating edges and reclamp them in this makeshift jig. A strip of masking tape, wax paper, or plastic between the joint and the top board will prevent gluing the top board to the frame parts. Assemble all four sides in this way.

When these joints are dry, glue and clamp the outside edges, then the inside edges, to the assembled face pieces. If

you don't have appropriate clamps, apply glue to the mating surfaces and then nail the edges in place with ¾-inch wire brads. You'll find that the mating surface

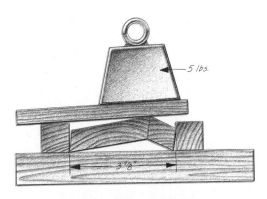

CLAMPING DETAIL

of the inside edge is a trifle narrower than the edge of the wide face. When gluing these parts together, position them so the extra width projects at the back of the frame. After the glue is dry, plane off the slight projection.

5 Miter the ends of the frame sides. Adjust the table-saw miter gauge to 45 degrees and test it by cutting a piece of scrap in half at 45 degrees. Turn one of the halves over and bring the two halves together forming a miter joint. They should be square to each other. If they aren't, adjust the miter gauge as necessary and retest until they do. Get the angle right at this stage or your mirror frame corners will not close properly.

When you're satisfied with the miter-gauge adjustment, miter the ends of the side assemblies. Shim the outer edge ¼ inch up from the saw table to position the parts correctly for the cuts. Make sure you cut the side assemblies to the overall lengths shown in the *Front View*.

6 Glue and nail the mirror frame together. The miter joints in the frame are held together primarily with glue. Fine finish cut nails help by holding the joints in alignment while clamping them. You don't need to use cut nails, of course. Modern wire finish nails will do the same job, they just won't look the same. You can clamp the joints with special corner clamps, with bar clamps (two vertically and two horizontally), or with a band clamp around the outside. If you don't have any of these clamps, you can wrap strong cord tightly around the outside, then pull it even tighter by inserting blocks of scrap wood between the cord and the sides.

Assemble the frame (without glue) on a flat surface, shimming up the outside edges the same way you did when cutting the miters. Drill slightly undersize holes for the 4d cut nails that will hold the frame together, positioning the holes as indicated on the *Front View*.

Apply glue to both surfaces of the joints, let it soak into the grain, then scrape off the excess. Apply fresh glue to at least one of the surfaces of each joint and reassemble the frame on the flat surface. Shim the outside edges again. Drive in the nails. You'll find it helpful while driving the nails to butt the short sides against a cleat clamped to the bench. Be careful not to smash the tips of the miters, though. When the nails are in place, apply clamping pressure.

7 Apply your finish. Carefully scrape off the squeezed-out glue, then sand the frame. Stain the mirror if you like, or let its own color mellow with age. Old pine develops a soft golden brown tone. Shellac or linseed oil would be historically correct final finishes. Apply your choice of finish to both the front and back to impede changes in the moisture content of the wood, then let the finish dry thoroughly.

8 **Install the mirror.** Put the frame front side down on your bench and fit the mirror into the rabbet. It should have about ⅛ inch to spare. Position the glue blocks around the inside edge of the frame as shown in the *Cross Section through Frame*. Put three along each short side and four along each long side. Scrape off the finish where the glue blocks will go, then glue the blocks in place. If you apply glue to a block and then rub it on the scraped area, you'll get an adequate bond without clamping.

9 **Attach the back and hanging hardware.** When the glue blocks are thoroughly dry, fit the back into the opening in the frame. The back rests on the glue blocks.

When you're sure the back fits properly, put a drop of glue on each glue block, put the back in position, and toenail it to the frame sides with ¾-inch brads.

To keep hammering to a minimum, predrill the brad holes using a brad with the head snipped off as a drill bit.

Most hardware stores sell a variety of hardware items for hanging pictures and mirrors. Select and install sturdy hardware; you don't want seven years of bad luck.

WINDOW VALANCE

No claims are made for the great antiquity of this design; it dates back to April 1993. The lines and style, however, are obviously far from new. It fits in well with a room full of country antiques and reproductions.

Several features of the design are worth noting. Closed on top, it helps protect curtains from dust. It hangs by means of finish nails in snug but not tight holes in the top of the window casing so it's easily removed for repainting and leaves no visible scars on the wall. It uses standard clothespole rod and hangers from the hardware store or lumberyard.

1 **Adapt the plans to your window.** The drawings show a valance for a window that measures 32⅜ inches from the outside of the vertical casings

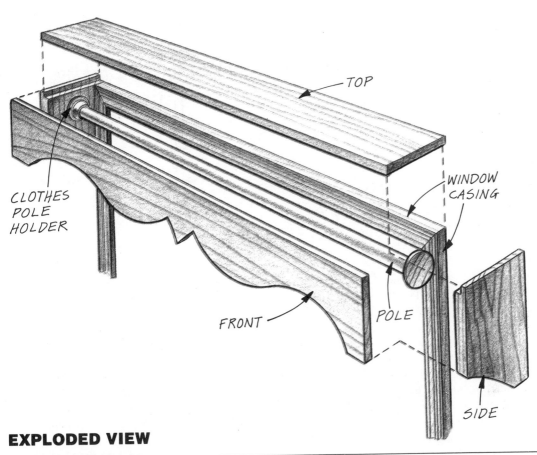

CLOTHES
POLE
HOLDER

TOP

WINDOW
CASING

FRONT

POLE

SIDE

EXPLODED VIEW

Part	Dimensions
CUTTING LIST	
Sides (2)	$\frac{3}{4}'' \times 5'' \times 7\frac{1}{2}''$
Front	$\frac{1}{2}'' \times 5'' \times X^* + 1\frac{1}{2}''$
Top	$\frac{1}{2}'' \times 5'' \times X^* + \frac{3}{4}''$
Pole	$1\frac{7}{16}''$ dia. $\times X^* + \frac{5}{8}''$

Hardware

1 pair, wooden clothespole holders. Available at hardware stores and building-supply stores.
3d and 4d finish nails

*X equals the window measurement from the outside of the vertical casing on one side to the outside of the
vertical casing on the other side.

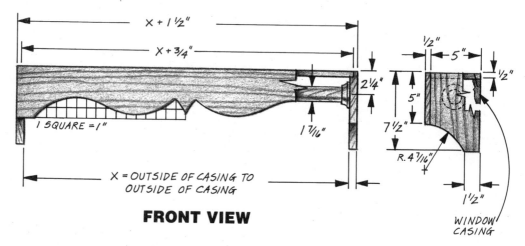

X + 1½"

X + ¾"

1 SQUARE = 1"

2¼"

1 ⁷⁄₁₆"

X = OUTSIDE OF CASING TO
OUTSIDE OF CASING

FRONT VIEW

½"

5"

½"

5"

7½"

R. 4⁷⁄₁₆"

1½"

WINDOW
CASING

END VIEW

on one side to the outside of the casings on the other side. This happens to be a not-uncommon size but no size can be said to be really common.

The valance can be adjusted 1 inch narrower or up to 3 inches wider by changing only the length of the straight part of the bottom edge of the front. If this range doesn't cover your window, don't give up. Wider or narrower windows can be accommodated by modifying the curves. Retain the overall height of the front and depart from the depth of the curves only with caution. Otherwise, simply draw curves to suit your taste. Then, calculate the lengths of the front and top as indicated in the Cutting List.

2 Cut the parts. The design uses ½-inch-thick stock for the front and top in order to keep weight down. Since most valances are painted, pine, basswood, or poplar are good choices, again to keep weight down. Cut the parts to the dimensions that you calculated and that are given in the Cutting List. Do all

the ripping to width at once, with the same fence setting, to ensure uniformity.

3 Cut the curves. Lay out a 4⁷⁄₁₆-inch-radius curve on card stock and cut it out. Mark off the ends of the straight portions of the front and bottom edges of the sides. Hold the card stock pattern up to these marks and trace the curve on both sides. Saw to the line with a coping saw.

Lay out the curves of one side of the front on card stock and cut it out. Trace the pattern onto the front and saw to the line. Clean up all of the saw marks with rasps and sandpaper.

4 Rabbet the sides. Lay out the rabbets as shown in the *Front View,* making sure you have a right side and a left side. With only two short rabbets to cut, it will be easiest to cut them with a saw blade on the table saw. Make the ⅜-inch-deep cuts in the inside surface of the sides first. Make sure you adjust the fence so the blade falls on the correct side of the rabbet edge. Readjust the fence and depth of cut and make the second cut with the stock on end and the outer surface against the rip fence.

5 **Fit the pole holders.** Position the pole holders on the sides as shown in the *Front View* and *End View* and mark their screw locations. Drill pilot holes, then screw the pole holders in place. The size of screw to use will depend on the particular pole holders you get; just make sure the screws won't exit the outside surface of the sides. Now unscrew them and set them aside.

6 **Assemble the valance.** Place a side in your vise, apply glue to the rabbet, and nail the top to it with 3d finish nails. Attach the top to the other side in the same way. Lay this assembly on your workbench and check that the sides are perpendicular to the top. Apply glue to the front edges of the top and sides. Position the front so the bottom edge is flush with the ends of the curves on the sides, then nail it in place. When the glue is dry, sand or plane the joints perfectly flush.

7 **Paint the valance.** Most valances, like most window trim, are painted; the two should match. First drive the pole-holder screws partway into their holes to plug them, then apply a primer, and paint to match the window trim.

Paint the pole and pole holders (assuming that you use wooden ones like the ones shown in the drawing) as well as the valance assembly. Let the paint dry thoroughly.

8 **Hang the valance.** The valance is not really nailed in place; it hangs on nails. To install it, first select a drill bit the same diameter as 4d finish nails. You want holes that will fit the nails snugly but not tightly. Now hold the valance in position on the top window casing as shown in the *End View*. Drill a hole through the valance top into the top edge of the casing and push in a nail. Make this first nail hole near the center so the valance will hang by itself while you continue. Now drill holes and push in nails about 4 inches from each end, and then about half way between the end nails and the center nail.

9 **Install the pole.** Typical wooden clothespole holders come in pairs; one part is closed all the way around, the other has an open portion so the pole can drop in. Screw the closed holder tightly in place. Screw the open holder just tightly enough that it isn't loose but not so tight that you can't turn it. Turn it so the opening is down. Put the curtains on the pole, insert the pole in the closed holder, then the open holder, then turn the open holder so the opening is up. Done with number one. If you're ambitious, do the rest of the windows in the house, then do the in-laws'.

CHERRY WALL SHELVES

There are a great many wall shelf designs, both contemporary and traditional, but few genuine antiques with the versatility and attractiveness of this one. It is big enough to provide generous storage and display space but won't totally dominate a wall. The variation in shelf width gives it a feeling of openness while the ½-inch-thick stock gives it some delicacy. The cherry provides plenty of strength.

1 **Select the stock and cut the parts.** The overall impression of this set of shelves depends to a large extent on the stock thickness. Since ½-inch-thick hardwoods are not commonly available, the parts will have to be cut from thicker stock. There are several alternatives:

• You or your hardwood dealer can plane 4/4 (four-quarter) stock down to ½ inch thick.

EXPLODED VIEW

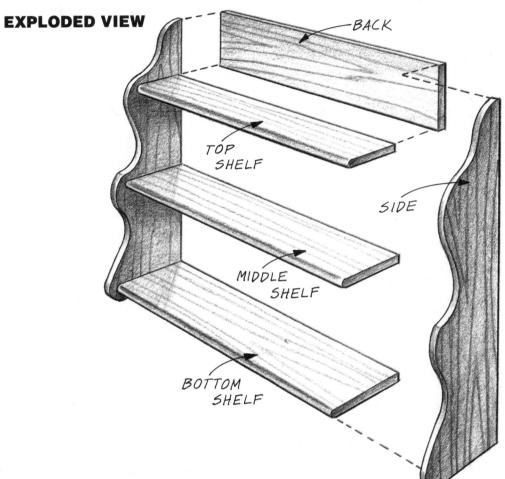

BACK

TOP
SHELF

SIDE

MIDDLE
SHELF

BOTTOM
SHELF

CUTTING LIST

Part	Dimensions
Sides (2)	$\frac{1}{2}'' \times 8\frac{3}{4}'' \times 25\frac{1}{2}''$
Top shelf	$\frac{1}{2}'' \times 5\frac{5}{8}'' \times 24''$
Middle shelf	$\frac{1}{2}'' \times 7\frac{1}{8}'' \times 24''$
Bottom shelf	$\frac{1}{2}'' \times 8\frac{1}{8}'' \times 24''$
Back	$\frac{1}{2}'' \times 6\frac{1}{2}'' \times 24''$

Hardware

2 brass flathead wood screws, #10 $\times$ 2½″

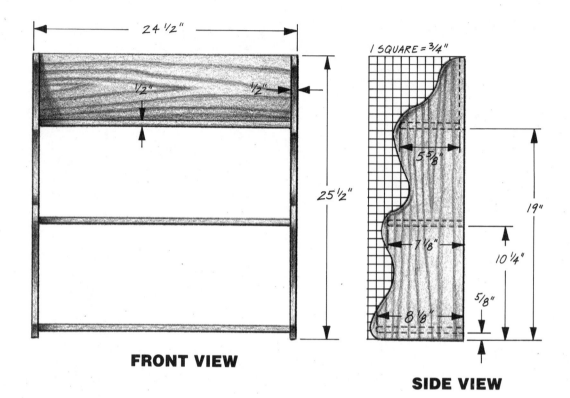

FRONT VIEW

SIDE VIEW

- You or a small professional wood-working shop can use a large band saw to resaw 5/4 (five-quarter) or 6/4 (six-quarter) stock.
- You can resaw 5/4 or 6/4 stock on the table saw by ripping from both edges with a thin-kerf rip blade, then finishing any uncut middle with a handsaw.

Plane the stock smooth, ½ inch thick, then saw it to the dimensions specified by the Cutting List. Be sure to cut each of the shelves and the back to exactly the same length. Use a stop block for accuracy when crosscutting them on the table saw.

2 **Rout dadoes for the shelves and back.** Lay out the dadoes for the

shelves on the inner surfaces of the sides. Keep in mind that the sides are mirror images, not identical. Rout the ½-inch × ³/₁₆-inch-deep dadoes with a ½-inch straight bit in your router. Guide the router with a straightedge clamped to the stock and remember that the three dadoes in each side are different lengths. Do *not* square the front ends of the dadoes.

Rout a ½-inch × ³/₁₆-inch-deep rabbet for the back in each side. Guide the router with the router fence attachment for these cuts.

3 **Round-over the front edges of the shelves.** Rounded-over front edges on the shelves fit the rounded front ends of the dadoes. You can round-over the shelf edges with either a ¼-inch-radius roundover bit in two passes, or in just one pass with a ¼-inch-radius bullnose bit. Make these cuts with the router fence on a hand-held router, or, for more control, with a table-mounted router.

4 Cut the sides to shape. Lay out the curved front edge on one of the sides. Fasten the two sides together with brads, hot melt glue, or double-sided carpet tape in the waste areas. Saw the curve with a coping saw, porta-ble jigsaw, or band saw.

Clean up the sawn edges with files and sandpaper. A sanding drum in a drill press can make quick work of the cleanup.

5 Assemble the shelving unit. Sand all the parts. On a flat surface, glue and clamp the shelves into the da-does in the sides. Make sure the assem-bly is square by checking that the diago-nals on the back are equal. Apply glue to the back edge of the top shelf and the rabbets in the sides, then clamp the back in place. The bottom edge of the back should be flush with the bottom surface of the top shelf.

6 Pin the shelves. The shelves are pinned to the sides with ³⁄₁₆-inch-square by 1-inch-long wooden pegs driven into ³⁄₁₆-inch-diameter holes. Drill two holes through the sides into each end of each shelf with a portable drill.

Rip the pegs from the corner of a piece of scrap cherry. To avoid the usual dangers of working with tiny parts on the table saw, adjust the blade height to just shy of ³⁄₁₆ inch but set the fence ³⁄₁₆ inch from the blade. Saw out the corner of the scrap by running first the edge, then the face against the fence. Since the blade height is shy of ³⁄₁₆ inch, the corner will still be attached to the scrap. Crosscut the scrap into 1-inch lengths. You can now break the pegs from the scrap. Pare off the corners on one end of each peg to make it easier to start the pegs in their holes.

Apply glue to the pegs and drive them into the holes. Driving square pegs into round holes makes a very tight dowel joint. Trim the pegs flush with the surface of the sides with a chisel and sand them smooth.

7 Finish the shelf. There are very few constraints on the kind of finish you can use on this project. As long as the finish is durable enough to stand up to the objects you'll be putting on the shelves, it will do. You can use a clear finish like shellac, lacquer, or varnish, or paint the shelves to fit your decor.

The simplest way to hang the shelves is with a couple of #10 × 2½-inch brass flathead wood screws. Decide exactly where you want the unit to hang, then locate the studs in the wall behind where you want the shelves. Lay out screw locations on the back 1 inch or so above the top shelf and positioned from left to right to line up with the centers of two studs. Drill and countersink shank holes in the back and drill pilot holes in the studs. Since brass screws twist off easily, you may want to thread the pilot holes with a steel screw before hanging the shelves with the brass screws.

SHELF WITH PEGS

A shelf and peg combination like this one is so universally useful it can be found in just about every woodworking tradition, and in every room in the house. The minor, decorative details may change with popular taste, but there is no improving on the basic design. The back board gives the shelf strength and support while providing a secure attachment for the pegs and a convenient place to screw it to the wall. The ends provide simple, solid support and an opportunity for a decorative touch. Build it from any stable wood you favor, hard or soft.

1 **Select the stock and cut the parts.** You'll notice from the Cut-ting List that the shelf board and end supports are easily cut from a surfaced 1 × 6 and the back board is easily cut from a 1 × 4. Cut these parts to the specified sizes. If you intend to turn your own pegs, make the blanks. The Cutting List gives a source of supply for turned pegs you can buy.

2 **Rout the edge bead on the back board.** Chuck a ¼-inch-radius tradi-tional beading bit in a table-mounted rou-ter. (This bit style is sometimes called a bullnose or full radius bit and may be specified by diameter instead of radius.) Recess the bit in the router-table fence so you can bead the edge with the front

EXPLODED VIEW

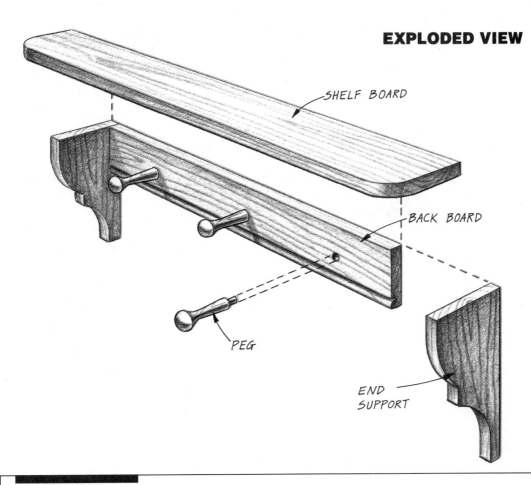

SHELF BOARD

BACK BOARD

PEG

END
SUPPORT

CUTTING LIST

Part	Dimensions
Back board	¾″ × 3½″ × 27½″
Pegs* (3)	¹⁵⁄₁₆″ dia. × 3⅜″
End supports (2)	¾″ × 5″ × 9″
Shelf board	¾″ × 5½″ × 36″

Hardware

6d wire finish nails *or* 5d fine cut finish nails. Available from Tremont Nail Company, P.O. Box 111, Wareham, MA 02571; (508) 295–1365.

*Turned pegs can be purchased from The Woodworker's Store, 21801 Industrial Blvd., Rogers, MN 55374-9514; (612) 428–3200. Available in maple (item #23366), oak (item #23374), and cherry (item #32382).

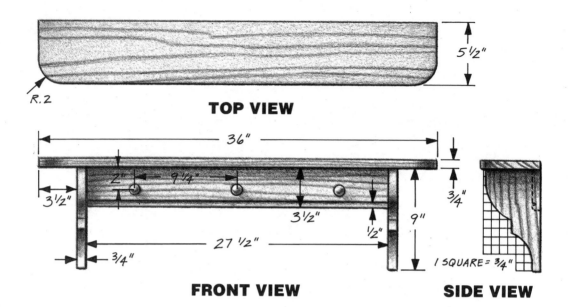

TOP VIEW

R.2

36"

3 1/2"

2" — 9 1/4"

3 1/2"

1/2"

27 1/2"

3/4"

9"

3/4"

5 1/2"

FRONT VIEW

SIDE VIEW

1 SQUARE = 3/4"

face of the stock against the fence. You can cut this bead with a molding head on the table saw if you don't have a router table.

3 **Bore holes for the pegs.** Lay out the peg holes on the back board as

shown in the *Front View.* If you are turning your own pegs, bore ⅜-inch holes for them and bore a scrap to use as a gauge when turning the pegs. If you bought your pegs, bore holes to fit their dowel ends.

4 **Turn the pegs on the lathe.** If you're making your own pegs, turn them to the dimensions in the *Peg Detail.* Sand the pegs before removing them from the lathe.

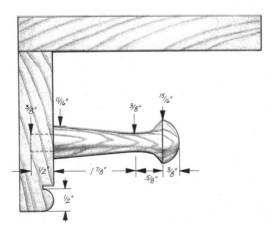

3/8"   1 1/16"   3/8"   15/16"

1/2"   1 7/8"   5/8"   3/8"

1/2"

PEG DETAIL

5 **Saw the end supports to shape.** Lay out the end-support shape on one of the blanks. Stick the two blanks together with double-sided carpet tape, then cut out the shape with a coping saw or band saw. Clean up the edges with files and sandpaper.

6 **Round the corners on the shelf board.** Lay out the 2-inch-radius rounded corners of the shelf board. Saw them to shape the same way you shaped the end supports. File and sand the corners smooth.

7 **Assemble the shelf.** Sand all of the parts. Glue and nail the end supports to the back board, then glue and nail the shelf board to the back board and end supports. If you nail with 6d wire finish nails, set the nails and fill the nail holes with wood filler. For a more original look, use 5d or 6d fine cut finish nails set flush with the surface of the wood. Predrill the nail holes through the end supports and the shelf board. Glue the pegs in the peg holes.

8 **Finish the shelf unit.** Most of the original old shelves of this sort were painted, as ours is. By applying a glaze over the paint and then wiping it off in the places that would receive natural wear, you can create a worn look. Natural finishes are also appropriate. If you use a light-colored wood, you may want to stain the shelf before applying a varnish or polyurethane.

WALL SCONCE

While few of us today have a daily use for candles for lighting, even fewer are immune to power outages caused by severe weather or accidents involving power poles. Wall-hung sconces holding a candle in a candlestand or a small oil lamp provide both down-home decoration and emergency utility. Make several and hang them in entrances, hallways, and perhaps the bathroom.

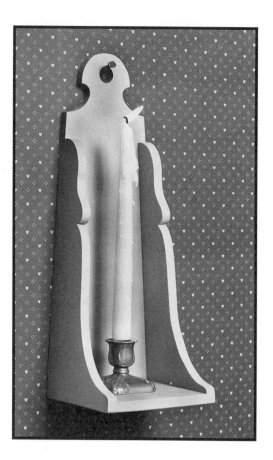

1 **Select the stock.** All of the sconce parts are ½ inch thick. Use poplar if you intend to paint your sconce like our prototype or use an attractive cabinet wood if you prefer a natural finish. If your dealer doesn't carry ½-inch stock and you don't have a planer, have the dealer plane the stock to thickness for you. Cut the back and bottom to the dimensions in the Cutting List but cut a single piece 5 inches × 13 inches for the two sides.

2 **Cut the shapes.** Make stiff paper patterns of the back and side shapes and trace them onto the stock. Both sides will fit on the 13-inch-long side piece; lay out both of them. Bore the ¾-inch-diameter hole in the back, then saw out the outline with a coping saw. Saw the side piece in half by sawing between the two layouts, then tape the two sides together and saw both to shape at once. Smooth the edges with rasps and sandpaper.

3 **Bevel the side and bottom edges.** Tilt the table-saw blade 3 degrees from vertical. Check that your miter-gauge bar is perpendicular to the miter-gauge fence, then bevel the cross-grain edges of the bottom and sides. Make sure that you don't shorten them while beveling them.

4 **Assemble the sconce.** Sand all of the parts. Glue the parts together

EXPLODED VIEW

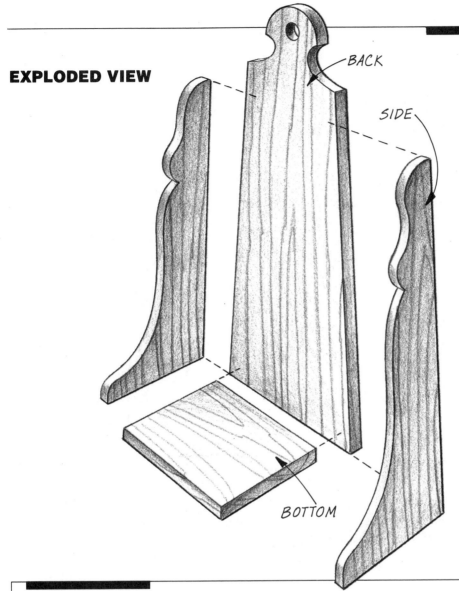

BACK

SIDE

BOTTOM

CUTTING LIST

Part	Dimensions
Back	½″ × 6″ × 16″
Sides (2)	½″ × 5″ × 12″
Bottom	½″ × 5″ × 5″

Hardware

4d finish nails

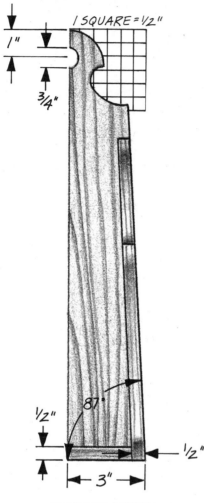

1 SQUARE = 1/2"

1"

3/4"

1/2"

87°

1/2"

3"

FRONT VIEW

1/2"

5"

1 SQUARE = 1/2"

16"

12"

SIDE VIEW

as shown in the *Exploded View,* holding them together for the time being with masking tape. Lay the assembly on one side and nail the side facing you to the bottom with 4d finish nails. Set the nails. Turn the assembly over and nail the second side to the bottom. Clamp one side in your bench vise and nail the back to it, then repeat for the second side.

5 **Complete the sconce.** When the glue is dry, remove the tape and sand off any smeared glue. Fill the nail holes on the sides. Apply a light-colored enamel, milk paint, or, if you prefer, several coats of an oil finish. See page 100 for more on milk paint.

PART SIX

SIMPLE PROJECTS

BOOTJACK

The demise of the bootjack in the last half century is, to say the least, a great misfortune. With untold thousands suffering from lower back pain and waist-lines increasing inexorably, the humble bootjack awaits its renaissance. Make a significant contribution to the comfort and convenience of society: Make a bootjack.

1 **Select sturdy materials.** Our prototype is solid American-grown oak; accept no less. Saw the ramp to the dimensions in the Cutting List but saw out a piece 3 inches (with the grain) × 6 inches (across the grain) for the foot.

2 **Saw out the ramp.** Lay out the shape of the ramp as shown in the *Bootjack Pattern* and saw it out with a coping saw or saber saw. Smooth the edges with rasps, spokeshaves, and sandpaper.

3 **Round the edges.** Chuck a piloted, ¼-inch-radius roundover bit in a table-mounted router and round-over all of the edges on both sides of the ramp. Round-over both sides of a long-grain edge and 2 inches of both adjoining cross-grain edges of the foot piece. Saw off the foot from the foot piece to the dimensions in the Cutting List.

EXPLODED VIEW

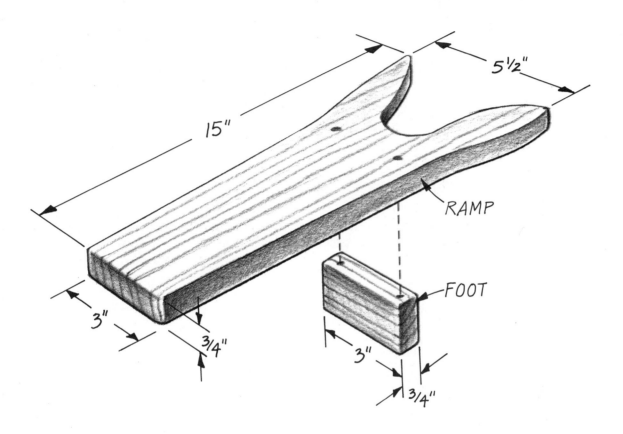

15"

5½"

RAMP

FOOT

3"

¾"

3"

¾"

CUTTING LIST

Part	Dimensions
Ramp	¾" × 5½" × 15"
Foot	¾" × 1½" × 3"

Hardware

2 flathead wood screws, #8 × 1½"

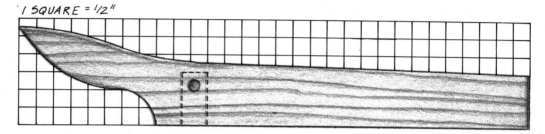

1 SQUARE = 1/2"

BOOTJACK PATTERN

4 Assemble the bootjack. Sand both of the parts. Apply glue to the unrounded edge of the foot, position it as shown in the *Bootjack Pattern,* and clamp it there. Drill and counterbore pilot and shank holes for #8 × 1½-inch screws, then drive the screws in.

5 Apply a weatherproof finish. When the glue from the assembly is dry, sand off any glue smears. Apply a good, durable polyurethane or exterior trim paint to the bootjack. Let the finish dry thoroughly, then revel in the conveniences of a bygone era.

QUILT RACK

A quilt rack is a pretty simple piece of furniture, but draped with a colorful quilt, it decorates the whole room. This rack is a good size and is soundly and thoughtfully constructed. The feet are made of chestnut for better wear, and the mortises and tenons in the pine uprights and crosspieces are all pinned. The feet are nicely shaped, and the uprights flare slightly at the bottom for strength. Chestnut is hard to find, but oak is a good substitute. Use a hardwood for the entire rack if you like.

1 **Select the stock and cut the parts.** Saw the feet and uprights to the dimensions specified by the Cutting List. Saw the crosspieces slightly wider and thicker, then plane them to the size specified.

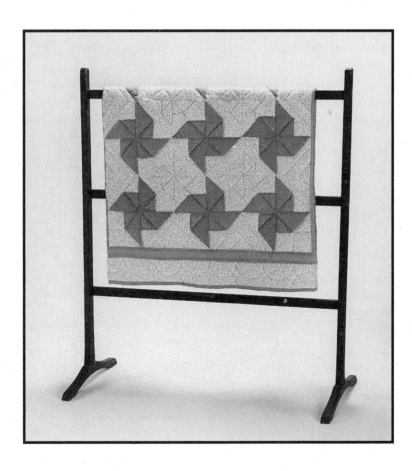

EXPLODED VIEW

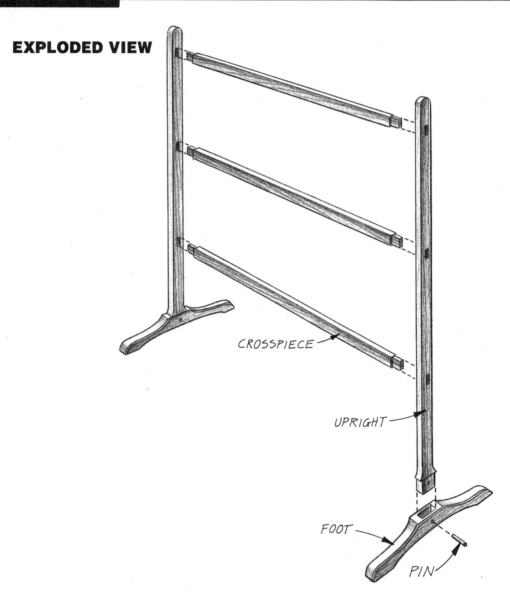

CROSSPIECE

UPRIGHT

FOOT

PIN

CUTTING LIST

Part	Dimensions
Feet (2)	$1\frac{1}{4}'' \times 2\frac{3}{4}'' \times 18\frac{3}{8}''$
Uprights (2)	$1'' \times 2'' \times 45''$
Crosspieces (3)	$\frac{5}{8}'' \times 1\frac{1}{4}'' \times 39\frac{1}{2}''$
Pins (8)	$\frac{1}{4}''$ dia. $\times 1\frac{1}{2}''$

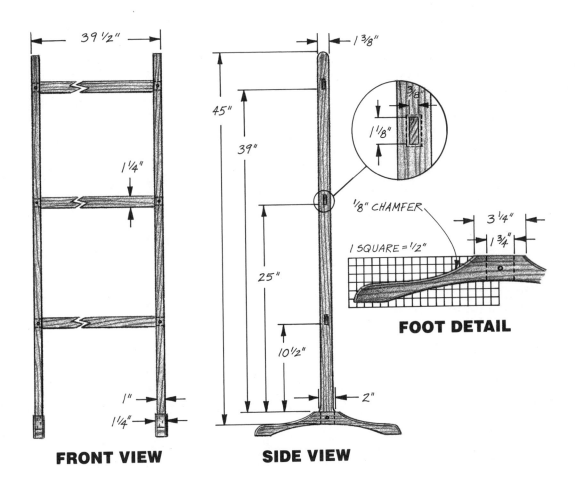

39 1/2"

1 3/8"

3/8"

45"

1 1/8"

39"

1 1/4"

1/8" CHAMFER

3 1/4"

1 3/4"

25"

1 SQUARE = 1/2"

FOOT DETAIL

10 1/2"

1"

2"

1 1/4"

FRONT VIEW

SIDE VIEW

2 **Cut the mortises.** Lay out the mortises in the feet and uprights as shown in the *Side View* and *Foot Detail.* The marking gauge is the preferred layout tool for this.

You can rout the mortises with a plunge router and a router fence attachment as explained in "Plunge-Routing Mortises" on page 18. Or you can drill the mortises with a ⅜-inch bit in a drill press, then clean up the sides and ends of the mortises with chisels. With either method, square the ends of the mortises with a narrow chisel.

The mortises in the feet must be at least 1½ inches deep but need not go all the way through since shaping the foot will open the mortises. Place a scrap of wood under the uprights when cutting these mortises to prevent splintering or damage to the workbench or drill bit.

3 **Cut the tenons.** Lay out the tenons to match the mortises, adjusting the dimensions as necessary if the mortises are not exactly as specified. Saw the shoulders first on the table saw. Butt

SHOP TIP: When joining parts with through mortises and tenons, allow a little extra length on tenon parts. Cut the shoulders in the correct position, making the tenons longer by the amount of extra length that you allowed. After you assemble the joints, trim off the protruding ends of the tenons. This procedure ensures that the tenons will be flush with the surface of the mortised pieces.

the end of the tenon against a stop block clamped to the fence to gauge the tenon length. Don't forget to change the blade height for the various shoulder depths.

Saw the tenon cheeks with a fine-tooth backsaw. Cut just to the layout lines but don't cross them. Check the fit in the mortises and pare the cheeks if necessary with a sharp chisel. The tenons should be snug in the mortises but you shouldn't have to force them.

4 **Lay out and cut the foot profiles.** If you have a band saw, lay out the foot profile directly on one of the foot pieces, stick the two pieces together with double-sided carpet tape, and saw out both of them as one unit.

If you don't have a band saw, saw the two feet separately. Twice the foot thickness is a bit too thick for a coping saw. In this case, make a pattern for the feet on stiff paper. Trace the pattern on each foot blank and saw them out with the coping saw.

In either case, saw only the top

profile of the feet for now; leave the bottom curve until later. Clean up the sawn edges with a fine rasp or round-face spokeshave and sandpaper. Chamfer the edges with a spokeshave, drawknife, or router and chamfering bit.

5 **Lay out and cut the upright profiles.** The flair at the bottom of the uprights strengthens the joint considerably. Cut them out the same way you cut the feet.

You may want to saw the long, straight portion on the table saw. Remember, however, that the table-saw blade cuts farther on the bottom where you can't see it than at the top where it's visible. Stop well short of where the curve begins.

Finish by cutting the curved portion, then smooth the sawn edges as you did for the feet. The edges of the uprights are not chamfered on the original.

6 **Assemble the uprights to the feet.** Sand all of the parts. Glue the tenons on the uprights into the mortises

SHOP TIP: The secret to sawing tenon shoulders so they match up perfectly is a table-saw miter gauge adjusted to a perfect 90-degree angle. You can check it by crosscutting a straight piece of wood, turning one half over, and butting the two sawn ends back together again. If the tightly butted halves no longer form a straight line, the miter gauge is off.

in the feet. Clean up any glue that may have squeezed out at the shoulders, then stack the two assemblies with the mortised sides of the uprights facing each other. Check that the bottom edges of the feet line up at the same time that the edges of the uprights line up. Tap them into alignment if they don't, then let the glue dry.

7 Saw out the bottom of the feet. Saw the remaining curve on the bottom of the feet. As you do so, you will be trimming the end of the tenon on the upright perfectly flush with the cutout. If you're careful to saw a fair curve here, there is no need to smooth out the saw marks; the surface will never be seen. Ease the edges a bit with sandpaper.

8 Assemble the crosspieces to the uprights. Glue and clamp the tenons on the crosspieces into the corresponding mortises in the uprights. Heavy bar clamps can distort an assembly like this by their sheer weight so clamp the assembly with lightweight band clamps or stout cord and tourniquets.

Stand the quilt rack on its feet on a flat surface and make sure all four feet rest on the surface. If they don't, the assembly is twisted. It will probably stay true if you simply untwist it by hand. If it won't, weight the feet while the glue dries.

Check that the assembly is square by checking that the diagonals are equal. If necessary, put a tourniquet on the long diagonal to square the assembly.

9 Pin the tenons. A light, open frame like this puts a lot of stress on the joints. Pinning the tenons reinforces them.

The pins should go through the center of the tenon cheeks. Lay out the ¼-inch pin holes and drill them with a bit with a spur, like a brad-point bit. Clamp a scrap of wood where the bit will exit to prevent tear-out.

The original pins were whittled from pine but hardwood pins will do a better job. Or you can use ¼-inch hardwood dowel. Bevel the leading edges of the pins, then glue and hammer them through the pin holes. Saw off the protruding pins as close to the surrounding surface as you can without scratching the surface, then pare off the remainder with a sharp chisel.

10 Complete the quilt rack. Final sand the quilt rack, softening hard edges. Stain is not a good choice for a quilt rack since it can bleed and may stain the quilt. An oil finish is unwise for the same reason. Shellac, lacquer, varnish, or polyurethane can all give you a tough finish and a professional result.

TOWEL RACK

The solution to some of life's problems is so simple and obvious that it can't belong to any particular style but is at home anywhere. This towel rack is an example.

The simple, straightforward construction of the rack makes it an evening's project at most. It then goes right to work drying towels and keeping them handy.

1 Cut the parts to size. Choose a straight-grained board for the back. If you work in strong hardwoods, make it ½ inch thick as shown in the drawings. If you prefer pine or one of the softer hardwoods like basswood or poplar, make it ¾ inch thick and make the ends 5¾ inches long instead of the 5½ inches shown in the drawing. Rip the back and stock for the ends to 6 inches wide.

EXPLODED VIEW

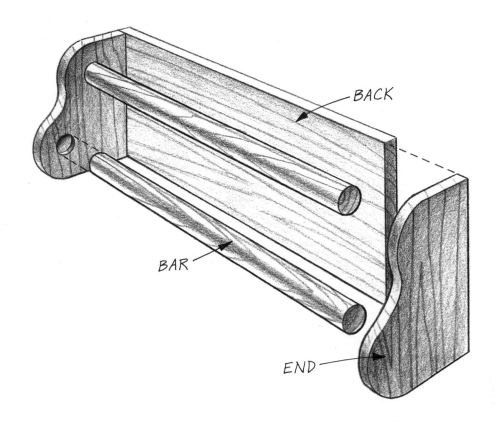

BACK

BAR

END

CUTTING LIST

Part	Dimensions
Ends (2)	$\frac{3}{4}'' \times 6'' \times 5\frac{1}{2}''$
Bars (2)	$1''$ dia. $\times 27\frac{1}{4}''$
Back	$\frac{1}{2}'' \times 6'' \times 27\frac{1}{4}''$

Hardware

6 finish nails, $1''$
#8 flathead wood screws

SIDE VIEW

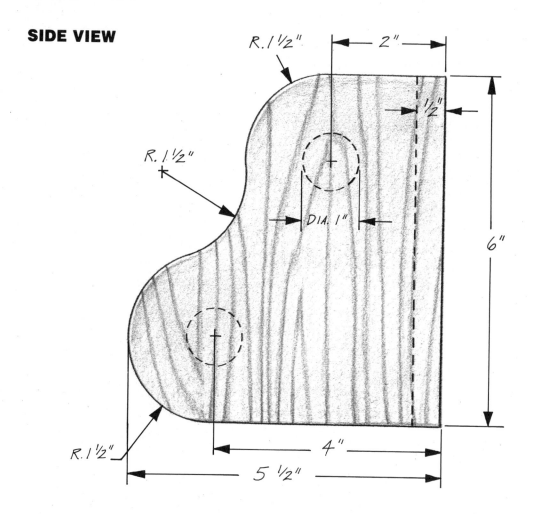

Crosscut the back and the 1-inch-dowel towel bars to length. All three should be exactly the same length. Crosscut the ends to 5½ inches long (or 5¾ inches as mentioned previously.)

2 Cut the ends to shape. Lay out the shape of the ends with a compass, marking the centers clearly for

when you will drill the 1-inch holes. Saw to the line with a coping saw, then smooth the sawn edges with a fine rasp and sandpaper. Bore the 1-inch-diameter holes ⅜ inch deep.

3 Rabbet the ends for the back. Adjust the table saw to cut ⅜ inch deep. Hold a scrap of the back stock against the rip fence and adjust the fence so the scrap just covers the teeth on the blade. With these adjustments, saw the first side of the rabbets with the ends inside-face down. Now hold an end on its back edge alongside the blade and raise the blade to the height of the first rabbet cut. Adjust the rip fence so there is ⅜ inch between the blade and the fence. With the ends on their back edge and the outside face against the fence, saw the second side of the rabbets.

4 **Assemble the rack.** Apply glue to the rabbets and the bar holes. Insert the bars in one of the ends, then fit the other end onto the bars. Fit the back into the rabbets, then clamp the assem-

bly from end to end. When the glue is dry, drive three 1-inch finish nails through each end into the back.

5 **Apply a finish.** Prime, then paint the towel rack to match the door and window trim in the bath or kitchen where you intend to hang the rack. Install the rack by drilling pilot and shank holes for #8 wood screws through the back and into studs in the wall. Countersink the holes, then drive in the screws. Use screws long enough to go through your wallboard or plaster and 1 inch into the studs. If you like, you can counterbore the screw holes and plug or fill and paint over them, or you can use brass screws and leave them showing.

MAGAZINE RACK

If your home needs a magazine rack, you know it. The country home of the eighteenth century had no such need, but this one will fit well with country antiques. Our prototype was made with recycled wide pine boards. Hardwoods would be just as appropriate.

1 **Select the materials.** The magazine rack, though a small project, requires wide materials. If you don't have wide stock, edge-glue, as explained on page 6. The sides of our prototype are 1/4-inch-thick, solid wood. Substitute plywood for these parts if you don't have

EXPLODED VIEW

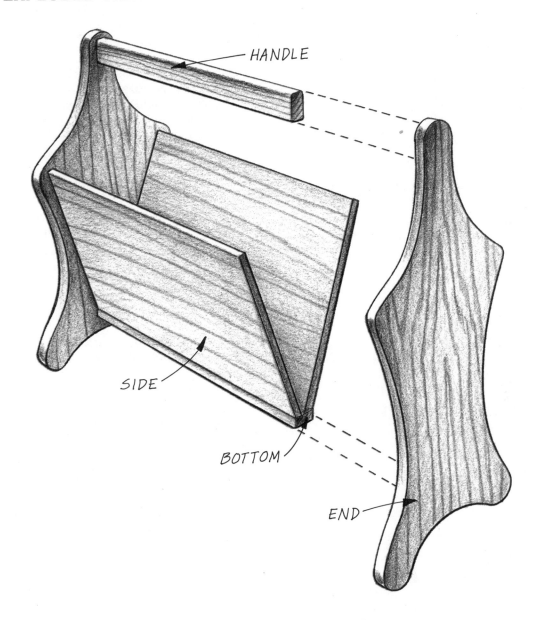

HANDLE

SIDE

BOTTOM

END

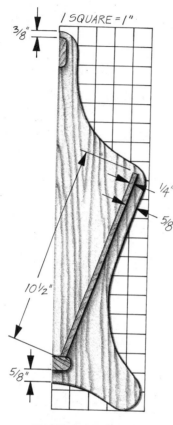

1 SQUARE = 1"

3/8"

1/4"

5/8"

10½"

5/8"

END PATTERN

a planer. Once you have the necessary width, cut the parts to the sizes specified by the Cutting List.

2 Rout side grooves in the ends. Lay out the shape of the ends as shown in the *End Pattern*. Include centerlines for the side grooves and the positions of the handle and bottom. Make sure the side groove layouts are identical on both ends.

For each side groove in turn, clamp a straightedge to the end blank half the width of your router base away from the centerline of the side groove. Guiding the router with the straightedge, rout the side groove ¼ inch deep with a ¼-inch-diameter straight bit. Square the ends with a narrow chisel.

3 Cut side grooves in the bottom. Hold the bottom in position on an end and mark the position of the side grooves on the bottom. Tilt the saw blade 21 degrees and adjust the depth of cut to ¼ inch. Adjust the fence so the

CUTTING LIST

Part	Dimensions
Ends (2)	¾" × 9¾" × 19¾"
Bottom	¾" × 2¼" × 14½"
Handle	¾" × 1½" × 14½"
Sides* (2)	¼" × 10½" × 15"

Hardware

6d finish nails

*Use either solid wood or plywood.

234

saw blade lines up with an edge of a groove and rip that edge. Readjust the fence and rip the other edge of the groove. If necessary, readjust again and remove the remaining waste. Repeat the operation for the other groove.

4 **Finish shaping the parts.** Saw out the ends with a coping saw and smooth the edges with rasps and sandpaper.

Chuck a ¼-inch-radius, piloted roundover bit in a table-mounted router and round-over all four long edges of the handle and bottom and the entire periphery, both sides, of the ends.

5 **Assemble the magazine rack.** Sand the parts, then apply glue to the grooves. Lay an end on your bench, with the grooves up. Insert the sides into the grooves in the bottom, then into the grooves in the end on the bench. Place the second end on top, fitting the sides into the grooves. Apply glue to the ends of the handle, then slip it into position. Drive two 6d finishing nails through the upper end into the handle and one into the bottom. Turn the assembly over and nail the other end to the handle and bottom. Check that the rack stands flat on a flat surface; give it a twist if necessary, then let the glue dry.

6 **Apply a finish.** Our prototype was stained a mellow, dark walnut and then oiled. Finish to your own taste; paint it if you like.

TREENWARE

Treenware, carved wooden cooking and eating utensils, can provide hours of enjoyment while carving and years of utility in the kitchen, all at negligible cost. Wooden spoons can be carved in endless variety, as primitive or as refined as you like. Carving them is an excellent way to become familiar with the tools and techniques of carving. The scraper shown is even simpler, not requiring a gouge, and is extremely useful for scraping Teflon pans clean while cooking.

The tools are simple: a knife, a gouge, a rasp, and a coping saw. The knife should have a blade no more than 4 inches long and a handle that will fit your hand comfortably. Keep the knife razor sharp for easy and safe carving. The gouge is one of those tools that you don't fully appreciate until after you have one, and then don't know how you ever

/ SQUARE = 1/4"

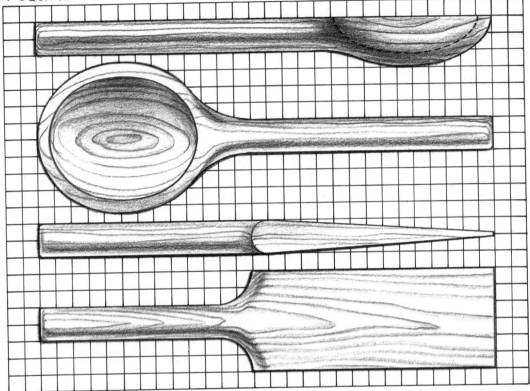

TREENWARE SHAPES

got along without one. For general carving work, an 8- to-10-millimeter gouge is a good choice. The rasp, an often overlooked hand tool, shapes material across the grain. The most versatile is the four-in-hand, a rasp with a flat side and a convex side, each side having a fine and a coarse surface, hence the name. A coping saw is used for cutting out rough shapes.

Experienced carvers will tackle just about any species of wood, but some species are particularly nice to work with. Basswood (linden) is a favorite for the ease with which it cuts and for its tight, uniform grain. Poplar and pine are also popular.

1 **Prepare a blank.** Begin a treenware project by cutting out a rectangular blank as thick, wide, and long as the item you want to carve. Draw the top view and side view onto the blank. Don't be compulsive about following the shapes in the drawings; they're there only to give you some idea of what these instructions are about. Sketch your pro-

---

CUTTING LIST

Part	Dimensions
Spoon	¾" × 2¼" × 7"
Scraper	¾" × 1½" × 7"

ject with fluid lines to suit your eye and your needs. If you're making a spoon, draw an outline for the hollow area.

2 **Hollow out the spoon.** Begin the spoon by clamping the blank to your workbench. Hold the gouge firmly with both hands, one on the handle the other on the metal shaft. Begin the cut well inside the outlined hollow area. Push the gouge with the grain, into the wood, but don't try to scoop back up again. You can only cut down into the wood. Repeat the cut from the opposite direction to remove the chip. Always cut with the grain, always take a little at a time, and hone your gouge frequently. Experiment. If you think you can cut across the grain, try it. If you think you can take a bigger bite, try it. You're not putting a fortune in lumber at risk. Carve the hollow in the spoon in this manner until it's as deep, wide, and long as you like.

3 **Saw out the top view shape.** Clamp the spoon blank in your vise and saw out the outline with the coping saw. Don't saw too close to the hollowed area; you can always carve away more but you can't put any back.

4 **Shape the handle and bowl.** The outside of the bowl of the spoon and the handle of the spoon must be carved at the same time to ensure that neither one dictates the shape of the other. Both are shaped with the knife.

The same basic rules apply here as with the hollow; cut with the grain and take a little at a time. Begin by cutting off the corners, then take smaller and smaller shavings as you approach final shape. The area where the bowl of the spoon meets the handle is quite different from the rest of the spoon. Both the top view and side view show concavity but a cross section in the same area is convex. Since the concavity is in the direction of the grain, you will have to cut from both directions to release a chip just as you did when hollowing out the bowl. Don't hesitate to reach for the convex side of the rasp while working this area.

While shaping the outside of the bowl, try to keep the thickness of the bowl as uniform as you can.

5 **Make the scraper.** The little Teflon pot scraper is even simpler than the spoon. Begin with the wedge-shaped blade. Saw out the side view of the blade, then plane the two surfaces.

Shape the handle and the transition between the handle and the blade the same way you treated the spoon.

6 Finishing. Don't. Sanding your treenware will simply remove the character of hand-carved utensils. Applying a finish is equally futile. Nothing that is safe for cooking or eating utensils will stand up to the abuse. If you insist on putting something on, use mineral oil; at least it won't turn rancid.

BOOKENDS

While these bookends are obviously not genuine country antiques, having been made with a router, they are ingeniously designed and go well with other country furnishings. The book supports themselves are joined to interlocking slides. The weight of the books on the slides holds them a constant distance apart.

The visible parts of the original are made of mahogany, while the hidden slide is made of pine. The small cleats on the ends hide the joinery.

1 Select the stock and cut the parts. The bookends don't require much wood but it does need to be thicker than ¾ inch. If your odds and ends around the shop are all too thin, glue face to face to get the required thickness. Prepare the cleats as one piece 4⅛ inches × 6⅜ inches and the remaining parts to the sizes specified by the Cutting List.

2 Shape the ends and cleats. Lay out and saw the rounded corners of the ends and cleats as shown in the *End View*. A coping saw will do fine. Smooth the cuts with sandpaper.

The edges of the ends are molded with a stepped or filleted roundover as shown in the enlarged detail of the *Top View*. The shape can be reproduced with a piloted router bit designed specifically to produce this shape or with a piloted bit that allows changing the diameter of the pilot bearing. You do need a piloted bit to follow around the corners of the parts.

Mold the edges all the way around the cleat piece on one side, then saw the

EXPLODED VIEW

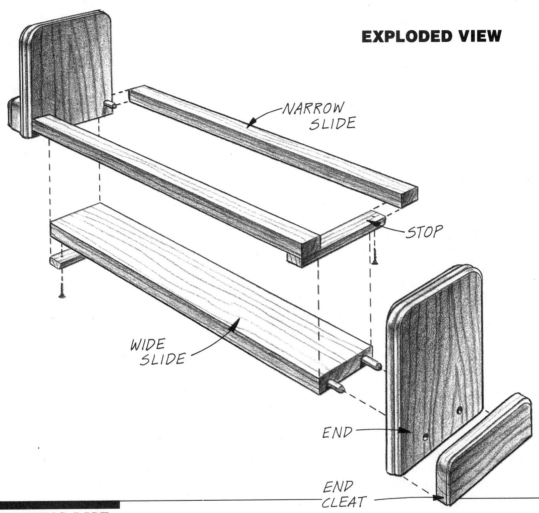

NARROW SLIDE

STOP

WIDE SLIDE

END

END CLEAT

CUTTING LIST

Part	Dimensions
Ends (2)	$1'' \times 6\frac{1}{2}'' \times 8''$
End cleats (2)	$\frac{7}{8}'' \times 2'' \times 6\frac{3}{8}''$
Stops (2)	$\frac{5}{16}'' \times 1\frac{1}{8}'' \times 5\frac{7}{8}''$
Narrow slides (2)	$\frac{7}{8}'' \times 1'' \times 24''$
Wide slide	$\frac{7}{8}'' \times 3\frac{3}{4}'' \times 24''$

Hardware

4 flathead wood screws, #6 $\times$ $\frac{1}{2}''$
4 dowels, $\frac{1}{2}''$ dia. $\times$ $2\frac{1}{2}''$

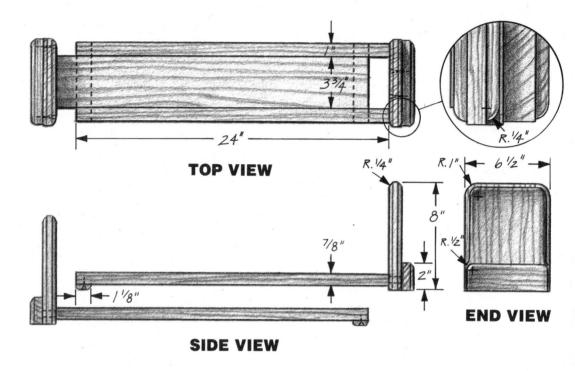

TOP VIEW

END VIEW

SIDE VIEW

piece into the required two cleats. Trace the cleats onto the ends in the position shown in the *End View.* Readjust the depth of cut of the router bit to the shape shown for the ends, then mold the side and top edges of the ends. Stop short of the traced outline of the cleats as shown in the *End View.* Mold the edges on both sides of the ends.

3 Assemble the slides. First sand the stops and slides. The narrow slides must fit alongside the wide slide with enough clearance to slide smoothly. Arrange them in position, slightly offset at the ends as shown in the *Top View,* with strips of poster board between the narrow slides and the wide slide. Tape

the assembly together, poster board and all.

One of the stops is glued and screwed to the two narrow slides, the other to the wide slide. Cover the wide slide with masking tape in the way of the stop that will fasten to the narrow slides. Cover the narrow slides with tape in the way of the stop that will fasten to the wide slide. The tape will prevent accidental gluing of the stops where you don't want it. Position the stops as shown in the *Top View,* drill and countersink pilot and shank holes for #6 × ½-inch flathead wood screws, then glue and screw the stops in place. Be a bit miserly with the glue.

Let the glue dry but don't remove the tape yet.

4 **Assemble the slides to the ends.** Clamp the slide assembly to your workbench. The end with the two narrow slides projecting should face you. Center an end at the end of the assembly and trace the position of the slides. Turn the end around so the tracings are facing you and again center it. Mark the centers of the slide tracings, then bore 1/2-inch-diameter dowel holes straight through the end and into the slides. The overall depth of the holes should be 2 1/2 inches. Saw a shallow groove lengthwise into the side of a couple of 1/2-inch × 2 1/2-inch dowels so air can escape when the dowels are driven into their holes; then apply glue to the dowels and drive them in.

Reverse the assembly on the bench and attach the other end in the same manner. Use two dowels positioned 3/4 inch in from the ends of the slide tracing.

5 **Attach the cleats to the ends.** Remove the tape holding the slide assembly together and disassemble the two slides. Squeezed out glue may have created some minor bonds between them but they should tap apart without trouble.

Glue and clamp the cleats to the outside of the ends. Make sure the cleats are flush with the ends on the bottom.

6 **Apply a finish to the bookends.** Finish sand the bookends removing any smeared glue. Apply at least two coats of a finish that dries hard and won't bleed onto your books.

Wax the slides to make them slide more easily.

KITCHEN SHELVES

Keeping stuff handy becomes more and more of a problem as the years go by simply because we have more stuff to keep handy. If you find yourself tempted to throw out half of the family heirlooms, don't. Instead, make a new one to house the old ones.

This simple shelf unit was designed to stand on a counter or a table against a wall, to fit comfortably in a traditional environment, and to be quick and easy to make. If you stand the shelves on a 36-inch-high counter, the top shelf will be just within reach.

Since a great many woodworkers modify published plans to suit their individual needs, this project was designed to be easy to modify. To change the overall width, simply go through the Cutting List and change the length of the shelves and back; they're all the same. Changing the thickness of the stock couldn't be easier; just change the diameter of the router bit used to cut the shelf dadoes and adjust the width of the back slightly. Since the drawings dimension the dadoes to their centerlines, a thicker shelf will still be in the right spot in relation to the curves on the sides. You could even add a shelf at the bottom and hang the unit on a wall instead of standing it on a counter.

1 **Select the stock and cut the parts to length and width.** As mentioned above, it is very easy to change the stock thicknesses for the project. The thicknesses shown are appropriate for use with a strong hardwood such as maple or oak and give a more delicate, refined look. If you are building with pine or poplar, ¾-inch stock would be more suitable and would give a more robust, rural look. Do use stock that is free of knots and straight-grained; you don't want the unbraced shelves to look like potato chips after a year or two.

Cut all of the parts to the length and width specified by the Cutting List. The shelves and back should be exactly the

EXPLODED VIEW

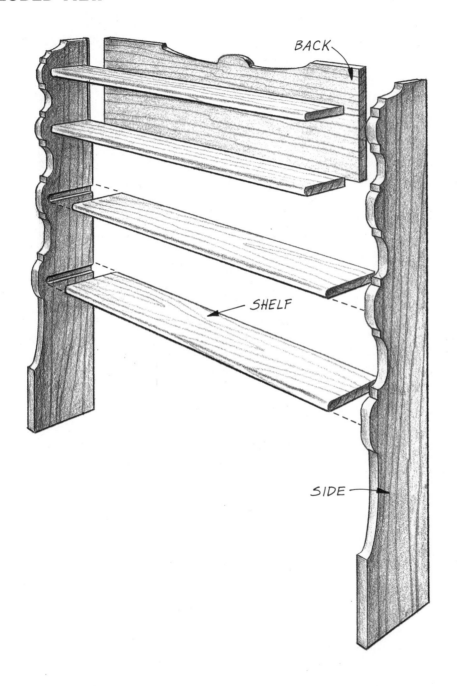

BACK

SHELF

SIDE

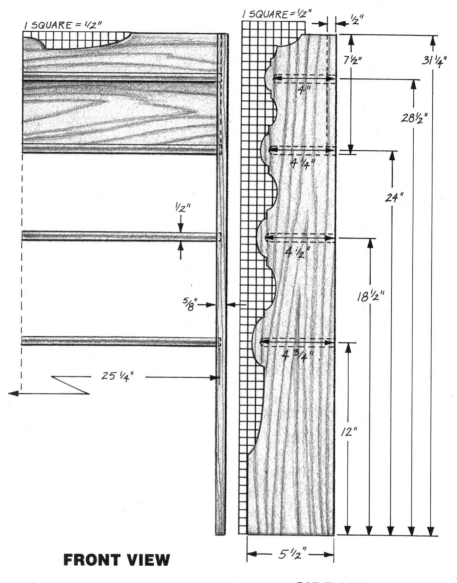

1 SQUARE = 1/2"

1 SQUARE = 1/2"

1/2"

31 1/4"

7 1/2"

4"

28 1/2"

4 1/4"

24"

1/2"

4 1/2"

5/8"

18 1/2"

4 3/4"

25 1/4"

12"

FRONT VIEW

5 1/2"

SIDE VIEW

same length so use a stop block clamped to a miter-gauge extension fence when cutting them to length.

2 Dado and rabbet the sides. The *Side View* gives the height of the dado centerlines above the bottom and the overall length of the dadoes. Lay out the centerlines and clearly mark the blind ends. Make sure you lay out a left and a right side, not two identical ones.

Chuck a straight bit with a diameter the same as the shelf thickness into your router. Adjust the depth of cut to ¼ inch. Clamp a straightedge to a side half the diameter of your router base away from a centerline and rout the dado. Depending on the style and condition of your bit and the power of your router, you may need to rout the dado in two passes, each removing ⅛ inch of depth.

Install the router's fence and rout the rabbet for the back. It's the same width and depth as the dadoes for the shelves.

3 Round-over the front edges of the shelves. Select a roundover bit with a radius equal to half the thickness of the shelves and chuck it in the router. Adjust the fence and depth of cut to cut a plain roundover with no fillets. Round-over the top and bottom of the front edges of all the shelves creating what is known as a bullnose as shown in the *Side View*. This bullnose should fit the rounded ends of the dadoes perfectly.

4 Cut the curves. Lay out the front edge and top end on the outside of one of the sides. If you happen to have a set of drafting templates for ellipses, you'll be interested to know that all of the curves are elliptical. If you don't, just sketch them out based on the grid in the *Side View*.

Clamp the two sides together and saw them out as one. A band saw with a narrow blade will be the easiest for this but a scroll saw or coping saw will do.

CUTTING LIST

Part	Dimensions
Sides (2)	⅝″ × 5½″ × 31¼″
Shelf	½″ × 4¾″ × 25¼″
Shelf	½″ × 4½″ × 25¼″
Shelf	½″ × 4¼″ × 25¼″
Shelf	½″ × 4″ × 25¼″
Back	½″ × 7½″ × 25¼″

Hardware

22 dowels, ¼″ dia. × 1¼″

Clean up the sawn edges with whatever works best for you. A round-bottom spokeshave, scraper, fine rasp, drum sander, or sandpaper on a flat or round block are all appropriate. Preserve the crispness of the outside and inside corners for the best appearance.

Lay out, saw out, and smooth the top edge of the back in like manner.

5 Assemble the shelves. The shelves are best assembled all at once so choose a glue with a long assembly time like liquid hide glue. Assemble the unit without glue first, to check the fit and familiarize yourself with the procedure, then do it all over again with glue.

Begin by adjusting a bar clamp to ⅛-inch-greater opening than the overall width of the shelf unit. Lay it, open jaws up, on a large flat surface. Apply glue to all of the dadoes, then assemble the two sides to the bottom shelf. Holding this unit together by hand, place it front edge down between the open bar-clamp jaws with one of the concave cutouts in the front edges straddling the clamp's bar. Don't tighten the clamp. Now insert the remaining shelves. The loose clamp will allow you to spread the sides enough to insert the shelves without scraping off all of the glue in the dadoes.

Brush glue onto the rabbets for the back and the back edge of the top shelf, then put the back in place. Check that all of the shelves are fully forward in their dadoes and that the back is flush with the bottom edge of the top shelf. Clamp the unit from side to side. Apply clamps only in line with the shelves and back,

not between shelves. If you don't have enough bar clamps, use band clamps or stout cord wrapped around the unit and tightened with a tourniquet. Clamp the back to the top two shelves.

Check that the assembly is square by checking that the diagonals are equal; check that it's flat by sighting from one side to the other. The back edges of the sides should appear parallel. Let the glue dry for a day, or at least overnight.

Reinforce the joints by doweling through the sides into the ends of the shelves and back. Use dowels with a diameter equal to half the thickness of the shelves. They should enter the ends of the shelves a distance equal to twice the thickness of the shelves. Applying these rules here, use ¼-inch-diameter dowels 1¼ inches long.

Use two dowels in each end of each shelf positioned one quarter of the shelf width from the edges of the shelf. Dowel the back in the same manner, then add a third dowel in each end of the back midway between the first two dowels. Trim the dowels flush with the sides.

6 Apply a finish. Shelves take a lot of abuse. You can choose a finish to resist wear or one that doesn't show it. Modern clear finishes like polyurethane are durable but show the scratches that do occur. Oil finishes don't show the wear as much but are not as easy to keep clean if you intend the shelves for the kitchen. If you choose paint, a good choice for a project of this character, use a good enamel, or milk paint as described on page 100.